LATINO TV

CRITICAL CULTURAL COMMUNICATION

General Editors: Jonathan Gray, Aswin Punathambekar, Adrienne Shaw
Founding Editors: Sarah Banet-Weiser and Kent A. Ono

Latino TV

A History

Mary Beltrán

NEW YORK UNIVERSITY PRESS

New York

NEW YORK UNIVERSITY PRESS
New York
www.nyupress.org

References to Internet websites (URLs) were accurate at the time of writing. Neither the author nor New York University Press is responsible for URLs that may have expired or changed since the manuscript was prepared.

Library of Congress Cataloging-in-Publication Data
Names: Beltrán, Mary C., author.
Title: Latino TV : a history / Mary Beltrán.
Description: New York : New York University Press, [2021] | Series: Critical
    cultural communication | Includes bibliographical references and index.
Identifiers: LCCN 2021011953 | ISBN 9781479868650 (hardback) | ISBN 9781479833894
    (paperback) | ISBN 9781479810758 (ebook) | ISBN 9781479830978 (ebook other)
Subjects: LCSH: Hispanic Americans on television. | Hispanic American television actors
    and actresses. | Hispanic Americans in popular culture. | Hispanic Americans—
    Ethnic identity. | Television programs—United States—History.
Classification: LCC PN1992.8.H54 B45 2021 | DDC 791.45/652968073—dc23
LC record available at https://lccn.loc.gov/2021011953

New York University Press books are printed on acid-free paper, and their binding materials are chosen for strength and durability. We strive to use environmentally responsible suppliers and materials to the greatest extent possible in publishing our books.

Manufactured in the United States of America

10 9 8 7 6 5 4 3 2 1

Also available as an ebook

For all of the Latina and Latino writers, producers, actors, and other creative professionals who forged a path as storytellers and performers in the television industry when none existed, and to all of those who will follow. Thank you for helping us recognize, love, and laugh at ourselves on the screen, and especially to dream. This book is dedicated to you.

CONTENTS

Introduction

Television and Latina/os' Place in the Nation

When we first started, when I first started, there was not the awareness there is today of the Latino presence, of the impact of who we are. Nor was there an openness particularly to who we were as possible people to be on your show.
—Jesús Treviño, producer of *¡Ahora!* (1969–70) and *Acción Chicano* (1972–74), writer, and director

The dominant culture gets to have complicated narratives in the media . . . but we're either cartel or we're squeaky-clean girls. The big, radical thing that I'm trying to do is to portray Latinas as complex human beings.
—Tanya Saracho, writer–executive producer of *Vida* (2018–20)

In early 2021, Latina/os in the US have a fraught relationship with English-language television, with ramifications seen in our tenuous place in the national imaginary.[1] We're often invisible—simply not included in the TV story worlds that US and global viewers passionately engage in. To begin to understand these dynamics, we might start with the 2015 Golden Globe Awards. When Gina Rodriguez, the Puerto Rican star of *Jane the Virgin* (2014–19), was awarded Best Actress in a Television Series—Musical or Comedy, she accepted the award with a poignant speech that underscored the importance of the series and her role even while Latina and Latino characters are still often left out of television story worlds. "This award is so much more than myself," she told viewers. "It represents a culture that wants to see themselves as heroes." Rodriguez expanded backstage that it helped Latina/o viewers "see themselves invited to the same party" that is American television.

1

As Rodriguez implied in her acceptance speech, while we've seen limited progress for Latina/os in richly drawn series such as *Jane the Virgin*, *Vida* (2018–20), *Gentefied* (2020–), and *One Day at a Time* (2017–20), they remain scarce, especially in lead roles in scripted narratives. When they do appear, it is often in skewed representations that depict them as sexier and more irrepressible than other people (think Sofía Vergara's Gloria Delgado Pritchett on *Modern Family* [2009–]), as more aggressive and criminal (as we've witnessed in series such as *Narcos* [2015–17] and *Breaking Bad* [2008–13]), or as less intelligent or otherwise unable to assimilate to the norms of Anglo American culture, as eternally goofy Fez—from an unknown, but clearly Latin American country—demonstrated in *That '70s Show* (1998–2006).[2] These patterns, which have structured much of the construction of Latinidad in US English-language television since its birth as a commercial medium in the late 1940s, and earlier in film and literature, have been broadly documented over the years by researchers and media advocates and in journalistic accounts.

These representational patterns are compounded by cultural norms and industry paradigms that have until recently largely kept Latina/os outside the professional roles that are focused on developing the stories that we watch for entertainment, escape, and inspiration. As statistics gathered by the Writers Guild of America and other studies of television professionals underscore, Latina/os are dramatically underrepresented as creators, writers, and producers. While they were 18.7 percent of Americans in 2020, they constituted just 4.7 percent of working television writers during the 2019–20 television season.[3] While the door to television writing and producing has cracked opened in recent decades, it is only slightly ajar, with just a small handful of Latina and Latino professionals employed in these roles even in 2021. Until recently, Latina/o cultural labor and the personal stories and perspectives of Mexican American, Puerto Rican, and other Latina/o writers and producers have seldom driven scripted English-language television.

The effects of all of these patterns are far reaching. The cultural forum of television, so central to national identity, has through exclusion from employment, erasure, and misrepresentation reinforced notions that Latina/os' place in the US mainstream is uncertain. For this reason, cultural citizenship and the struggle to achieve it is one of the central concerns of this study. Cultural citizenship describes a social group's participation in symbolic acts of citizenship, which both empower that group and signal their inclusion in the mainstream. Individuals enact it, among other things, through engagement and leadership roles in social institutions, through voting and holding political office, and in making and consuming media.[4] It should be noted that cultural citizenship rests on status and voice being shared by the dominant group. For Latina/os in the US, the continuing struggle to achieve it is tied to the histories of US Latina/o communities experiencing racism and disenfranchisement, or as Hector Amaya describes it, "citizenship excess," by which white Americans over the last centuries have experienced an excess of the rights and privileges of citizenship and Latina/os have experienced a deficit.[5] These dynamics are reinforced by patterns of representation and by the media industries themselves. Claiming a voice and telling our stories in the entertainment media, and pushing for greater Latina/o empowerment and agency within the media industries, thus both reflects and reinforces Latina/o cultural citizenship.

Gloria Anzaldúa raised the same point in her inimitably poetic fashion with her concept of *haciendo caras*, or "making face."[6] Anzaldúa writes of how empowerment is achieved through women sharing their own stories and truth (their own "face" in the world), rather than letting themselves be described and understood through the stories of others. I bring this to bear on understanding that Latina/o television storytelling that is especially impactful, and often more commercially successful, is truthful, culturally and otherwise, to Latina/o experience, history, and perspectives. *Haciendo caras* also includes the plural: "making faces," or content that challenges others. It's the look "that says 'Don't walk all over me,' the one that says, 'Get out of my face.'"[7] This dynamic underscores that resistance and activist stances are also part of cultural citizenship, and often are part of a group's history of survival and resilience within the United States.

Even so, Latina/os in the United States have a long history of not being able to "make face," linked to their early exclusion from participating in the production of English-language film and later television. This study traces the slow but incremental growth of Latina/o cultural production in US television and the negotiations that this has entailed.

A growing number of Latino and Latina series creators (showrunners, in industry speak), producers, and other creatives are bringing Latina/os into television story worlds and beginning to tell their own stories and produce and promote Latina/o programming. These efforts have necessarily involved navigations, and at times battles, within the industry and in society, to advocate for Latina and Latino narratives as worthy of a spotlight in national and local television. In *Latino TV: A History*, I survey these histories and the resulting television narratives over the decades in broadcast, cable, and digital television that have offered glimpses of Latina/o lives and perspectives.

I should insert a disclaimer here: I don't mean to imply that nuanced and appealing Latina/o narratives are necessarily only created by Latina/o writers and media makers, or that Latina/os can only tell Latina/o stories. A project such as this one requires making generalizations under the broad umbrella of Latinidad writ large; my intention is not to essentialize Latina/o creators and writers, who are not by any means a monolith who automatically create and produce mediated narratives that come across as relatable to a majority of Latina/o viewers. However, it has been borne out over the last seven decades of US television that it has usually been Latina/o creators who care about Latina/o narratives and about telling them with veracity and affection. Regardless of the creator's ethnic background, progress in Latina/o television can be understood as storytelling with sincerity to a specific Latina/o community from the estimation of that community. In foregrounding the concept of cultural sincerity, there's another term that I avoid here, "cultural authenticity," which involves agreed-upon images and narratives and can result in a caricature of a community.[8] There can be a fine line between representation that comes across as sincere to a creator's vision and community and representation that comes across as a politically correct (or, for that matter, insulting) facsimile that stereotypes a community, however. Even for Latina/o creators, this is another minefield that they navigate in telling their and their community's stories.

Understanding the terrain and impact of television storytelling for Latina/os both as viewers and as cultural laborers is particularly important today because of the hostile political climate that Latina/o citizens and immigrants are facing in 2021. In 2016, after Donald J. Trump was elected president of the United States, in large part by stoking white supremacist ideologies and sentiments, the US took a decisive turn toward more entrenched anti-Latina/o and anti-immigrant sentiment and policies. Deportations, the inhumane detention and treatment of Latin American children and families seeking asylum, and hate crimes against Latina/os rose sharply. All of this makes starkly clear the importance of representation. Mediated narratives showcase, reinforce, and challenge popular notions about Latina/o individuals and communities, while a lack of representation on and behind the screen obscures the realities of our experiences, denying Latina/os a place in the imagined mainstream of the nation. Trump and his cheerleaders at Fox News while he was president often emphasized nightmarish images of Latina/os as criminals, gang members, and people with problems. The presence of a Gina Rodriguez or George Lopez on our screens, in contrast, helps dismantle those ugly characterizations. Misrepresentation, in intent and effect, robs Latina/os of their humanity and can harm the self-esteem of Latina/o youth. Conversely, when given opportunities to tell our own stories, Latina/os are able to use television to educate viewers regarding our active and influential place in the nation and national history, to empower ourselves, and to feel valued. To put it more succinctly: How Latina/os are depicted and given a voice in scripted television makes a difference in their lives and futures.

This brings us back to the overlapping topic of Latina/o cultural citizenship. Cultural citizenship is linked to participation in the popular culture, which is constructed primarily by the dominant members of the group. Viewers absorb valued American ideals through media texts such as television story worlds—in other words, through the characters that they return to week after week or in a few nights of binge viewing. Our favorite series construct a fantasy community that effectively offers us lessons on who is a valued citizen and who isn't. As Kristal Brent Zook said, "It's about who we allow to dance inside our heads, and why."[9] So, whose stories are told in our television worlds? Who are the heroes and heroines, held up as intriguing, loveable, and compelling? Which characters are fully realized, rather than cardboard villains and sidekicks? And who are our storytellers? Exploring the histories of Latina/o television narratives and the authors of those narratives sheds important light on how Latina/os have been included (and more often not included) in the television industry and the country writ large.

I'm indebted in this work to a number of scholars who have studied how media narratives and industry practices have not just depicted Latina/os but played a role in how they're positioned in the American imagination. In my research I've relied on the work of Chon Noriega, Angharad Valdivia, Charles Ramírez Berg, Dolores Inés Casillas, Arlene Dávila, Isabel Molina-Guzmán, María Elena Cepeda, and many others.[10] I also build on scholarship that has explored individual television series featuring Latina/o protagonists, and that has documented the underrepresentation of Latina/os in television and in professional roles.[11] Surprisingly, while a few scholars have studied US television series with major Latina/o characters and themes, a broad history of Latina/o representation and authorship in television has yet to be written. In this study I begin to excavate this history, tracing how television narratives and their production dynamics behind the scenes constructed Latina/os and Latinidad for US audiences and how creative professionals have played a role in forging them.

I argue that television is not just a cultural forum, as Horace Newcomb and Paul Hirsch posited in their seminal essay in 1983, but a cacophonous theater of competing story worlds and visions of the nation.[12] In this storytelling battleground for meaningful inclusion, representation signals not just a place in popular culture, but also citizenship—with all of its associated protections and rights—and status. It includes telling our own stories, as opposed to merely being depicted through others' visions.

As I detail in the chapters that follow, this has only gradually become a possibility, as more Latina/o families have entered the middle class and younger generations are achieving the education and training that makes it possible to enter the realms of screenwriting and media production. It also involves a revolution of industry mindset and culture. The production culture of the television industry and its written and unwritten policies and practices have clearly influenced the possibilities for Latino and Latina employment and professional advancement. These struggles continue as I write this introduction in 2021.

But first, we need to learn how we got here. I endeavored in this study to uncover the series and writers, producers, and actors that have had a major impact on Latina/o representation in US television across seventy years of television history. Among these television histories is that of the first Mexican American TV gunslinger—based on a real-life figure—the subject of the Disney children's Western series *The Nine Lives of Elfego Baca* (1958–61), and the first Chicano and Puerto Rican public affairs series, among them, *¡Ahora!* (1969–70) and *Realidades* (1971–77), produced by activist-minded Chicano and Puerto Rican producers, respectively. I explore a score of failed series with Latino and Latina protagonists in the 1970s, 1980s, and 1990s as artifacts of programming that was produced with little or no Latina/o creative input or attention to Latina/o audiences. Finally, I examine how in more recent decades Latino and Latina showrunners such as Dennis Leoni, George Lopez, and Gloria Calderón Kellett made their way into the industry and bridged the diverging interests of their personal vision, their network, their audience, and others with interests at stake with respect to television about Latina/o characters and communities. In large part through their navigations of these competing interests and their own creative efforts, we are beginning to witness changes in how Latina/os are imagined, by the television industry and beyond. *Latino TV: A History* brings to light these previously submerged histories.

Come Quick! Looking for Latina/os on TV

What ends up on the screens in front of us has a profound impact on our sense of belonging and the belonging of other groups in our communities and nation. We're typically not even aware of it, however. As a kid growing up in Seattle, Denver, and Southern Illinois in the 1970s and early 1980s, I didn't think a lot about the fact that there was almost no one on television who looked like me or my mixed Mexican and German and English American family. My Mexican mother had made a choice over a decade earlier to prioritize her four children speaking perfect, unaccented English after a teacher's mistreatment of my oldest brother for speaking Spanish at school; she stopped speaking Spanish at home. As a result, the world of Spanish-language television wasn't open to me. I instead watched reruns of *Gilligan's Island* (1964–67) and *The Mickey Mouse Club* (1955–59), and shows like *The Brady Bunch* (1969–74), all series in which the characters having adventures had fair skin and nondescript accents. Latina/o Americans simply didn't exist. I noticed but didn't really connect with the few exceptions, like flamboyant Spanish American musician and personality Charo, who appeared regularly on *Hollywood Squares* and occasionally lit up the screen on nighttime talk shows with her exaggerated, broken English and sweet, flirtatious style. (She was always willing to play up her foreignness for laughs, with an ebullient "Cuchi-cuchi!"—her catch phrase—but was also a virtuoso flamenco guitarist).[13] The only Latina or Latino characters that I remember from that time are cheerful and funny Mexican American mechanic Chico, played by Freddie Prinze on *Chico and the Man* (1974–78), Puerto Rican–Jewish high school student Juan Epstein, played with comic absurdity by Robert Hegyes on *Welcome Back, Kotter* (1975–79), and earnest dance student Coco Hernandez, portrayed by Erica Gimpel on *Fame* (1982–87). Despite the fact that of the three actors performing, only Prinze was of Latina/o descent,[14] these characters and their narratives stuck out because they looked a bit like me and reminded me of my Mexican American family and Mexican relatives. Most of the time as I watched television, that wasn't the case.

While we've witnessed a small blossoming of creative and compelling new Latina/o television series in recent years, for decades this scarcely seemed possible. The evolution of Latina/o televisual representation over the last seven decades tells us a great deal about how Latina/os' place in the national imaginary has remained largely static even while we have grown in numbers in the US. In the 1950s, Latina/os were seldom seen outside of *I Love Lucy* (1951–57) and Western series, making a performer's appearance or guest starring role an event that would have people rushing to call their *hermanas* to turn on their TV sets; Latina/os were tallied as only 2.8 percent of Americans at the time. They have grown steadily since—to 6 percent of Americans in 1980, 13 percent in 2000, and almost 19 percent in 2020—making them the largest non-white ethnic group in the country. By 2045, it is estimated by the US Census Bureau that Latina/os will be 24.6 percent, a fourth of the population.[15] Nevertheless, the percentage of Latina/o or Latin American television characters has shifted only slightly across these decades. A recent study that examined ethnic and racial representation in television, the aforementioned *Hollywood Diversity Report 2019*, found that in 1,316 broadcast, cable, and digital series of the 2016–17 season, Latina/os were just 6.2 percent of scripted broadcast series characters, 5.3 percent of cable series characters, and 7.2 percent of streaming series characters.[16] Clearly, we haven't come far since the days of *I Love Lucy*.

Latina/o underrepresentation on and behind the screen was, and sometimes still is, exacerbated by misunderstandings among network executives regarding Latina/os' language preferences and related media habits. In studies of Spanish-language radio and Spanish-language advertising and television, respectively, Casillas and Dávila make strong cases for Spanish as a key node of historical and ongoing cultural connection within Latina/o communities and for first-generation Latina/o Americans in particular.[17] This continues to be true; 47 percent of Latina/o respondents reported in a 2020 study by digital media company H Code that they consumed at least some Spanish-language entertainment and news media in their daily lives.[18] But 30 percent of all respondents reported that they also consumed English-language media daily, while 53 percent engaged only with English-language media, underscoring the importance of English-language television to Latina/os and the popular construction of Latinidad, especially in recent years. Given that Latina/o Americans are particularly youthful, with a median age of thirty in 2019 compared to forty-four for white Americans, the media habits and interests of younger Latina/os also are and will be increasingly influential.[19]

Meanwhile, however, Latina/os ourselves are often divided and confused about our identities and cohesion as a racialized ethnic group. As individuals with histories in the United States, Central and South America, and the Caribbean, and with widely distinct appearance, racial identities, economic status, and so on, Latina/os often are more different from than similar to one another. The fact that there is no one ethnic label we all embrace is just one of the indicators. While "Hispanic" has lost favor with many academics, it still is popularly used as a personal label by many people, including many of my students from South Texas. Others prefer "Latino," while scholars in particular have taken up the more gender inclusive "Latina/o" or "Latino/a," which underscore that women are included, or "Latinx" or "Latiné," which are gender fluid and have become popular especially on college campuses and with younger adults since the late 2010s. The more politicized terms "Chicano," "Chicana/o," and "Chicanx," rooted in the 1960s–70s era of the movement for Mexican American civil rights, also are used as a personal identifier, especially by individuals with an affinity to these ongoing social and political battles. Many Americans aren't sure of which term to use or why; the reality is that they are all "correct" and a matter of personal choice.

In recent years, Latina/os have grown as a consumer market and an audience that advertisers and media producers can no longer ignore. With a purchasing power of more than $1.5 trillion in 2017, Latina/o millennials are becoming a driving force in the economy, with a swathe of marketing and media companies helping advertisers to reach them. Latina/os and particularly the large young adult generation are increasingly essential to the survival of media providers in the US, and English-language television, including broadcast, cable, and digital programming, is a key medium within these dynamics.

Critical Approach and Methods

With a focus on the evolution of Latina/o representation and storytelling in US English-language television, this study chronicles many of the influential series and their creators over the last seven decades, as well as examining the industry climate for Latina/o creative professionals since the 1950s. My research combines textual analysis of relevant episodes, promotional texts, and tie-ins with linked cultural artifacts, interviews with Latina and Latino media professionals, and discourse analysis of television criticism and news media discussions focused on Latina/o series, writers, and producers. Given that industry dynamics and employment patterns tended to block Latina/o employment and cultural production in the first decades of television, my early chapters focus most heavily on representation and on relevant production concerns, rather than on authorship. With respect to theoretical grounding, my analysis is rooted in turn in cultural studies, television studies, and Latina feminist studies scholarship, and is guided in part by research on media production cultures. It views television as a conduit of creative and political expression, as a medium that plays a role in uniting diverse Latina/os as an imagined community, and as a cultural forum where ideas about our cultural communities have been enacted, reinforced, and challenged on a national scale.

In the case of older series and series that never aired or were quickly canceled, copies of episodes at times were not preserved or archived, an illustration of the common lack of preservation of television and film artifacts of the Latina/o experience. I was able to locate and watch episodes of some of the series at the UCLA Film and Television Archive, the Library of Congress, and the Paley Center for Media in Los Angeles, as well as those saved on videotapes and DVDs or uploaded to YouTube. I also was able to locate a handful of scripts and videotaped interviews with television professionals archived in library collections at UCLA, the Wisconsin Center for Film and Television Research, and elsewhere. For series that were not preserved, my research involved the detective work of seeking out whatever extant traces I could locate, whether an image, credit sequence, or promotional bumpers (brief commercials for a television series) that had made their way to YouTube, Google Images, or eBay; mentions in interviews by the showrunner or star; or reviews in newspapers or trade journals. I also searched for and studied production documents when they were available. Although these materials were usually not preserved, I did find some items archived in the UCLA Libraries Special Collections, USC's Cinema and Television Library, the UCLA Chicano Studies Research Center, and the Wisconsin Center for Film and Television Research. Additional information on the production of series that were a part of my study was located in books on screenwriting, on television pilots and failed series, and in autobiographies, as well as in the digital archives of television columns that ran in local newspapers and trade publications such as *Variety* and *The Hollywood Reporter*.

Perhaps most importantly, I conducted interviews with television producers, writers, and actors involved with the series I studied whenever possible. The creative professionals that I was able to interview over the last several years in connection with this project included (alphabetically) Cristela Alonzo, Gloria Calderón Kellett, Enrique Castillo, Natalie Chaidez, Henry Darrow, Luis C. Garza, Mike Gomez, Dan Guerrero, Christy Haubegger, Bel Hernandez, Brenda Herrera, Ruth Lansford, Dennis Leoni, Luisa Leschin, Ruth Livier Nuñez, Katie Elmore Mota, Peter Murrieta, Rick Najera, Dyana Ortelli, Susan Racho, Luis Reyes, Dailyn Rodriguez, Paul Rodriguez, José Luis Ruiz, Tanya Saracho, Pepe Serna, Jesús Treviño, Ligiah Villalobos, JoAnne Yarrow, and Richard Yniguez. In addition, I relied at times on digital archives of interviews that professionals relevant to this project gave to the

Museum of Broadcasting, the Academy of Television Foundation, or another entity focused on preserving television history. Further information about the interviews is located in the appendix. Particularly for professionals who began working in television and film in the 1970s, the stories of their experiences were heartbreaking with respect to the dismissive and at times cruel climate in which they had to work. This book serves as a testament to these professionals' strength, resilience, and talent.

One of my major challenges in this research was in narrowing its scope. I realized early on that I could not study every relevant series in depth. To maintain a clear focus, I narrowed my research to scripted narrative programming for adult audiences, with a few caveats. I made two exceptions, in my exploration of Western series targeting children and families, the subject of chapter 1, and in examining Chicana/o and Latina/o public affairs shows of the late 1960s and early 1970s in chapter 2. I did so because of the importance of these series to later Latina/o television depictions and authorship. I also wasn't able to expand my study to Latina/o participation in televised professional sports like baseball or the more performative arena of professional wrestling, where they've often made a mark, and I chose not to explore unscripted or reality programming, where Latina/os have at times played prominent roles.

I then homed in on case studies that I felt best illuminate the evolving construction of Latinidad in television and the evolution of their employment as writers. I chose case studies based on which series were the most emblematic of influential trends in a specific era, whether episodes and extratextual materials were accessible, and whether I might be able to interview a producer or cast member or access interviews conducted by others. In choosing episodes to analyze in depth, when I had many to choose from, I favored those that focused in some way on Latinidad broadly, on a specific Latina/o community, or on Latina/o perspectives, and those that were particularly representative of the series premise and lead characters' roles in relation to the narrative. For this reason, I focused heavily on pilot episodes, given how important pilots and their ratings are to networks' programming decisions and how they serve as an introduction to a series and its protagonists.

Much of my focus ends up being on Mexican American representation and participation in television. This is because lead characters over the decades have until recently been mostly Mexican American, also the largest Latina/o national origin group.[20] Considering that the construction of Latinidad in US media culture has often entailed an awkward conflation of Latina/o groups, with Mexican American culture the most defining, an emphasis on these depictions sheds useful light as well. I also focus on Puerto Ricans and Latina/os of Cuban, Central American, and South American descent as they arise in the histories I uncover.

Latina/os in Television's First Years, and Overview of Chapters

To begin this chronology and to give an overview of the chapters that follow, it is helpful to examine how Mexican Americans and other Latina/os were positioned in relation to the medium in its first years, the late 1940s and early 1950s. This is the era in which television broadcasting—led by just four networks, CBS, NBC, ABC, and a now lesser-known network, Dumont—was a new phenomenon; American households were purchasing their first television sets. Meanwhile, white and Latina/o Americans often lived in sharply divided cities and regions, the result of de facto segregation that reinforced Mexican American and Puerto Rican marginalization in education, employment, and politics and made it very difficult for them to join the middle class.[21] It likely comes as no surprise, then, to learn that Latina/os were also not employed as creative professionals in television's first full decade.

Despite the television industry's eventual consolidation in Los Angeles, home to the largest Mexican American community in the nation, it was generally a closed shop to Mexican Americans and other Latina/os.[22] Given that the television networks were offshoots of radio networks, film studios, and film production companies and thus were already steeped in the employment cultures of Hollywood, Latina/os were not considered viable to hire in entry-level positions as writers or other creative professionals. There were also no Latina/o executives at the networks or individual stations—with the major exception of Desi Arnaz, the Cuban actor and musician who starred in *I Love Lucy* (1951–57) and became the president of Desilu Productions in 1950. These employment patterns were linked to dynamics not only of cultural exclusion but also of class and educational attainment; few

Mexican Americans and Puerto Ricans, the majority of Latina/os in this decade, were able to attain the education expected for employment as a television professional.[23] While better off economically than in previous decades, most could not dream of entering the work force of television creatives. As the guilds and talent agencies expanded to include the first television professionals, Latina/o employment simply was not a concern of the leadership of these organizations. Latino and Latina performers also seldom appeared on screen in 1950s and 1960s family sitcoms or variety shows, genres that factored heavily into the new medium's imagining of the nation.

An important exception was *I Love Lucy*. Desi Arnaz and Lucille Ball, his Anglo American wife in the series and in real life, became beloved stars akin to America's "first family" when their sitcom became a hit and as they integrated Ball's pregnancy and the birth of their son into the storyline. Arnaz's Cuban, rather than Mexican American, heritage and fair skin allowed him to be seen by US audiences as a classy foreigner rather than a stigmatized ethnic American. While Arnaz's role as Ricky Ricardo did demand that he exaggerate his accent, Ricky was also a successful musician and businessman; his character in fact was "straight man" to Lucy, his daffy and unpredictable wife. Arnaz and Ball also had creative control of the series. Arnaz became executive producer and the first Latino television executive as president of their production company, Desilu, in 1950. He was an important figure, and an anomaly, as a series creator, performer, and television executive.

Aside from *I Love Lucy* and television Westerns, Latino and Latina performers and characters were seldom seen in 1950s or 1960s programming. As mentioned earlier, they rarely performed on variety shows or as characters in family sitcoms. A few film stars, among them Anthony Quinn, Ricardo Montalbán, and Katy Jurado, were exceptions to the rule in occasional guest starring roles and rare lead roles in anthology drama series.[24] These series, popular in the 1950s and 1960s, presented teleplays, often written by famous playwrights and novelists, that were broadcast as stand-alone narratives each week. Less famous actors might be found in the TV Western. In series like *The Cisco Kid* (1950–56) and *Bonanza* (1959–73), most played bumbling cowboys and servants, typically with broken English and a servile demeanor, or more immoral Mexican criminals. A few fair-skinned Latino heroes, cowboys, and vigilantes of great integrity also appeared in roles reminiscent of Hollywood's Latin Lovers of the late 1920s and Good Neighbor musical films in the 1940s.

This is where I began my study. These narrative patterns in 1950s children's TV Westerns, and their lessons on Latinidad for US audiences, are the subject of chapter 1, "1950s: Border Heroes: Kids' TV Westerns and Mexican American Marginalization." In this chapter, I explore how Latina/os were depicted in *The Cisco Kid* (1950–56) and *The Nine Lives of Elfego Baca*, and connections to the submergence of Mexican American histories in national cultural memory. I begin with *The Cisco Kid*, which featured the heroic exploits of the eponymous Spanish-Mexican vigilante, and Pancho, his less intelligent Mexican American sidekick. Adapted from radio and film by Ziv Television, it paved the way in many respects for what would later become sedimented patterns of Latina/o portrayals. I ask how this series and the ideologically similar *The Nine Lives of Elfego Baca* taught American youth and adults a version of American history that underscored the exceptionalism of "whiter" Latina/os and European Americans. *The Nine Lives of Elfego Baca*, a family miniseries produced by Walt Disney Productions for *Walt Disney Presents* (1958–61), was notably based on the exploits of a real-life Mexican American gunfighter and lawyer in New Mexico, although it submerged Baca's Mexican American ethnicity after the first episode. Finally, I find a critique of these narrative patterns in a surprising place, the animated Hanna-Barbera series *The Quick Draw McGraw Show* (1959–62). In my conclusions, I highlight the power of parody to critique patterns of established ethnic hierarchy, underscoring how even long-term depictions and historical erasures can be challenged.

In the chapter 2, "1960s–70s: By Us, For Us: Chicana/o and Nuyorican Activist Television," I relate the story of the first Chicana/o and Latina/o producers and writers in television. This was in the late 1960s and early 1970s, as a number of activists agitated for media industry reforms, often beginning with their local public television stations and commercial network affiliates, and began to work as producers of public affairs series focused on their communities. I examine the first television programs created and produced by Chicana/o, Nuyorican, and white television producers for local Mexican American, Latina/o, and other audiences. These included the first Mexican American drama series, *Canción de la Raza* (1968–69), produced by the Los Angeles PBS affiliate KCET; the first Mexican American public affairs shows, *¡Ahora!* (1969–70), *Fiesta* (1969–70), and *Periódico* (1969–70), produced and aired in Los Angeles, Tucson, and San Antonio, respectively; and the first Puerto Rican show, *Realidades* (1971–77), in New York City. These were prompted by activists and public television staff who demanded that the medium include Chicana/o and Puerto Rican voices for the first time, and by a benefactor, the Ford Foundation, that funded several of these series. They inspired similar programs at network affiliate stations in Los Angeles, New York, and a few other cities. My research into this blossoming of early Latina/o television included interviews with several producers of these series. I explore how they negotiated the obstacles they encountered as they pushed local stations, the growing system of public television, and later the Corporation for Public Broadcasting to better address the needs of Latina/o communities. While these series for the most part did not survive beyond the 1970s, they offered an important showcase and training ground for Latina/o self-representation on television.

Given how Latina/os were able to make these inroads in public television, I next turn to commercial television in these same years. While network programming began to reflect younger Americans' growing interest in social issues, including race relations (with an emphasis on black and white Americans), generational clashes, and the women's movement, Latina/os seldom appeared in these story worlds, and Latino and Latina writers were not offered entry or training to work on these series. In chapter 3, "1970s: Always the *Chico* (and Never the Writer)," I illuminate the industry lore and practices behind these dynamics as I examine several dramas and situation comedies that featured Latina/o lead characters. In particular, I study two series in depth, *Viva Valdez* (1976), which flopped, and *Chico and the Man* (1974–78), which was successful for a few years and made a star of its Puerto Rican and Hungarian lead actor, Freddie Prinze. For these few examples of Latina/os in 1970s story worlds, I engage in critical analysis of series episodes and study their production and promotion, as well as responses by critics and audiences. Both series notably did not choose to hire Latina/os to serve in writing or producing capacities, despite complaints from the actors in the case of *Viva Valdez*, and from viewers and media advocates in the case of *Chico and the Man*. I examine how they were they constructed for American viewers and the impact of the exclusion of Latina/os in creative roles.

Some industrial shifts, however minute, were nevertheless in motion, as series began to be developed in the 1980s and 1990s around a handful of Latino and Latina comedians and actors, and a few creative professionals were given opportunities. These deals did not lead to hit series or even to a long-running series, however, for reasons that I interrogate in chapter 4, "1980s–90s: 'What Works for TV': Series that Tried, and Failed." Here, I examine these failed Latina/o-centric series and pilots, with an emphasis on *a.k.a. Pablo* (1984) and *First Time Out* (1995) as illustrations of common strategies and misfires in the 1980s and 1990s, respectively, and how the networks viewed Latina and Latino characters, stars, creatives, and viewers. I find that these series, constructed almost entirely by non-Latina/o writers and producers, were hampered by industrial logics that viewed Latina/o characters and actors only narrowly and discounted the creative input of the few Latino and Latina creatives and consultants hired. Norman Lear's *a.k.a. Pablo*, starring Paul Rodriguez as Paul Rivera, was a notable exception with promise. In all, these series are instructional regarding the network practices and mindset that got in the way of more fully realized and appealing programming with Latino and Latina leads.

Further shifts began to be felt in the new millennium, as Latina/os had grown dramatically as a television audience. In the 2000s, a small number of Latino and Latina professionals were working as staff writers, and the first Latina/o creators and executive producers had a chance to produce successful series. These showrunners had to pull off a major balancing act in pleasing their networks and Latina/o and non-Latina/o viewers while also remaining true to their own vision for their series, however. In chapter 5, "2000s: By Us, For Everyone: Latino Storytellers Enter TV's Mainstream," I examine Latino-led series with respect to these dynamics, as a handful of male writers executive produced series that ran for multiple seasons. My case studies are three particularly influential series: *Resurrection Blvd.* (2000–02), helmed by Dennis Leoni; *George Lopez* (2002–07), executive produced in part by its eponymous star; and *Ugly Betty* (2006–10), created and co-executive produced by Silvio Horta. In particular I highlight how these creators' mining their own childhood memories and cultural experience enriched and provided compelling nuance to their narratives, while network dictates at this time still pushed them to put white audiences first in their storytelling.

The final chapter of the book is set only a decade later, in the 2010s, but reflects new possibilities for Latina/o cultural production and television in recent years. Latinas have been leading a wave of culturally specific and intimate programming that centers on complicated, relatable, and empowered characters; these series include *One Day at a Time* (2017–20), *Vida* (2018–20), *Gentefied* (2020–), and *Los Espookys* (2019–). Chapter 6, "2010s: The Latina Wave and Other Trends," explores the impact of Latina writers and showrunners whose narratives include feminist and culturally resistant content. The Latinas who led popular series on cable networks and streaming television in this decade include Gloria Calderón Kellett, Luisa Leschin, Dailyn Rodriguez, and Tanya Saracho, while Cristela Alonzo's experience as the first Latina to serve as writer, executive producer, and star of her own series (*Cristela* [2014]), is instructional as well. I examine Alonzo's *Cristela*, Calderón Kellett's *One Day at a Time*, and Saracho's *Vida* as case studies of the constraints faced by and possibilities for Latina-led and -focused television narratives. I find that all routinely challenged traditional norms of gender, race, family, and sexuality, even as they affirmed and entertained viewers.

Finally, in my conclusion, "'Dear Hollywood': The Ongoing Struggle for Latina/o Television," I address the implications of my findings and the ongoing battle over Latina/o television representation and authorship. Given that Latina/os often still struggle to find entrées into the industry and promotion to roles as series creators and executive producers, I conclude by asking why there has been so little progress on these fronts and what can be done to turn this around. I highlight interventions that are aiming to bring in and support Latina and Latino creatives, from the Latinx Pilot TV Project, which aims to shine a light on the most compelling new Latina/o pilot scripts each year, to informal professional groups that are working to build support and create community within the television and film industries. Like my sources, I find hope in the new storytellers who are just beginning to put their voices and stories out there.

1

1950s

Border Heroes: Kids' TV Westerns and
Mexican American Marginalization

For American families watching *Walt Disney Presents* on ABC on October 3, 1958, it may have been hard to imagine that they were witnessing the first Mexican American television hero. In the show's introduction before the first episode of *The Nine Lives of Elfego Baca* (1958–61), Walt Disney poured a barrel of shiny bullets on the floor to tease the "4000" that a lynch mob of cowboys used, fruitlessly, to try to kill Baca, a real-life lawman in a small town in New Mexico in 1884. As Disney told viewers, Baca shocked everyone when he walked away from the assault without a scratch, the first of many impressive feats of his illustrious life. The episode kicked off a ten-episode miniseries loosely based on the exploits of the real-life legend, a former peace officer, lawyer, and politician known for standing up for the rights of his fellow Mexican Americans.

The Nine Lives of Elfego Baca was one of a few popular children's Western and adventure series with Latina/o main characters in the 1950s and early 1960s. It may be surprising to learn of these series, considering that it's a rare occasion when a television narrative focuses on a brave and capable Latina or Latino hero even today. These series included *The Cisco Kid* (1950–56) and *The Nine Lives of Elfego Baca*, the main case studies in this chapter, and the Disney adventure series *Zorro* (1957–59), which included a number of narrative parallels, but in a sword-fighting adventure context. The Hanna-Barbera animated series *The Quick Draw McGraw Show* (1959–62) also subtly parodied some of the tropes and patterns of all of these series, showcasing the counter-hegemonic potential (and delightful humor) of satire that critiques the racialized expectations embedded within the Western genre.

The distinctive characters of these series carried a heavy burden of representation because of Latina/o invisibility in other popular television genres in late 1940s, '50s, and '60s.[1] Aside from Desi Arnaz in *I Love Lucy*, discussed in the introduction to this book, Latina/os were almost never seen in family comedies, variety shows, or dramas in these decades.[2] And while Latina/o characters in film Westerns would usually not be a point of pride—they were typically incorrigible criminals, simpleminded servants, or hapless peasants—in *The Cisco Kid* and *The Nine Lives of Elfego Baca*, the Latino protagonists were depicted as heroic, even while their sidekicks possessed less admirable traits. What lessons of Latinidad and Latina/o cultural citizenship were conveyed in these constructions? Analysis of these series reveals how television and other media narratives played a role in the submerging of Mexican American histories, particularly of violence and marginalization experienced by Mexican Americans and Mexicans in the years in which the narratives were set, all while packaged as lighthearted children's and family entertainment. It also underscores the impact of the dearth of Latina/os in the television industry in the 1950s and early 1960s; all of these series included no Latina/o creative input in their development or production.

The success of these series was linked in large part to the popularity of the genre. The children's radio, film, and now television Western, which targeted white American boys in particular, aimed to convey "lessons in patriotism, fairness, and other traditional values designed to protect them from communism and juvenile delinquency in an era of rapid change," as Gary A. Yoggy notes.[3] In these adventure stories, "good always triumphed over evil, crime did not pay, and the hero was invariably brave, just, kind, smart, and tough."[4] What was less often questioned was how goodness was subtly and not so subtly equated with whiteness, while US histories of systemic violence against non-white groups were obscured. In radio and television narratives that loosely adapted mythology about the Texas Rangers, for instance, including *The Lone Ranger* (1933–56 radio; 1949–57 television) and *Tales of the Texas Rangers* (1950–52 radio; 1955–58 television), the Rangers were celebrated as heroes, while a cultural amnesia regarding the Texas Rangers' systematic anti-Mexican violence was encouraged.[5] *The Cisco Kid* and *The Nine Lives of Elfego Baca*, while uniquely focused on Mexican American protagonists, also rewrote history in similar ways.

Needless to say, executives of the networks, which in this era were NBC, CBS, ABC, and Dumont, and producers appear to have paid little attention to Mexican American and other Latina/o viewers in these years. This likely was due in part to presumptions about their small numbers within their audience. While Mexican Americans had a substantial presence in some Southwestern cities, in 1950 they were tallied by the US Census Bureau as only 2.5 percent of Americans, although this was likely an undercount.[6] Some Latina/os also consumed some or all of their media in Spanish, making it easier for the English-language networks to disregard them, although some certainly watched English-language television and were among the purchasers of the first television sets.[7] Regardless, they were an afterthought at best in English-language TV programming decisions.[8]

It was within this social and industrial context that *The Cisco Kid*, about a vigilante of Spanish-Mexican descent and his Mexican American sidekick, became the first TV Western that was a smash success with young American viewers and with families. Produced and broadcast in syndication by Ziv Television, it helped sell television sets and encouraged the greenlighting of adult TV Westerns by the last half of the decade.[9] It and other children's TV Westerns presented a particular picture of Mexican Americans in the 1800s, however. That picture rested on seeming contrasts constructed between whites and Latina/os, and between Latina/os of primarily Spanish heritage versus those of indigenous heritage. The clear appeal of this bifurcated representation established a paradigm still felt in contemporary Latina/o media images and narratives.

How did children's Westerns that centered on Mexican American protagonists affect the way Latina/os were viewed by the wider American audience? In my exploration of *The Cisco Kid* and *The Nine Lives of Elfego Baca*, I work to uncover their appeal, how they might have inspired children's play, and what they ultimately "taught" young Americans about Mexican American history and American identities. I also explore Disney Productions' construction of US history and ideals through its Elfego Baca merchandising and the Frontierland section of Disneyland theme park. Finally, I examine an animated series popular with adults as well as children that cleverly lampooned the children's Western: Hanna-Barbera's *The Quick Draw McGraw Show*. Its main characters, Quick Draw McGraw and Baba Looey, offered a satirical take on *The Cisco Kid*. Baba Looey, a mule costumed in manner reminiscent of Pancho in *The Cisco Kid*, is smart and wily, especially in comparison to his companion, the hapless horse gunslinger Quick Draw McGraw. With broad humor, it exposes the discursive schisms of the distinctions set forth in *The Cisco Kid* that denigrate Latinidad when it's paired with mestizo heritage and broken English.

The lessons taught through series such as *The Cisco Kid* had a broad and lasting impact on Latina/o authorship and cultural citizenship. These series and characters established still-influential patterns for imagining Latina/os in television story worlds in relation to national histories and, behind the scenes, for who had the ability and right to be national storytellers. They unfortunately positioned Mexican Americans (and by extension, all Latina/os) at the borders of American civic life, even while showcasing a few Latino protagonists' integrity and valor.

Westerns and Latina/os as "Foolproof" Entertainment: *The Cisco Kid* and *Zorro*

Mexican Americans faced a number of economic and cultural challenges in the 1950s, particularly throughout the Southwest, as historians such as Rodolfo Acuña, Vicki L. Ruiz, and Eric Avila have well documented.[10] These included political disenfranchisement, labor discrimination, and inferior schooling for children, issues that advocacy groups such as the League of United Latin American Citizens (LULAC) and the GI Forum called attention to and tried to combat.[11] Latina/os also had virtually no voice and negligible representation within the larger national popular culture, in films, radio programming, and now television programming. It was in this period that *The Cisco Kid* made its way to television, alongside *Hopalong Cassidy* (1948–52), *The Lone Ranger* (1949–57), and dozens of other, now less-known Western-themed children's shows that aired in the late 1940s and 1950s. These adventure dramas, which adults also enjoyed, now can seem almost interchangeable. Their "good" characters typically never faltered, their villains were purely evil, and each episode contained a problem or conflict that the heroes resolved within the half hour. However, *The Cisco Kid* was unique for making the hero Mexican American—but ambiguously so.

The Cisco Kid (1950–56) continued an already popular narrative pattern from film and radio, the pairing of a Spanish-Mexican gentleman vigilante and a mestizo sidekick who provided comic relief. In doing so, its writers were following a long and lucrative path of adaptation of the narrative from its original source, a 1907 O. Henry story, "The Caballero's Way." Over two dozen Cisco Kid films had been produced since 1914, while a successful radio version had been broadcast since 1942. Notably, in O. Henry's story, the Cisco Kid was an Anglo Texan who in fact brutalized and murdered Mexicans for amusement.[12] Film adaptations quickly altered this; a more positive characterization began in the late 1920s with the casting of Warner Baxter as Cisco in *In Old Arizona* (1928).[13] Cisco further morphed into a Latino Robin Hood type when he was played by Spanish and Cuban actor Cesar Romero, by Mexican actor Gilbert Roland, and by Duncan Renaldo, of Romanian descent, in the twenty Cisco Kid films that followed. Cisco's companion was added to the narrative beginning in 1928.[14]

This more lighthearted Cisco Kid story clearly appealed to children and adults, to which advertising-turned-broadcasting impresario Frederick Ziv took notice. Ziv and Walter Schwimmer at the Frederick W. Ziv Company purchased the story rights for both radio and television in 1942, despite the fact that television wasn't yet a national medium. The Ziv Company, then located in Cincinnati, Ohio, produced it as a radio series, with Ziv writing the first scripts. He aimed to maximize the action and drama and to make Cisco a hero that listeners would admire. As he stated, "I had to show why he helped the poor, and helped those who had no friends."[15] The series then was sold by the Ziv sales force to over 50 radio stations around the country; it aired on radio from 1942 to 1956.[16]

Ziv proved brilliant at promoting the *Cisco Kid* radio series. Employees of Interstate Bakeries, the show's first sponsor, wore sombreros and pins that read "Ask me about CK!" in the weeks leading up to the premiere. Children were given *Cisco Kid* pins to wear, and later convinced their parents to buy Cisco Kid toys, outfits, and products. Another promotional campaign, the Cisco Kid Triple S Club, taught the show's fans about "safety, scholarship, and strength"—and good behavior at home, at school, and in the community.[17] The merchandising and promotional campaigns helped make the series a household name. By 1948, Ziv had become the most prolific producer of radio programming outside of the networks, producing game shows, talk shows, and adventure dramas. *The Cisco Kid* was so steadily successful that Ziv decided it would be the first series the company would produce for television. He commented in an interview in 1975 that he chose it because he knew it could appeal to a broad cross section of viewers.

> We did not do highbrow material. We did material that would appeal to the broadest segment of the public. And they became the big purchasers of television sets. And as they bought television sets, the beer sponsors began to go on television. And the beer sponsors, for the most part, wanted to reach the truck and taxi driver, the average man and woman. . . . The Western is an almost foolproof entertainment vehicle.[18]

While Ziv found the narrative an easy sell because it emphasized action, it cannot be ignored that it featured two Mexican American buddy protagonists, which was unique in both radio and television at the time. Ziv was effusive about the show's appeal—and showcased the high-intensity sales drive that was part of his image—in an interview with Daniel Herbert Levoff. He said that both children and adults were drawn to *The Cisco Kid* because it contained

> not just excitement—not just law and order—but humor, romance, adventure, drama, heart appeal. It's a rampage or roaring adventure! . . . The Old West never dies! It lives forever in the heart of every American—in the imagination of every American kid—in the patriotism of every red-blooded American—in the pride of every woman (many of whose ancestors crossed the prairies in covered wagons).[19]

It's striking that patriotism is underscored by Ziv; this clearly was considered an *American* story. Levoff, after conducting several interviews with Ziv in 1969, points out that the Southwestern setting and Mexican elements of the narrative were also deemed as adding color and excitement, as well as a potentially romantic element for adult female viewers. The appeal of the Latin Lover characters and actors who played them in 1920s films, as described by Charles Ramírez Berg in his scholarship on Latina/os and Hollywood films, was likely quite similar.[20]

Ziv relied heavily on successful elements of the film and radio versions of *The Cisco Kid* in adapting the narrative to television. The pilot was produced in 1949, and the series went into regular production in 1950, with Interstate Bakeries as sponsor. A number of screenwriters of the *Cisco Kid* film serials, including several women, adapted their scripts as television episodes for the program's first season.[21] Ziv also chose to cast Duncan Renaldo and Leo Carrillo, who had played Cisco and Pancho in several films, despite their ages. Renaldo was in his 50s and Carrillo in his 70s at the time, making them older than many actors in similar roles. As noted earlier, Renaldo was of Romanian descent. He was an orphan who had grown up in part in Spain; he falsely claimed Spanish heritage in some interviews.[22] Carrillo was Spanish American, but often confused as Mexican American because his family had lived in California for generations. The confusion of labels attached to both actors reflected a common lack of knowledge of Mexican American history among journalists at the time.

The pilot, "Boomerang," aired in the late afternoon on September 5, 1950, on local stations around the country. Strangely, it begins without a great deal of introduction to the main characters, undoubtedly counting on young viewers (and their parents and grandparents) to already be familiar with them. It jumps right into a story of Cisco and Pancho contending with bandits impersonating them to commit a series of bank robberies. Jailed when they are mistaken for the impostors, the duo have to break out and capture the actual thieves to prove their innocence. The episode includes all the trademark elements expected in a *Cisco Kid* story: clear contrasts between a brave and honest Cisco and timid and less moral Pancho played up for excitement, adventure, and laughs; moments in which they ride their horses, Diablo and Loco, across "Western" terrain; a pretty young woman from whom Cisco gets a kiss by the end of the story; and the final refrain that ended every episode, Pancho and Cisco teasingly chiding each other with an "Oh, Cisco!" "Oh, Pancho!" as they ride off to another adventure.

Throughout the program's six seasons, Renaldo and Carrillo repeated their characterizations from the *Cisco Kid* films. Cisco and Pancho are close friends who are almost polar opposites; we're schooled in these differences in a number of ways. They have contrasting body types (Cisco is lithe, Pancho is portly), costumes, and commands of English, with

Figure 1.1. Duncan Renaldo and Leo Carrillo as the Cisco Kid and his companion Pancho in a promotional photo for *The Cisco Kid* (1950–56), roles they also played in films prior to the television series.

clear racialized and classed connotations that are at the heart of the narrative itself. In the series, Cisco wears the heavily embroidered jacket and tight-cut pants of the Mexican *charro*, in contrast to the cowboy or *vaquero* (a lower-class livestock or horse wrangler) outfit worn by Pancho. Cisco's outfit thus clarifies that he is not associated with the racialized labor and economic histories linked to Mexican Americans in the US Southwest. The reinforcement of Spanish domination of indigenous Mexicanidad is a subtle but palpable element of these constructions.[23] The distinctions between the two characters don't stop there. Cisco speaks like a well-educated and well-to-do gentleman, with proper English usage and just a hint of a Spanish accent. Pancho, on the other hand, has a strong Hispanic accent, and constantly butchers English, favoring solecisms (He was known for saying "Let's went!" whenever he and Cisco face danger) and malapropisms (among them, "I will keep an eye

on him like peeping Tomcat"). This falls in line with how accent and dialogue historically were used in radio narratives and other media forms
to signal character's ethnicity or race, through reinforcing stereotypical
associations. As Shilpa Davé notes, these choices and their significance
for audiences were "intertwined with social and political relations and
part of larger cultural formations."[24] In this case, viewers are being in-
structed that a particular command of English is tantamount to American cultural citizenship.

In addition, Pancho is shown as not equal to Cisco in other meaningful ways. He is often timid while Cisco is brave (as in his line "Let's went
before we find ourselves dancing at the end of a rope. Without music!"
in "Boomerang"). While Cisco is attractive to young, beautiful (white)
women, and is forever romancing them—at least, long enough to steal
a kiss—Pancho often appears to be running away from them. Pancho
also has to be pushed by Cisco to not give in to his impulses for petty
thievery, as when he has to be warned by Cisco to keep his eyes—not
his fingers—on money in the sheriff's safe in "Boomerang." These narrative, video, and audio logics ultimately taught American viewers about
Cisco's inclusion in the American pantheon of heroism and Pancho's
converse inability to assimilate to American culture.[25] There were occasional moments that reversed these patterns, however. Pancho was
not always presented as unintelligent. In fact, there are a handful of
episodes in which his foresight proves helpful. The friendship between
Cisco and Pancho was also portrayed as warm and genuine, which was
perhaps why adults who became fans in their youth fondly remember
their interactions.

Additionally, there is a clear ambivalence about Mexican American
subjectivity expressed in the series, despite the presence of Pancho and
Cisco. To examine how Mexican American communities and characters
are depicted in the series, I searched for roles and guest stars with Spanish names or surnames. Surprisingly, by this measure at least, only seven
of the 156 episodes included Latina/o guest roles or cast Latina/o actors.
Of those that I did find, most depict Mexican Americans as meek townspeople in need of Cisco and Pancho's help or as underdeveloped criminals, whose reasons for stealing or hurting others are never revealed. In
"Thunderhead," Cisco and Pancho come to the aid of Mexican American
tenant farmers being mistreated by the overseer of the land. While the

farmers are unable to help themselves, Pancho does get to handily knock out a guy with a frying pan in this episode. Mexican American characters are similarly either passive and helpless or ruthless criminals in "The Bell of Santa Margarita," in which a town's lucky bell has been stolen by a Mexican man named El Puma (Cougar) and his gang. I should note that throughout the show's run, most of its many villains are white. This is mitigated, however, by well-developed and "positive" white male and female characters in each episode. That isn't the case for Mexican Americans and Mexicans, aside from Cisco and Pancho as heroic figures. The young women presented as love interests are white as well.

Other elements of series episodes contribute to a sense of ambivalence and confusion regarding Mexican American characters. When relatives of Pancho are included in story lines, it is in a decidedly awkward fashion. In "The Puppeteer," Pancho's Uncle Gitano, the titular puppeteer, tells his nephew that he's about to perform at a "grand fiesto" (mispronunciation his) in his town. White actor Raymond Hatton as Gitano (Spanish for Gypsy) has a vaguely Italian appearance and odd accent, and he and Carrillo come across more like strangers than uncle and nephew. A similar disconnect with the warmth of many Mexican American families is evident when another family relationship is depicted in "Not Guilty" and "Horseless Carriage." Both feature Mexican American comic actor Jose Gonzalez-Gonzalez as Jose Gonzales de la Vega, Pancho's nephew.[26] Short, tan, and with mestizo features, Gonzalez-Gonzalez lends authenticity to the role, in stark contrast to Carrillo's facsimile of a Mexican American. The family connection is not believable, but Gonzalez-Gonzalez does add youthful energy to his episodes. Cast as a comic figure, in "Not Guilty" José needs to be protected by Cisco and his uncle after he has witnessed a murder and is going to testify against the murderers. He is offered more leeway to present his own comedy style in "Horseless Carriage," in which he shocks Pancho when he appears in a friend's "borrowed" automobile—only to have it stolen by thieves and used in a bank robbery. Gonzalez-Gonzalez portrays José as a charming but goofy young man (a pretty young white woman in fact says he's "rather cute") in need of rescue by his uncle and Cisco. He has a shining moment as well, when he tricks the criminals and grabs one of their guns, saying "Ha! José is smart, too!"

Finally, "The Devil's Deputy" notably includes a rewriting of Mexican American history when Pancho poses as a town's new marshal. It in fact is a performance of a performance, brought about when a corrupt white businessman mistakes him for a small-time criminal he had hired to impersonate the town's law enforcer; at Cisco's behest, Pancho keeps up the act so they can end the swindle. In a turn that can only be described as historical fantasy, the white townspeople are completely free of racism in their embracing of Pancho in this policing position despite his inability to speak English well; his ability to shoot bottles out of the air—four at once with the surreptitious help of Cisco—may have played a role. The narrative thus presents a false history of Mexican American inclusion in the US, while Pancho's shortcomings reinforce their marginalization. The episode is confusing mélange of implied acceptance and stigmatization of Mexican Americans, as can be said for the series as a whole.

Despite the ways in which the series effaced its own cultural roots, the series and its merchandising did stretch the archetype of the American hero, if only slightly, to include male adventurers of Latin descent. Ziv produced and sold *Cisco Kid* comic books and toys, clothes, Viewmaster reels, and countless other items, even bread labels emblazoned with images of Renaldo and Carrillo in character (one, for example, reads "A new *Cisco Kid* adventure: Pancho's Big Day!"). The company created a merchandising division in 1956 to take on this work, even as they stopped producing new episodes. And the series, its stars, and even the horses that played Diablo and Loco were a huge hit with its young fans. They asked their parents to purchase Cisco Kid toy guns and other memorabilia and flocked to promotional events to see the stars and horses in person. One such event, at a Detroit grocery store in 1951, drew a reported 64,000 youth and adults hoping to meet Renaldo.[27] What is not known is how *The Cisco Kid* may have directly influenced the ideas of American viewers. Mexican American writer Nash Candelaria writes in the short story "The Day the Cisco Kid Shot John Wayne" that for him and his friends in New Mexico, of all of the Western heroes, "our favorite was the Cisco Kid" because he had been played by Gilbert Roland, Cesar Romero, and Duncan Renaldo.[28] In other words, they knew Cisco was Mexican like them, unlike Hopalong Cassidy and so many others.

Kids not looking for Latino role models might miss Cisco's (if not Pancho's) ethnicity, however. This was quite possible because Mexican

American identity and culture is generally submerged in episode narratives and series promotion in favor of a more raceless ethos. As Kay Sanford, *Cisco Kid* account manager for Bing Crosby Productions, Inc., which purchased the rights to the series from Ziv in 1964, noted to Rouse, "The storylines shunned blood-thirsty violence and irreverence, but concentrated on wholesome, good-natured entertainment for junior and granddad alike."[29]

The Latino crime-fighting duo formula was soon to be repeated, in the Disney children's swashbuckling adventure series *Zorro* (1957–59). *Zorro*, like *The Cisco Kid*, already had proven successful as an entertainment vehicle. It had been adapted to film at least eight times and in multiple film serials.[30] Zorro also was a Robin Hood type, this time in 1820s California, when it was under Spanish colonial control. Spanish protagonist Don Diego de la Vega, soon to take on the mask of Zorro, also is a horseback-riding vigilante who helps oppressed people in need. *Zorro* also paired the gallant hero with a comic (and in this case, mute) sidekick, Bernardo, who presumably was also Spanish. In addition, it posed a more swarthy and foolish character, Sergeant Garcia, in contrast to Don Diego. In this regard, *Zorro* owes allegiance to the racial conventions of the Western, through which white characters always possess more intelligence and integrity than Mexican or Indigenous characters, clarifying the need for the "white" heroes to prevail and ultimately lead the new West.

Zorro was in the works for several years at Disney Productions before airing on television in 1957. Reportedly Disney decided to make it more appealing for the youth audience by foregrounding comedy as well as action.[31] Norman Foster, who had directed Disney's hit *Davy Crockett* series and had lived in Mexico for several years, was chosen to helm the early episodes. Foster's experience may have led to a warmer portrayal of Mexicans, mestizos, and Indigenous people (they were not yet Mexican Americans in this historical era) than the series would have presented otherwise, but it did not bring a higher standard of authenticity to the casting or the accents of the characters. Mostly non-Latina/o actors were cast in the many Spanish and mestizo Mexican roles. They included Italian American Guy Williams (born Joseph Armando Catalano) as Don Diego/Zorro, while Gene Sheldon (Eugene Search) was cast as Bernardo, Zorro's servant and companion. Henry Calvin (born Wimberly Calvin Goodman) was cast as the oafish Sgt. Lopez Garcia. The one recurring lead cast member of Mexican nationality (but of Spanish and Welsh descent) was George J. Lewis, who played Don Diego's father, Don Alejandro. While the historical setting would call for characters to speak Spanish, they instead spoke accented English with a few Spanish words thrown in.[32]

On October 10, 1957, the series debuted with "Presenting Señor Zorro." Set in El Pueblo de Nuestra Señora la Reina de los Ángeles (early Los Angeles) in 1820, it introduced Don Diego de la Vega, returning after three years attending a university in Madrid. He discovers that a corrupt political leader has taken control of the region. He and his valet, Bernardo, decide to secretly fight the corrupt regime. Don Diego will pretend to be a bookish nerd to fool the regime into thinking he is harmless while he fights in disguise as Zorro. His servant, in turn, will act deaf as well as mute. In this manner they try to help Don Alejandro and the rest of the community. The episode introduces Captain Enrique Sánchez Monastario, the self-serving commander who has taken control of the community, and Sgt. Garcia, the comic relief of the series.[33] Garcia sees himself as a friend of Don Diego and dreams of capturing Zorro for the reward money. The jokes are always on him, however. His lack of common sense and weakness for food and drink are constants throughout the series.

In differing ways, *Zorro* and *The Cisco Kid* both reflected and reinforced the imagined "fantasy heritage" of California, a term coined by Cary McWilliams to describe the popular emphasis on and romanticization of the state's Spanish colonial era.[34] McWilliams, writing in the 1940s, pointed to the many festivals honoring Spanish heritage throughout California at the time. As he elaborated, the appeal of this mythology was its submergence of uncomfortable facts regarding race and class relations for Mexican and indigenous Americans. For instance, while Spanish Americans, whose ancestors had subjugated Mexicans and indigenous people during the mission era, began to be included in California civic life after the turn of the twentieth century, Mexican Americans were still typically shut out. The stark contrasts between The Cisco Kid and Pancho, and Don Diego and Sgt. Garcia, in countless films, radio, and now television episodes make more sense if one thinks about how they comfortably echoed and reinforced this fantasy history. As McWilliams notes, "By a definition provided by *Californios* themselves, one who achieves success in the borderlands is 'Spanish'; one who doesn't is 'Mexican.' "³⁵ Similarly, *The Cisco Kid* and *Zorro*, through their pairing of "good" and "bad" Latinos in the form of Cisco/Pancho and Zorro/ Sgt. Garcia, enact a pedagogical process. These depictions ultimately teach viewers that Mexican Americans of darker skin tone, indigenous features, shorter height, and accented or less-than-perfect English are "Mexican" (and *not* American), are less intelligent and unable or un-willing to assimilate to American life, and, as a result, are unfit be part of the American mainstream. This contributed to the subjugation and marginalization of Mexican Americans as not true citizens and rightful leaders of these communities.

Perhaps unsurprisingly, Leo Carrillo is mentioned in McWilliams's scholarship on fantasy heritage. Described in the late 1940s by McWil-liams as "the man on the white horse," Carrillo is mentioned as a *Cali-fornio* who periodically would lead a retinue of riders performing as Spaniards through downtown Santa Barbara as part of the annual Fiesta celebration.³⁶ McWilliams points out the irony of Carrillo doing so, as a Spanish American famous (in films prior to this TV series) for por-traying Mexican Americans in a way that supported the subjugation of Mexican Americans of mestizo and indigenous descent in the country at large, actually reinforcing the erasure of Mexican American history through supporting the myth of Spaniards having had more influence on California's history. And it is striking, considering the obfuscation also of Mexican American history and experiences in *The Cisco Kid*, and the series' links to other fantasy heritage narratives.

American Heroism, According to Disney: *The Nine Lives of Elfego Baca*

The enduring patterns of representation reinforced in these series make Walt Disney Productions' *The Nine Lives of Elfego Baca* all the more intriguing. Elfego Baca's story is not one that we might normally expect to air on network television, even today. Baca, who lived from 1865 to 1945, had led a colorful life as a gunman, sheriff, attorney, and failed politician in New Mexico. Born in Socorro, New Mexico, in 1865, he was Mexican American and had spent much of his life working to help Mexican Americans get fair treatment in New Mexico and his later home of El Paso, Texas. A statue of Baca stands in Reserve, New Mexico, in honor of his heroism when he was trapped by the group of white cowboys who attempted to end his life with the "4000 bullets" of the legend. Most Americans living outside New Mexico were unaware of him, which makes Disney's memorialization all the more remarkable.[37]

It turns out that Davy Crockett had something to do with it. In 1954, Disney's *Davy Crockett* (1954–55) miniseries was a surprise hit. Children around the nation loved the adventure narrative about the Western legend of the 1820s. This was despite the fact that Crockett was much older than his character in the miniseries, preferred to be called David, and dressed like a gentleman rather than in buckskins. At their kids' behest, parents of fans of the miniseries bought countless coonskin caps, Davy Crockett toy guns, and other merchandise. It was in aiming to replicate the cultural and financial success of that series that Walt Disney assigned researchers in the late 1950s to find similar legendary heroes to further populate the Disney empire. They found three such heroic figures whose stories were turned into miniseries that aired on alternating dates on Walt Disney's Sunday night show in these years: "Texas John" Horton Slaughter, Francis Marion, also known as "the Swamp Fox," and Elfego Baca, the lone Mexican American in the group.

While it was an unusual move on Walt Disney's part to produce a series with a Mexican American protagonist, it doesn't appear that Mexican Americans were brought on as writers or consultants. The production also cast non-Latina/os in most of the Mexican American roles. For the lead, the production cast Italian American actor Robert Loggia. Loggia said in an interview with Leonard Maltin years later that he was given leeway by Disney to play the character as he saw fit. "Walt said, 'How do you want to play him?' I said, 'He's Mexican American. If he's gonna be the All American Boy, call him Jack Armstrong. He's gotta have that [Mexican] ethnicity.' And Walt went with it, so I played him with a definite accent and celebrated his ethnicity."[38] Lisa Montell, of French and Polish descent, was cast as Anita, the Mexican American woman who becomes Elfego's girlfriend. Italian American actress Annette Funicello, of *Mickey Mouse Club* fame, had a showy role in a few episodes as Anita's younger sister. Only a few Latina/o actors were cast. Mexican actor Rodolfo Hoyos Jr. (called "Rudy Hoyas" on an archived call sheet), who played an older relative of Elfego's, was the best known of these actors.[39]

Figure 1.2. Robert Loggia and Lisa Montell as Elfego Baca and his love interest, Anita Chavez, in the television miniseries *The Nine Lives of Elfego Baca* (and a Buena Vista Productions theatrical film later cut from the miniseries).

Walt Disney Presents had established Walt Disney as a maestro of American entertainment and proto-educator on US history for American families with children. Much of this image was established from the introductions he provided each week, often dressed in accordance with the genre or theme of that week's episode. It was in this role that on October 3, 1958, Disney dressed as a frontier sheriff to introduce the story of Elfego Baca, as noted in this chapter's introduction. After presenting the bullets that failed to fell Baca, Disney referred to him as the "Lighthearted adventurer, and lightning-fast gunfighter, but always on the side of justice. . . . Mexican Americans, whose lives he always defended, called him 'the man who couldn't be killed!'" In doing so, he subtly linked Baca to other American heroes that his company had lionized. He then introduced a trio of white male musicians, who sang a soulful folk song about Elfego Baca, with a chorus that went, "And the legend was that, like *el gato*, the cat, nine lives had Elfego Baca!"[40]

The episode begins in the small town of Frisco, New Mexico, in 1884 as Baca, a handsome, fair-skinned, clean-cut, and quietly confident young man, comes to visit his friend Sangano, only to find that Charlie McCarty, a white cowboy, is drunkenly shooting up the town and scaring its Mexican residents. When the justice of the peace is too afraid to stop him, Elfego deputizes himself (saying "We are American; same as they are") and calmly arrests the man. A mob of armed cowboys who work with McCarty try to coerce Baca to release him, however. Angered when that fails, they start shooting at Baca. They chase him into a townswoman's modest adobe shack, which they shoot up in a siege that extends overnight. Facing what would seem to be certain death, Elfego is composed, brave, and a good shot. He later thanks a religious figurine of Nuestro Señora Santa Ana in the shack, as he and it remain unharmed. The townspeople, meanwhile, can only watch anxiously from a nearby hill. The shack's owner, a comely young woman by the name of Anita Chavez (Lisa Montell), is the one villager who stays to see how he fares through the night. Amazingly, he walks out the next day untouched.[41] When Elfego later faces murder charges in court for killing four men during the assault, despite having acted to protect the community, he reacts by saying "Que barbaridad." Told to "Speak English!" he answers, "I only said, what a barbarity." While there are many Mexican Americans in the court room, watching, the jury is all white men (in real life they were Mexican American), and Elfego's case seems precarious.[42] However, he's found not guilty. The music swells, a blend of Mexican and big-band music; we're meant to see this as an example of white American progressivism, as he is able to go home. When Elfego later calls on Anita to pay her for the damage to her shack, he tells her that he plans to become a lawyer to help their people. He bravely faces the armed cowboys one more time, and is victorious even after their leader tries to shoot him in the back. Elfego hears him and shoots him in the arm instead, saying, "Remember if there's one to be tried and one to be buried, I'm going to be the one that's tried."

Elfego Baca thus was established through the narrative as a Disney-style American hero—as using violence only when necessary, as naturally smarter than his enemies, and as brave and resourceful. While he is

Mexican American, he is depicted primarily as raceless or simply as white after this episode. He is shown to see only actions, not race. For example, he later corrects the greedy behavior of his own Uncle Arturo, who has been charging local residents inflated prices on alcohol and food at his saloon and grocery store. While this episode constructs Elfego Baca as a heroic protector of his fellow Mexican Americans, over time, after he is elected sheriff of Socorro and is studying law, his focus becomes policing particular standards of behavior. He is reduced to just another lawman bringing "order" to New Mexico in later episodes, when his ethnic identity appears more ambiguous. In his introduction to episode 2, "Four Down and Five Lives to Go," Disney says Baca defended "pioneers," not mentioning that it was Mexican Americans that the real-life Baca was committed to avenging.[43] In the episode, Baca as sheriff is asked by the governor's office to arrest a "countryman" (a Mexican man) known as El Sin Verguenza (The Shameless One), who stole from and killed a mining company's paymaster. Baca follows the man to Mexico. After a chase on horseback and a shoot-out, he's able to capture him, force him back over the border, and arrest him. When Mexican American residents come to his jail to extract their revenge, demanding El Sin Verguenza for committing another murder, he won't do it. "You're not human beings anymore, you're a mob!" he tells them. However, in his absence the jailed men have shot his deputy and escaped. Baca again has to go after El Sin Verguenza, and finally kills him in a shoot-out. Being a hero here means vanquishing a Mexican menace *and* calming unruly Mexican Americans.

The casting of Annette Funicello as a Mexican American teen, Chiquita Bernal, in episode five, "Attorney at Law," was part of the further dilution of Mexican American presence and subjectivity in the series. In this episode, Baca helps Chiquita and her three siblings through aiding their father, who is being framed for a bank robbery he didn't commit. However, the casting of Funicello (and of Robert Loggia and other non-Latina/o actors) symbolically negates a sense of Mexican American subjectivity within the episode, along with empathy for the continuing inequities experienced by Mexican Americans in New Mexico at the time. Once again, a Mexican American hero is reduced to calming a Mexican American threat.

As Ferenc Morton Szasz notes, the series downplayed both Baca's ethnicity and the discrimination experienced by Mexican Americans.[44]

The publicity for the series, which in particular had targeted local news-papers, bears this out. Elfego Baca's actual legendary life was often em-phasized in Disney Productions' press releases. Joe Reddy wrote one as a laundry list of reasons why Baca was an exciting television hero for young viewers. This list began detailing that Elfego Baca "1. Was born on a baseball field, 2. Was captured by Indians, 3. Was a youthful associate of Billy the Kid," and that he "4. Held off 80 gunslingers for 33 hours, killed 4 of them, and was acquitted twice for murder."[45] The four-page memo includes no mention of his Mexican American ethnicity or of his work on behalf of his fellow Mexican Americans in New Mexico. With only a few exceptions, mostly in cities with large Mexican American popula-tions such as Albuquerque and San Antonio, newspapers also almost never mentioned Elfego Baca's ethnicity in their stories on the series. Some mistakenly described him as Spanish American or misidentified Robert Loggia as a Latin American actor.[46] Given the confusion and mixed responses in how newspapers discussed the series, it's unclear whether audiences would have realized Baca was Mexican American.

These obfuscations express ambivalence regarding whether Mexican Americans fit within the accepted history and constructed ideals of cul-tural citizenship of the United States. A typical Disney hero who uses "guile, not gunfire" to meet his goals, Baca's story was used to support an American mythology that our history has always been built on actions and ideals of fair play.[47] Contrasts are constantly set up, however, be-tween Baca, as brave, capable, well-spoken in English, and willing to do whatever it takes to combat lawlessness and to protect the innocent, and the other Mexican Americans and Mexicans that he encounters. Mean-while, the production team was constructing and reinforcing notions of Latinidad through its casting, costuming, and dressing of the sets used (for example, production materials at the Disney archives required that "Spanish" female extras have long dark hair and wear black shoes).

The Nine Lives of Elfego Baca did well enough that Elfego Baca toys and other merchandising followed its broadcast. American boys and girls could buy Elfego Baca holsters, toy guns, dime novels, and com-ics, and thus were given license to embody the Mexican American gunslinger and do-gooder in their play. As J. G. O'Boyle describes it, "in 1959, when the words *Hispanic, Latino,* and *Mexicanos* had yet to supplant the ethnic slur *wetback,* we re-enacted Baca's siege over and over. . . . It never occurred to us that there was anything odd about imitating a Mexican American hero whose rise to fame began by shooting it out with a mob of white cowboys."[48] A real-life Mexican American hero immortalized on television was a pioneering first, despite the fact that Baca's ethnicity was largely left unstated after the first episode.

Walt Disney's "imagineered" world of Disneyland adds another layer to how Elfego Baca might factor in to American children's play at this time. Notably, when *The Nine Lives of Elfego Baca* premiered, Disney Productions had recently opened its first theme park, Disneyland, in Anaheim, California. Its Frontierland section housed Disney's version of American history, including performances by actors who depicted such figures as Davy Crockett, Mark Twain, and, for several years, Elfego Baca.[49] His presence was important given that indigenous and Mexican American characters were typically absent or confined to the background at Frontierland, highlighting the borders of Disney's American history. The only clear Mexican American presence aside from Baca during these years were The Gonzalez Trio, two brothers and a sister who played traditional Mexican music in a small gazebo in the middle of Frontierland, and Casa de Fritos—a "Mexican" restaurant known for a completely inauthentic dish, Frito chili pie, using Frito-Lay's Frito corn chips.[50] Mexican Americans were consequently positioned as having a place in US civic life in relation to music and food, but not to the nation's history or hegemonic ideals of valor and justice at stake in the adventures of Frontierland.

Walt Disney Productions' films and television series of this period are now known for submerging elements of American history that might have been troubling to his young white viewers and their families; these dynamics are even more evident in the "happy place" he aimed for Disneyland to be as a tourist destination.[51] A wide swathe of scholars have written over the years about the implications of Disneyland's sanitization of the past.[52] Its five parks avoided acknowledging histories of conquest, slavery, or of racial and class inequities. For example, in the park's Hall of Presidents, "the plight of native Americans and of blacks after the middle of the last century is not mentioned; instead, we find references to freedom, the rights of individuals, and the dignity of 'man.'"[53] Attention to discrimination experienced by Mexican Americans would be particularly disturbing to Disneyland's version of US cultural memory; a whitewashed Elfego Baca apparently was as far as it could stretch in these years.

Erasure and Exceptionalism in Children's TV Westerns

The children's Westerns examined in this chapter had a complicated and profound impact. They constructed the first Latino television heroes, and clearly were enjoyed as such by American youth, Latina/o and non-Latina/o alike, in the 1950s and early 1960s. However, they also encouraged a complex misrecognition of the presence and impact of Mexican Americans in US history. This was fitting with the era, a time of what appears to be intense stigmatization of and ambivalence toward Mexican immigrants and, by extension, Mexican Americans. In 1942, the United States and Mexico had ratified the Mexican Farm Labor Agreement, known popularly as the Bracero Program. This agreement created provisions for Mexican workers to legally come to the US for farm jobs that Americans were not filling because of World War II. There was a backlash from some Americans, including laborers who feared Mexican workers would permanently take jobs away and farmers who feared it would inflate workers' wages.[54] In addition, the Supreme Court ruled in 1947 that Mexican American children had the right to attend city's primary public schools as opposed to inferior "Mexican schools" in *Mendez v. Westminster School District*, and in 1954's *Hernandez v. Texas* that Mexican Americans deserved the same rights as white and black Americans. Repercussions could be seen in Operation Wetback, with stigmatizing language front and center in its title, which President Dwight D. Eisenhower initiated in 1954. It enabled the forced deportation of undocumented Mexicans and some Mexican Americans, particularly in Texas and California. It was short-lived, but it broadcast support for the continued marginalization of Mexican Americans and erasure of Mexican American voices in US politics and popular culture.

Meanwhile, the televisual tales of the Cisco Kid, Don Diego de la Vega, and Elfego Baca conveyed a comforting fantasy version of national history, particularly when paired with Mexican and Mexican American companions and counterparts of mestizo heritage who are always comic or hapless in contrast. In place of Mexican American men and women who fought political and economic disenfranchisement, we have ethnically ambiguous gentlemen who protect white Americans and occasional pitiable Mexican Americans, and who fight Mexican villains in a substitution for cultural history. Elfego Baca, for instance, protects new "Americans" from evil Mexicans in the later episodes of the series, a far cry from the experiences of his real-life inspiration. These series and their promotional texts thus ultimately elided contemporary Mexican American political and cultural citizenship, even while they depicted a few Western heroes of Latina/o heritage.

These series and other television Westerns also offered stories and stances that relayed American ideals, as children elaborated on their narratives of heroism, law and order, and rightful citizenship. Using toys, costumes, and other merchandise linked to their favorite shows, American kids engaged passionately in Western play. Children would act out and repeat these scenes in their imaginations and on playgrounds; the effects, while subconscious, were likely profound. And Mexican American kids were not immune to their appeal. It's notable that Nash Candelaria remembers that he and his friends loved playing The Cisco Kid, rather than The Cisco Kid and Pancho. But what might *The Cisco Kid* have imparted to them if they or their parents looked or sounded more like Pancho than Cisco? A takeaway might have been that only a subset of Mexican Americans or other Latina/os would be able to enter the privileged space of whiteness (and thus full citizenship)—as long as they did not complain about the marginalization of others who were less lucky.

This isn't to say that no one behind the scenes or watching television in those days was questioning children's Westerns' assumptions, however. Surprisingly, *The Quick Draw McGraw Show* (1959–62), produced by the Hanna-Barbera animation company, offered a sharply satirical twist on the usual good/bad, Cisco/Pancho pairing. I remember watching reruns around 1970—it was funny, and for once the joke wasn't usually on us. It paired Quick Draw McGraw, an anthropomorphic horse gunslinger, and his burro sidekick, Baba Looey. Both were voiced by Daws Butler with distinctive accents that gave life to the goofy "white" cowboy and his English-butchering but *smart* Mexican American companion. Thus, while it's modeled in part on the The Cisco Kid duo, it

Figure 1.3. Baba Looey and Quick Draw McGraw in "Mine Your Manners," *The Quick Draw McGraw Show* (1961).

upends those expectations. Michael Maltese, known for his sharp wit, wrote most of the episodes, as head of the story department for Hanna-Barbera, based on characters created by animator Ed Benedict. While Baba Looey is regularly discounted by villains who judge him merely by his size or accent, he often gets the upper hand.

Unable to compete with larger animation companies like Disney and Warner Brothers, Hanna-Barbera was the first to give television a shot in the late 1950s. With *Quick Draw, The Huckleberry Hound Show* (1958–61), and *The Yogi Bear Show* (1961–62), they became known for creating humorous characters appealing to both adults and kids because of their satirization of American culture. *The Quick Draw McGraw Show*, for instance, spoofed popular Western films and television series. In this regard, Baba Looey is the sidekick to Quick Draw McGraw and speaks in an exaggerated broken English (he calls Quick Draw "Quicks-draw," for instance), but his similarities to Pancho or Sgt. Garcia stop there. Baba Looey is quietly confident, jaunty, and above all clever, while Quick Draw is earnest, egotistical, and dumb. Luckily, Baba Looey can easily defend himself and Quick Draw. And he is no dummy. In "Bad Guy Disguise," he has to pretend to be a baby but uses this guise to shoot the bad guy in the face, time and again. (It's an incredibly violent show, with the fantasy conceit that characters are never permanently hurt.) In "Masking for Trouble," the villain, Sundown Sam, says to Baba—they're the same size—"Maybe you'd like a nice punch in the nose!" Baba simply responds, "No. But you have one!" This is followed by a loud boing as his hoof bops the guy's nose. Baba Looey also constantly foresees and warns Quick Draw of potential danger or embarrassment; he's always right, though Quick Draw seldom heeds his advice. (A common refrain from Quick Draw is "I'll do the thin'in' around here . . . and do-o-on't you forget it!"). Indeed, one of the running gags is that Quick Draw constantly blunders because he won't listen to Baba Looey. In some episodes Baba is also cunning, tricking villains and Quick Draw alike. In "Slick City Slicker," Baba Looey dresses up like a hotel bellhop in order to help Quick Draw arrest the Raindrop Kid, a criminal hiding out at the hotel. In this role, he's easily able to trick the Raindrop Kid—and Quick Draw—into thinking that they're stuck to the ceiling by nailing the furniture to the actual ceiling. They're then incapacitated as they obsessively try to jump "back" to the ceiling, where they think they belong. In "Baba Bait," Baba is able to catch a robber, the Masked Mosquito, after Quick Draw cannot. The episode ends with Baba now the confident sheriff, while Quick Draw is being carried away from town.

The show's satire thus offered a clever parody and convincing critique of the Mexican American erasures that undergird the earlier children's Westerns, even while the visual appearance of Baba Looey appears to reinforce their mythology. As Jason Mittell notes, Hanna-Barbera began the "kidult" trend of animated series meant to appeal to both youth and adults "by specifically aiming the visuals and the 'wacky' sound effects at the 'moppets,' and the dialogue at adults."[55] In this case, adults who saw through the thinly veiled discourses of white superiority and Mexican American stigmatization of children's Westerns could enjoy the satirization of these discourses in *The Quick Draw McGraw Show*.

Sadly, however, this critique was not sustained throughout Baba Looey's tenure as a Hanna-Barbera character. He's a lobotomized version of his former self when he and Quick Draw reappear on television over a decade later, in a 1973 children's series called *Yogi's Gang*, produced after Hanna-Barbera had been sold to Taft Broadcasting Company in 1966. *Yogi's Gang* brought together former Hanna-Barbera characters as a crime-fighting gang under the leadership of Yogi Bear, in a half-baked attempt to exploit their previous popularity. It posed Quick Draw as a dull but capable cowboy and Baba Looey only as an embarrassing remnant of a more politically incorrect era; it appears he was judged by his costume rather than by his intellect in the original episodes. He is seldom on screen, almost never speaks and is drawn with less facial detail than during the original series; as a result, his intelligence and mischievous spirit are no longer conveyed. The power of individual television storytellers to animate Latina and Latino characters, literally and figuratively, to various ends, and of satire and critical authorship on viewers' ideas and attitudes is starkly illustrated in Baba Looey's final, pitiful reappearance.

This was only the first full decade of what might be termed Latina/o television, however. Latina/o cultural production was soon to have a stronger impact on television in later decades. I return to these themes and topics, given their importance to Latina/o representation and story-telling in television's later decades, in the chapters that follow.

2

1960s–70s

By Us, For Us: Chicana/o and Nuyorican Activist Television

In the 1970s, Latina/os began to break the patterns of invisibility in programming and behind-the-scenes television work, at least at the regional level in some parts of the country. Chicana/o and Puerto Rican activists demanded access to lead and participate in local television productions while also fighting for better conditions and protections for their communities.[1] It was no coincidence that these activists were the first generation to grow up with television and with greater access to a college education; as a result, they were well aware of the powerful impact of TV images and narratives and also believed strongly in Chicana/os' and Latina/os' right to *hacer caras*, in the words of Anzaldúa, to shape their own images and narratives in film, television, and popular culture. Some of these individuals, using the tools of film and video cameras and production studios, were the first to fight for Latina/o self-representation on television.

Taking advantage of 1960s political shifts that created openings for television programming that served minority communities, these producers launched low-budget but ambitious Chicana/o and Latina/o-oriented programs at public televsion and network affiliate stations. A number of non-Latina/o television professionals and funders from outside the community also contributed to the birth of Chicana/o and Latina/o television, necessitating complex negotiations and cultural education among shows' production teams, casts, and crews to produce these shows and keep them on their local broadcast schedules. In this chapter I survey this complicated emergence with a focus on the first Chicana/o and Latina/o shows, their producers, and their ultimate impact on Latina/o television and cultural production in later decades.

The first Chicana/o television series included but were not limited to *Canción de la Raza* (KCET, Los Angeles, 1968–69), *¡Ahora!* (KCET,

1969–70), *Fiesta* (KUAT, Tucson, 1969–70), and *Periódico* (KLRN, San Antonio, 1969–70). A few years later, the Puerto Rican and New York Latina/o series *Realidades* (1971–77) was produced at WNET in New York City. All but *Canción de la Raza* fell within the public affairs show genre, featuring news, discussions with city officials and arts and advocacy organization representatives, musical and other performances, and historical and cultural segments; *Realidades* also showcased narratives in some of its episodes. In response to political and local pressure, in the next few years the ABC, CBS, and NBC affiliate stations in Los Angeles also agreed to air at least one Chicana/o series. All similarly addressed topics of relevance to the Mexican American community through interviews and discussions and through producing short documentary and occasional narrative segments. These series included *Unidos* (1970–71) and *Reflecciones* (1972–73) at ABC affiliate KABC, *Impacto* (1970–74) at NBC affiliate KNBC, and *The Siesta Is Over* (1972–73; renamed *Bienvenidos*, 1973) at CBS affiliate KNXT, now KCBS. Another Puerto Rican and pan-Latina/o-focused series that was produced and aired in these years was *La Plaza* at WGBH Boston, beginning in the mid-1970s and continuing until recent years.

To illuminate what these series contributed to Latina/o cultural production and representation in television in these years, I examine the first of these series and the social and industrial shifts and determined individuals that brought them to life. Building on Chon Noriega's excellent study of Chicana/o media advocacy and media policy shifts that gave birth to the Chicana/o public affairs series and subsequently to Chicana/o cinema, I work here to closely examine the making of these series and their impact on subsequent Latina/o television productions and professionals.[2] These series, notably, were inspired by, produced in, and consumed in local community settings, and later contributed to the growth of pan-Latina/o media advocacy and production; illuminating how these productions originated and were developed and received by audiences thus is valuable to understanding of the evolution of Latina/o television across the decades.

A number of questions have guided this exploration. What were the goals of the first producers of programming for local Chicana/o communities and the Nuyorican and Latina/o community of New York City, and what kinds of shows did they produce? What obstacles did they encounter, and how did they negotiate those obstacles? And finally, there is much to learn about the long-term impact of this programming on local communities, on the commercial television industry, and on future Latina/o portrayals and authorship. I pose these questions with regard to *Canción de la Raza*, *¡Ahora!*, *Fiesta*, *Periódico*, and the first iteration of *Realidades*, and the local and national contexts in which they were funded, envisioned, and produced. As a part of this examination, I focus in depth on these first series, which began in Los Angeles, Tucson, San Antonio, and New York City, respectively, as they established common goals and expectations for Latina/o television produced *by and for* local Latina/o communities.

The Seismic Shifts that Created Space for Chicana/o and Nuyorican Voices

The activist producers who worked on the first Chicana/o and Latina/o series were aided by a number of overlapping social developments that took place on the national level in the mid- and late 1960s. Among them was legislation passed by President Lyndon B. Johnson, who established several laws that supported the birth of Chicana/o and Puerto Rican television. The Civil Rights Act of 1964 set the stage for the Equal Employment Opportunity Commission (EEOC) to scrutinize the media industries regarding their lack of diverse employment. Likewise, in 1967, the Public Broadcasting Act created the Corporation for Public Broadcasting (CPB), a private nonprofit corporation that supports and serves as the steward for national public broadcasting. President Johnson, as he signed the Public Broadcasting Act into law, gave a speech about television's importance for the future of the country. "Television is still a young invention. But we have learned already that it has immense—even revolutionary—power to change, to change our lives," he argued. ". . . So today we rededicate a part of the airwaves—which belong to all the people—and we dedicate them for the enlightenment of all the people."[3] Also important for early Latina/o television, the Federal Communications Commission (FCC), the entity that oversees US broadcasting and mass communication services, established the Prime-Time Access Rule in 1970. This policy, meant to limit the monopoly of the three major networks over television production, specified that local stations could not air network-produced programming in the first hour of prime time. This fueled an interest in and opening on the part of stations to produce local programming that would fulfill this mandate.

The Ford Foundation was also an important benefactor of Chicana/o and Nuyorican television in these years. It established and funded National Educational Television (NET), the precursor to the Public Broadcasting Service (PBS), in 1963 through consolidating a number of organizations focused on educational television and partnering with educational stations.[4] Its goal in these efforts was to create a national system of public broadcasting, including a network of local affiliate radio and television stations.[5] Toward this goal, NET's shows were meant to model the impact that public television could have in ameliorating social problems, particularly those experienced by minority communities. The Ford Foundation's efforts apparently were motivated in part by the findings of the National Advisory Commission on Civil Disorders, better known as the Kerner Commission, which had been tasked in 1967 by President Johnson with examining the root causes of race-related protests that took place in several major cities earlier that year.[6] The commission's 1968 report pinpointed a social divide related to the marginalization of African Americans and other minorities in the United States, with the media an influential component. This lent support to educational television's charge to serve minority audiences (with African American audiences given particular focus) and to the EEOC's investigation of the film and television industries' lack of diversity among its employees.[7] In this time period, as the Ford Foundation increased funding for public television stations and programming. In conjunction with its efforts to provide uplift to black communities and other communities of color, it also provided funds for a few Latina/o-oriented programs to be produced at local public television stations.[8]

Meanwhile, Chicana/o activist and advocacy groups were forming in Los Angeles, San Antonio, Washington, DC, and other cities, with goals of eradicating television, film, and advertising images that they deemed denigrating stereotypes, Chicana/o employment in the media industries, getting to offer input on television and film scripts, and other goals. Puerto Rican activists similarly organized in New York City. Los Angeles, home of television network corporate offices and also a large Latina/o population, in particular, was home to several advocacy groups focused on Mexican American and Latina/o media representation, including Justicia, CARISSMA (the Council to Advance and Restore the Image of the Spanish Speaking and Mexican American), and Nosotros, an actors' advocacy group. The 1969 Supreme Court decision in *Office of Communication of the United Church of Christ v. FCC* notably affirmed the right of community members and activists to file "petitions to deny" license renewals if a station neglected to serve public interest when the public included an ethnic community. Chicana/o and Puerto Rican advocacy groups took up such petitions as a common tactic, in addition to network and advertiser boycotts, sit-ins at stations, letters to networks and major newspapers, and other actions.[9]

Convinced that having a voice and positive representation in the media offered "the swiftest and most crosscutting vehicle for change" on other civil rights fronts, Chicana/o activists convened and gathered at conferences in 1969 and the early 1970s to establish group goals and strategies regarding representation and inclusion in television, film, and the news media.[10] These included a conference in Southwest Texas, the Midwest Chicano Media Conference, and a national Chicano Media Conference in New York City in 1970. The goals established at these gatherings included studying Mexican American representation and its impact, learning the fundamentals of media production and how to use news and entertainment media effectively for movement goals, becoming familiar with FCC policies in order to challenge station practices, and agitating for Chicana/os to be employed in the media industries and allowed entrance into college training programs.[11] Agreeing on these goals and actions likely involved negotiations among those who felt the television and film industries would always marginalize Chicana/os, and others who felt that they could change the Hollywood media industries from the inside once they gained entrance; these were schisms that some of my sources recalled in interviews.[12] One result of the Chicano Media Conference also was the establishment of the National Chicano Media Council, a first effort to unite multiple advocacy groups for more effective negotiations with the television networks and other industry entities.[13] Later this council merged into a pan-Latina/o group, the National Latino Media Council.

A tangential but equally influential development related to Chicana/o media activism and the EEOC hearings was a concerted push for students of color to be admitted into film production programs in Los

Angeles for the first time. In 1968, the New Communicators program was established at the University of Southern California and funded by the Office of Economic Opportunity, targeting African American, Latina/o, and Asian American students. While it did not last beyond a year, Jesús Salvador Treviño, who went on to become one of the early instrumental Latina/o television producers and later a filmmaker and television director, was among its students. In addition, the UCLA's Ethno-Communications Program, which operated from 1968 through 1973, enrolled a diverse group of students of color and hired graduate students of color as teaching assistants.[14] A number of Latina/o media producers who ultimately worked in television were students or teaching assistants in the program; these filmmakers included Susan Racho, Luis C. Garza, Sylvia Morales, José Luis Ruiz, and David Garza.[15] Racho noted in an interview that she became involved as a producer of the KABC series *Reflecciones* in part because of her Ethno-Communications ties, for instance.

The First Chicana/o TV Drama: *Canción de la Raza*

It was in this era and in relation to these kinds of interventions that the first Chicana/o series was produced with a primarily Chicana/o audience in mind at the Los Angeles PBS television station KCET. *Canción de la Raza* (*Song of the People*), funded by the Ford Foundation, depicted a family in East Los Angeles facing challenges and cultural issues typical for Mexican American Angelenos of the time. The Ramos family consisted of a mother, father, and five children, including three children in high school, a son fighting in Vietnam, and a daughter married to a Chicano man who wanted to ignore their heritage and assimilate in the suburbs. The drama aired locally at 3:30 p.m. and 7 p.m. each weekday. While it was considered a success by the Ford Foundation and KCET, little information has been preserved about the series, and researchers are only able to view the first of the sixty-five episodes that were broadcast.[16]

The producers of *Canción* were all Anglo employees of KCET who hoped to involve Mexican American residents in the creative process of producing a drama for their community. Dr. Richard S. Scott, head of the station's human affairs division (and a medical doctor), served as

executive producer and project director of its Ford Foundation grant.
Scott and Charles R. Allen, then KCET's vice president for programming, said in *Television Quarterly* in 1969 that the production neces-
sitated a cultural education of the part of both the Anglo producers and
the Mexican American actors and crew members, who had no previous
experience in television. The production began with a 1968 proposal
by Scott and other KCET personnel to include and target the 1.5 million Mexican American residents in Los Angeles with a bilingual drama
in telenovela format that would be both educational and entertaining,
addressing relevant social issues and providing links to community resources. In establishing these goals, Scott and the producers had no research on Mexican Americans as television viewers to guide them, as in
this period just prior to the founding of Chicana/o studies and television
studies as academic disciplines, almost none had been conducted.[17] Still,
they argued that there was a need to target their Mexican American
community because it was "isolated in the lowest end of the socioeconomic scale" and by language differences.[18] David Davies, the Ford program officer focused on public broadcasting in 1968 under the direction
of Fred Friendly, then the Ford Foundation's advisor on media-related
grant funding, chose to fund the production proposal with a $625,000
grant.

Given the go-ahead, the producers began reach out to the Mexican
American community. KCET encouraged local residents to audition
for roles and apply for production positions through announcements
disseminated to Spanish-language media outlets, community organizations, and the drama departments of local schools and colleges. Ultimately, producers hired almost 100 Mexican Americans as actors or in
creative or administrative positions.[19] Because most of the individuals
interested in performing lacked experience, KCET organized a six-week
actors' workshop led by experienced actors Francisco Ortega, Natividad
Vacío, and Victor Millan, who also would subsequently direct a few episodes of the series. Ultimately, the show cast both professional and non-
professional actors.[20] Among them was Richard Yniguez, then a college
student, who played one of the brothers and would go on to a busy,
multi-decade career in television and film.[21] Two Mexican American
writers, Richard Duran and Abel Franco, also worked on the production. As Yniguez recalls about the production, it was challenging for the

Figure 2.1. The cast of *Canción de la Raza*, produced at KCET Los Angeles. Standing, from left: Robert De Anda, Priscilla Garcia, and Richard Yniguez. Seated: Mike De Anda and Tina Menard. ©1968 Ford Foundation Collection. Courtesy of Rockefeller Archive Center.

actors, as they all were learning how to perform for television cameras during the busy shoot for the sixty-five episodes. Yniguez noted that some of the directors, all white except for Ortega, Vacío, and Millan, at times treated the actors with condescension.[22]

When the production team, including producer Charles Polachek and director Lamar Caselli, held community discussions at local organizations and interviewed leaders about the interests, needs, and concerns of Mexican Americans in the area, it tried to reassure community members that this wasn't a "Hollywood based" project that would disappoint them.[23] Harold Mendelsohn, a social psychologist at the University of Denver, also designed audience research for the series. His team of bilingual researchers spoke with Mexican American residents in the area.[24] They spoke of wanting *Canción* to address issues relevant to their lives such as Chicana/o activism, school and employment inequities, police brutality, drug abuse, managing a low-income budget, and responding to the farmworkers' grape boycott.

The production team also created a component devoted to communicating directly with their viewers. Edward Moreno (also known as Eduardo), who had been program manager of the Spanish-language radio station KALI, came on as a community relations consultant. Among other things, Moreno presented to community groups about the series. *Linea Abierta* (*Open Line*), a call-in line staffed by two bilingual social workers, was established for community members; viewers were encouraged to call in during *Canción*'s mid-way break and after each episode. According to Scott and Allen, over 800 individuals called during the thirteen weeks that the series aired. While most of the calls initially were complaints that the series didn't feel authentic for various reasons, over time viewers were more likely calling with suggestions for characters and story arcs or to ask for advice on how to deal with issues, such as immigration problems, that had arisen in the show. The producers also created a talk show that replayed calls on issues of strong interest and brought in community experts and leaders to discuss them.

Scott and Allen note the difficulties the production team and cast experienced as they worked to cohere as a group and tape the shows despite differing work styles, such as a desire to stick to a set schedule on the part of the Anglo KCET staff and a looser, less stringent style on the part of some of the Mexican American actors and crew. The KCET team had to learn to adjust. The producers and supporting Mexican American organizations also benefited from building trust over time, beers, and unstructured conversations. In a *TV Guide* story, Carolyn See implied that the Ford Foundation's expectations were another challenge for the program's writers and producers to navigate, citing an anonymous Hollywood adviser to the production. The adviser stated that *Canción*'s production team wanted the series to have an open-ended conclusion that emphasized the ongoing social problems that Mexican Americans face. This, however, was nixed by Ford, which wanted its funded program to support an optimistic, and safely liberal message, rather than one that was more overtly political. "The Foundation wants to tell the ghetto about community action. But they don't want to tell it too much," the adviser joked.[25] It's notable that the chief philanthropic benefactor of Chicana/o public affairs programming wanted to promote messages of social uplift but not of radical resistance.

Canción de la Raza's first episode debuted locally on Monday, October 14, 1968. The episode opens to what appears to be real-life video footage from the 1968 East Los Angeles high school "blowouts," historic walkouts by Chicana/o students in the Los Angeles area protesting racial inequities at their high schools.[26] In stark footage, police officers are shown hitting student protesters with billy clubs. This is interrupted by an intertitle announcing the new series. It features two eagles, one with a snake in its mouth as is featured on the Mexican flag, and an acknowledgment that the program was made possible by the Ford Foundation. With Spanish guitar playing in background, a Mexican American narrator, likely Eduardo Moreno, finally introduces the series as "la melodía y letra de un pueblo digno muy orgulloso" ("The melody and lyrics of a dignified, very proud people").

The narrative then opens on an older Mexican American mother in a modest but well-tended home. She dusts a Virgin of Guadalupe figurine, does the sign of the cross, and continues dusting things in the living room. Her teen daughter, Maria Elena, comes home distraught. She says she was part of the blowouts and that it was terrible; the police were violent to the student protesters. Her mother asks why the students left their schools. "For the schools! For better teachers, better everything," Maria Elena responds. Hearing that the police hit their brother David, her older brother Roberto promises to find out what happened to him. Their mother is scared for David, but only thinks to pray about it. Cut to another part of the city: David and his friend Chuy have slipped away from the police into an alley, but David is bleeding from a head wound. Despite David needing medical attention, Chuy wants them to hide longer. He gives David some pills that he describes cryptically as "pain killers." Then Chuy hears police officers nearby and runs away. David, now under the influence of pills that have him confused and sedated, isn't able to follow. He manages to get into a phone booth, where he calls home. Maria Elena answers, but he passes out before he can speak. "Hello? ¿Quién es? [Who is this?] Hello!" she frantically shouts, but David cannot hear her in just one of the many melodramatic moments of the episode.

Maria Elena, the chief protagonist of the episode, asks her mother to stop praying so that she might help find David. They argue, as her mother is fearful of challenging the schools or the police, while Maria Elena believes in protesting as an activist strategy for Mexican Americans. "We need to do things for ourselves," she tells her mother. "We need to get together and get strong." She continues, talking about the blowouts: "We were all for each other. We were standing up for the first

time. Imagine, mama; for the first time, the Chicanos spoke out!" Maria
Elena and Roberto later find the phone booth where David called from,
but he's nowhere to found. At the close of the episode, however, David
has made his way home. He passes out again, this time on the living
room floor of the Ramos house, in a cliffhanger ending that demands
viewers to watch the next episode to learn his status.

In a coda, the man who introduced the episode, presumably Moreno,
speaks in Spanish directly to the audience. He notes that the series aims
to highlight real issues and problems that Mexican Americans face,
from a Mexican American perspective. He also calls attention to the
importance of education for improving the lives of Mexican Americans,
noting "Cada cabeza es un mundo," (a popular phrase that translates as
"Each mind is a world of its own," or "Every person has their own perspective"). In all, over its season run, the bilingual family drama pulled
in a substantial number of local viewers—12.6 percent of the Mexican
American community in the Los Angeles region, or 223,000 residents.[27]

With respect to *Canción*'s impact, 83 percent of Mexican American
viewers in Los Angeles County interviewed by Mendelsohn's team of
researchers ranked the series as being of the same or higher quality than
other shows they liked watching, while 57 percent said they had gained
useful knowledge from it.[28] Low-income viewers (with a $4,000–$5,000
annual income at that time) were especially appreciative of the show.
Scott and Allen also touted its Mexican American cast and crew members, some of whom went on to other media productions, while two
Chicano writers and three associate directors (all male) were able to join
the writers' and directors' guilds afterward. Finally, they pointed to the
friendships they forged with Mexican Americans and their new knowledge of Mexican American culture as a result of working on the series.

Because of its local ratings and being deemed by its researchers to
have had a favorable impact on viewers, the Ford Foundation funded its
distribution in 1969 to other public television stations in cities with substantial Latina/o populations, including San Francisco, Denver, Houston, and New York City. The grant also paid for modest promotional
budgets and one-day workshops by Moreno on outreach to Latina/o
residents. *Canción* was not as successful as it had been in California,
however. Puerto Ricans in New York and New Jersey reported that they
didn't relate to the Mexican American family, while Mexican Americans

in other parts of the country found the differences in dialect and the social issues addressed unappealing.[29] The foundation took from this experience that a presumption of Latina/o homogeneity could prove disastrous to national programming. Their funding plan after this appears to have kept this in mind, as the next Ford-funded series for Mexican American, Puerto Rican, or Latina/o viewers were all programs with a local or regional focus.

Serving the Community with Two Chairs and a Camera: The First Public Affairs Shows[30]

In 1969, a year after *Canción de la Raza*'s qualified success, the Ford Foundation established a $5 million New Television Programming grant program, which earmarked funding for programming targeting communities of color. Scholars of public broadcasting such as Ralph Engelman argue that establishing a national public television system was a driving objective of the foundation.[31] In prior years they had awarded grants to educational stations to improve their production capacity and to create national distribution channels; it's useful to point out that this was a very real challenge in this period before satellite and digital technology. Ford also had a commitment to ameliorating problems related to the racially lopsided media industries, which had been a focus of the Kerner Commission's report. To this end, New Television Programming grants funded productions and research teams proposing to serve African American, and occasionally, Chicana/o communities.[32] The stations that received funding for a Chicana/o series were KCET in Los Angeles, which produced *¡Ahora!*; KLRN in San Antonio, for the production of *Periódico*; and KUAT in Tuscon, which produced *Fiesta*. *Periódico*'s and *Fiesta*'s proposals included plans for research to survey their Mexican American community members' interests and reception to the new series, perhaps a motivating factor in their grant approvals. The cultural memory of these series is preserved for the most part in a handful of photos, in the summaries and evaluations written by their producers and researchers that worked with the production teams, and in news coverage. Copies of episodes of these series for the most part were not preserved by their stations or producers, in this era in which cash-strapped public television stations typically reused videocassettes on which they had shot local programming. I was able to obtain only one episode of *¡Ahora!* and to view a compilation of clips from its other episodes as I was conducting this research.

Of the three Chicana/o series, *¡Ahora!* has received the most attention from scholars over the years because of the influential role that it ultimately played in the birth of Chicana/o cinema.[33] Beginning in September 1969, *¡Ahora!* was taped at KCET's studio in East Los Angeles and broadcast at 7 p.m. each weeknight. Claudio Fenner-López produced the series, while the project director was Eduardo Moreno, who had played an influential role managing community relations for *Canción de la Raza*. Hosts and producers of the series were Moreno, Jesús Salvador Treviño, in his first job at the station, and Esther Hanson. Importantly, it was the only Chicana/o public affairs series at this point in time created *and* led by Chicana/os. As KCET describes its goals on its website, citing Treviño:

> The purpose of this series is to explore the history, the culture, the artistic achievements, and intellectual thought of our people, La Raza. Our historical presence in the development of this country has been denied. We at "¡Ahora!" affirm our identity as a people unique in world history. The empires of our forefathers stretch throughout the Americas long before the first European immigrants came to Veracruz or Plymouth Rock. Through our veins runs the blood of our Spanish father and our Indian mother. We are a new people. We are La Raza. This is our history. The history of the early Indian civilizations. The history of Mexico. The history of La Raza in the United States.[34]

As noted by Elson Trinidad at KCET, the production of the series was unique; it was shot in an East Los Angeles studio with a large window to the street that offered passersby full view of the production process. The first episode modeled the variety of topics that the program would explore in its 175 installments; it included discussion with members of the Mexican American Education Commission and the League of Mexican American Women, a spotlight on artist Daniel Ramirez Aguilar, and a performance by children at the Park Vista Headstart.

Treviño, the series co-producer, said that *¡Ahora!* and *Acción Chicano*, which he also later produced, "Covered everything from

Figure 2.2. Jesús Treviño, seated on the left, co-producer of ¡Ahora!, KCET Los Angeles, confers with stage manager Parke Perrine prior to an interview with photographer Rudy Rodriguez, on the right, on the set in 1970.

sit-ins—broadcast live—to talk shows, to music, to theater productions. We covered all aspects of the political scene going on at the time but also a lot of the cultural aspects of it."[35] They also put a lot of emphasis on Mexican American history, and on Latino literature. The importance of Mexican American producers leading the way in these efforts cannot be underestimated, he added.

> This was a first. This was the first time anyone had bothered to document the lives of Latinos. And it came at a time when the Spanish television stations were just recycling telenovelas from Mexico, and there was virtually no local programming to speak of in Spanish-language television. We became the exemplar of what could happen, because although we [Latina/os] were English-based, [it was unique that] all of the participants were speaking English. It did signal what could happen. The television was handed over to Latinos to talk about Latino issues.[36]

Unfortunately, as noted above, most of the episodes of the series have not survived. One of the few episodes that has been preserved,

Figure 2.3. The opening credits of Chicana/o public affairs series *¡Ahora!* (1969–70, KCET) consisted of a montage of photos focused on Mexican and Chicana/o history and culture, ending with this image of a young Chicano in school.

"The Image: Part 1," was the first of a three-part series broadcast in 1970. Treviño wrote and produced the episode, which was directed by Victor Millan with a majority-Latina/o crew. It opens with the *¡Ahora!* credit sequence. This is a quick montage of photographs. They initially are historical images: Aztec sculptures, peasant fighters of the Mexican Revolution, lynched Mexican Americans, and a string of Mexican American political leaders, mostly men and a few women, over the decades. These are followed by a montage of contemporary photos, of children, Mexican American musicians, Cesar Chavez, the Teatro Campesino theatrical troupe, and Chicana/o political leaders and activists. The series title, *¡Ahora!* finally appears, over a photo of Mexican American children in school.

The episode opens on a minimalist sound stage, with a large-scale drawing of a Hollywood-style Mexican bandido in the background; he wears a large sombrero and a toothy, foolish grin. Metallic film canisters are strewn on the floor, and a larger-than-life paper facsimile of celluloid film, including frame after frame of a bandido, frames each side of the set. Treviño, the show's host, introduces this episode on how "Mexicans and Latins" have been depicted in films. He looks like a young professor as he reads from his notes. Treviño begins with overviews of the careers of silent film actors, including Ramon Novarro, Conchita Montenegro, and Gilbert Roland. Photographs from the actors' films fill the screen. The types of characters to which they were confined were Latin Lovers and "greaser" villains, he explains, adding that these characters as a result were often linked in American viewers' minds to Mexican Americans as a whole. He references scholarship on the nature of prejudice to argue that these persistent images reflect a subconscious racism toward Mexicans/Mexican Americans in American culture. Moving to sound films, he summarizes the career highlights for Latina/o actors from the 1930s through the 1960s. Treviño again analyzes the significance of these depictions and how both positive and negative stereotypes worked through white American anxieties. "We find that [Latina/os] have played bandits, roly-poly buffoons, Latin Lovers, Indians, sleepy Mexicans, and of course the Mexican spitfire. There have been exceptions, but these actors have been of the stature of an Anthony Quinn, actors who have prevailed in spite of the typecasting." Treviño then turns to the rare films that have featured Latina/o main characters. With film stills illustrating, he notes a handful of 1950s–60s social problem films that had depicted Mexican Americans with sensitivity and realism: *The Lawless* (1950), *The Ring* (1952), and *The Trial* (1962), and particularly *Salt of the Earth* (1954). But these films "pale in comparison to the number of films that have stereotyped the Mexican American," he adds.[37]

Turning to the subject of media advocacy, Treviño says that Mexican American activists had picketed the Academy Awards two months earlier to protest racist depictions, especially in *The Wild Bunch* (1969) and *Butch Cassidy and the Sundance Kid* (1969), and a failure to cast Latina/o actors in Latina/o roles in films such as *Che!* (1969).[38] Mexican Americans were becoming angry about how they and their children were being depicted, he notes, and connects this to studies by Tomás Martinez demonstrating the significance and impact of negative imagery in advertising.[39] As he speaks, ads fill the screen. One depicts a sleepy Mexican next to a TV set, the item being promoted. Other examples

include Frito-Lay's Frito Bandito and ads portraying Mexicans as criminals or as having exceptionally smelly perspiration. Treviño concludes
that it was commonplace in that period to depict Latina/os as objects
of ridicule and scorn. Because of protests, the Frito Bandito was being
phased out, but the film industry was not undergoing a similar change.
In all, the episode illustrated the passion, intense work, and research that
went into episodes of ¡Ahora!

While much of the scholarship on Chicana/o television has focused
on the important work of this early programming at KCET, Periódico
and Fiesta are important to study as well precisely because they were produced and broadcast far from the television capitol. KLRN's Periódico, in
contrast to ¡Ahora!, served Mexican Americans in South Central Texas.
The half-hour series, which aired Tuesday evenings and Sunday after-
noons, was hosted by Guillermo "Memo" Lozano, Willie Velasquez, and
Olga Garcia Brown, produced by Terrel L. Cass, and directed by Ro-
lando Morales. Unfortunately, none of these participants helped to write
the only published summary of the production experience.

In a chapter for Broadcasting and Social Action: A Handbook for
Station Executives, KLRN producer Frank Duane notes that KLRN
staff brainstormed about a potential Mexican American program in a
series of meetings with local organizations and members of the Mexican American community.[40] The discussion was often heated regarding whether the community needed its own show and what its content
should include. Duane notes with some paternalism, as he likely did
in his proposal, that the series would serve a region with perhaps the
highest concentration of Mexican Americans in the country, many of
whom struggled "in a social limbo," not assimilated into the national
culture and facing the erosion of their culture and economic disadvantage.[41] Notably, the message here, while seemingly sympathetic in
tone, judges Mexican Americans as unable to help themselves. This is
tempered by Duane's statement that KLRN built the show around the
premise that "Mexican-Americans have a beautiful heritage and they
should be proud."[42]

KLRN's proposal claimed that Periódico's Mexican American staff
would lead the production. Duane admits that this was at times hard
to accomplish. They decided to not impose language requirements on
the program—participants could choose to speak Spanish or English.

Differences in knowledge of television production also had an impact on the production, especially at first. He claims that the Mexican American cast and crew at times at times needed help to master their roles or, if going on the air, to express their thoughts. The show's producers found that Mexican American youth and college students who participated, on the other hand, were much more articulate and comfortable speaking on the show. Duane notes they came to better understand how differences in cultural capital played a role in these dynamics. "People who spend their lives in communications and who make daily professional use of the First Amendment's guarantee of Freedom of Speech tend to forget that they are exercising an ability as well as a right," he noted. "It is a sobering lesson in the limits of democracy to deal with people who have nurtured a different ability, the ability *not* to show, or say, what they think."[43]

On September 17, 1969, *Periódico* premiered on KLRN, featuring a discussion of whether the public schools were cheating Mexican American youth out of a quality education. Later episodes focused on such subjects as San Antonio's involvement in the federal Model Cities program, school busing, Chicana/o student walkouts at Lanier High School, language barriers for Spanish speakers in the city, and practical issues such as job seeking and taking advantage of Social Security benefits.[44] Guests included poet and professor Moisés Espino del Castillo, classical guitarist William Torres, and a rock band, The Highlighters. Other episodes similarly balanced a focus on news and relevant social issues with segments featuring Mexican American creative artists, musicians, and scholars.

Fiesta, which aired in the Tucson, Arizona, region, bore many similarities to *Periódico*. E. B. Eiselein, then a media anthropologist at the University of Arizona in Tucson, served as the production's head researcher. He designed and led a bilingual research team that surveyed Mexican American residents as the series was being planned and later evaluated *Fiesta*'s impact. In a 1974 book, Eiselein, along with Wes Marshall, program manager at KUAT and fellow professor in Radio-Television, John Thomas Duncan, director and co-producer of *Fiesta*, and Raul Gámez Bogarín, the host and co-producer, usefully summarized their work on the production and what they learned from it.

Similar to *Periódico*, most of *Fiesta*'s preproduction team was non-Latino. The production team made a point to hire Hector Gradillas, who had worked on another Radio-TV project with the Mexican American community as a consulting producer, however. In a short afterward to the book, Gradillas discussed how he came to trust that the producers would listen to suggestions from the Mexican American community. For example, it was Gradillas's suggestion, based on their initial survey, that their set design and program format be modeled after an intimate backyard party. Gradillas also recommended the hire of the show's hosts and newsreaders. Still, the show sometimes struggled to integrate the Anglo production team and Mexican American cast members and guests who were used to working on Spanish-language productions. Similar to *Periódico*, the *Fiesta* team had to make "cross cultural adaptions" to overcome differing cultural mindsets, including adapting to what they referred to as "*hora mexicana* (Mexican time)", a more relaxed conceptualization of the strictness of the work schedule on the part of some of the Mexican American cast and crew.[45] On the other hand, the team found when attempting to hire Mexican American college students that they often were not able to lure them away from better-paying jobs.

Much of *Fiesta*'s content was focused on entertainment, interspersed with occasional news and information segments, to keep the series appealing to its audience. Their twenty half-hour episodes included performances by Mexican American and Mexican musical artists and bands, folk dancers, and theatrical groups, and news segments on topics such as bilingual and adult education, Las Posadas (days of pre-Christmas events celebrated by some Mexican Americans), receiving benefits from the Veterans Administration, and the experience of Mexican American students at local colleges. Their study found that it reached 60 percent of its target audience, and that half of these viewers continued to watch it throughout its season run.[46] Respondents also reported that they felt cultural pride and at times were motivated to take action on the topics addressed in *Fiesta* episodes. The research team and producers ultimately declared the series a success, although they acknowledged that they could have done a better job "had we begun the project knowing the audience as well as we do now."[47] If they could do it all over again, they elaborated, they would put more focus on Mexican American history and consumer education, hire more Mexican American employees to train in production, push for more integration between their show and the KUAT news departments, and do more to promote the series. It's notable that the Anglo participants received at least as much education about Mexican American culture and issues through their work on the series as the Mexican American target audience did, which speaks to the general invisibility of Mexican Americans in mainstream culture at the time. Despite the positive impact of this and the other Latina/o public affairs series, after the Ford Foundation grants were exhausted, the local public television stations generally let them quietly end.

"It was about a Counter Narrative": *Realidades*

In this same time period but across the country in New York City, *Realidades* (WNET, 1971–77) was established at the juncture of the Puerto Rican art movement and activism in the 1960s and 1970s. Puerto Rican and other artists of color formed the Art Workers Coalition in East Harlem in the late 1960s to protest the Vietnam War, the exclusion of Latina/o art from museums, and other activist causes. Members were also often involved in Puerto Rican activist organizations such as El Comité, which fought for the independence of Puerto Rico and the freedom of Puerto Rican political prisoners, the Puerto Rican Student Union, the Real Great Society youth collective, and the Young Lords, a revolutionary social service and activist organization with chapters in Chicago and New York City.[48] In 1970, this activist spirit was instrumental to the formation of Taller Boricua (Puerto Rican Workshop), an artists' collective that also focused on community improvement. Among the artists involved were Marcos Dimas and Julio Rodriguez. Community activists José García, Esperanza Martel, Blanca Vázquez, Humberto Cintrón, and hundreds of others demonstrated against their public television station, WNET/13, in 1972. As Vázquez, also a founding editor of *Centro*, the print journal that accompanied *Realidades* in these years, described their efforts, "It was about a counter narrative [to how the mainstream media was depicting Puerto Ricans]. . . . *Here*'s what it means to be working class people of color . . . from a colonized state."[49]

Humberto Cintrón at the time was the director of Community News Service, a small nonprofit news service focused on journalism about Puerto Ricans and other residents of color in Manhattan, as well as on activism supporting the Puerto Rican community. In his mid-30s, with a master's degree in urban studies, he was older than some of the other activists. José García, a friend of Cintrón's who was a filmmaker and cinematographer, had asked if he would take part in picketing WNET. Previously, García had contracted with WNET to air his film adaptation of the venerated René Marqués play *La Carreta* (*The Ox Cart*), about a Puerto Rican *jíbaro* (peasant farmer) family forced to migrate to New York City. The play implicates the US government and corporations for the severe poverty on the island and the trauma suffered by its people. After a community screening, WNET refused to air it, however, considering the material too controversial. When García's protest went nowhere, he asked for help from various community organizations. In support, Community News Service and other allies decided to picket the station to challenge its decision, calling in other activist groups throughout the city to join them.[50] "Under a banner reading '20% Hispanic population, 0% programming,' some 250 people demonstrated outside the station, including sympathetic WNET staff."[51] It became a multi-day, growing demonstration, and was considered an important social event for all self-respecting artists and activist-minded Puerto Ricans. When the protest didn't have the desired effect, they decided to "sit in" at the WNET offices. Cintrón noted to Christopher Bell, "We took them off the air by going in and [sitting] in the studio. We closed the door and said, 'That's it. Nothing will be aired on Channel Thirteen.' Then, Channel Thirteen decided they would talk with us."[52] Apparently the growing protest was not good for WNET's image, particularly as a public television station. While they still didn't air *La Carreta*, station executive vice president John Jay Iselin agreed WNET would fund and produce a weekly Latino cultural series.

Iselin decided to hire Cintrón, whom he had never met, to serve as executive producer of the series, given his experience with Community News Service and social service organizations in the city, not realizing that he had been one of the demonstrators. (In an absurd turn, the station staff told the picketing Cintrón, who offered his services, that they had no interest in hiring him because they hired "Humberto Cintrón." They discovered their mistake the next day). Cintrón then hired a production crew of twelve people for *Realidades*; they included García, who worked as the show's producer, nine other Puerto Ricans, a Venezuelan, and a Brazilian.[53] Julio Rodriguez, one of the production team, noted in a 2019 retrospective discussion of the series that they typically decided as a group what subjects they would explore.[54] WNET gave the group funding for fifteen episodes, which they stretched into nineteen, in addition to airing *La Carreta*, the film that had sparked so much controversy.

Given its interest in serving the entire Latina/o community, the team decided to make the series bilingual, with subtitles in both Spanish and English. They produced episodes on issues affecting the Puerto Rican and broader Latina/o community, such as bilingual education, the election in Puerto Rico, the "New Latin Woman," and Puerto Rican veterans. They also included a major focus on the arts, with segments on poets, fine art, dance, and theater. For example, "Your Collective Expression," an episode produced by Marcos Dimas and Larry Vargas, focused on Taller Boricua and Puerto Rican art and artists; the episode was later nominated for an Emmy. Dimas and Vargas also produced "Mestizajes," centered on the complexities of mestizo heritage and racial identity and on Puerto Rican, Mexican American, and Cuban American identities and experience.[55]

News coverage of the series was generally positive, emphasizing the important function of Latina/o leadership and cultural production in challenging stereotypical representations of Puerto Ricans and other Latina/os. As Cintrón noted in the (New York) *Daily News*, "If we do nothing else this year, at least we will present the views we have and the perception of the world through our eyes rather than studies of the community by others."[56] In *The New York Times*' coverage of the series, television critic Beatrice Berg described it as the "first show dealing with this important part of the population of the metropolitan area, which has until now been all but ignored in television programing."[57]

A unique and influential aspect of the series' home at WNET was a bilingual (Spanish and English) film and television production class offered at the station that was open to all community members; it was taught by film professional Lillian Jiménez and others. As Marcos Dimas describes it, it was an important "generative" mechanism.[58] Dimas was one of several local activists who produced segments of *Realidades* or other shows after going through the training.

Many of the individuals who worked on *Realidades* and the African American–focused WNET series *Tony Brown's Journal* over the years were able to get their start through this training. Raquel Ortiz, who went

Figure 2.4. From right, Humberto Cintrón, executive producer of *Realidades* (1971–77), producer Marco Dimas, and Esperanza Martel and Julio Rodriguez, community activists who supported the series, in 2019 at the "*Realidades* Revisited" panel at Taller Boricua/Puerto Rican Workshop in New York City.

on to become a busy producer on Latina/o subjects for WNET and then WGBH in Boston (where she produced the long-running Latino series *La Plaza*), is another prime example.

Some of these activists later formed the Puerto Rican Media Action and Education Council, as Julio Rodriguez shared in a "*Realidades* Revisted, 1971–1977" panel at Taller Boricua/Puerto Rican Workshop in New York City on July 6, 2019. The Council was focused on increasing Latina/o visibility in the US mainstream media and employment behind the scenes. Fairly quickly they began using petitions to deny license renewals as a major tool in these efforts. Humberto Cintrón has noted in interviews that he and his colleagues used this strategy to negotiate with stations to hire correspondents of color and better represent communities of color. For instance, J. J. Gonzalez and David Diaz were hired at New York–based news shows, while Raquel Ortiz began working on Latino-focused series and films at WGBH Boston.[59] José Rivera, an attorney from the Puerto Rican Legal Defense Fund, assisted them with this process ("Until we picketed the Ford Foundation," Julio Rodriguez noted, because they were funded in part by the foundation). Producers of color at WNET also trained activists from around the country on how to launch their own station license challenges. An offshoot of this work was the founding of the National Latino Media Coalition with Chicana/o advocacy groups in 1975.

Despite the hard and often thankless work, the individuals who were a part of these production efforts and advocacy spoke at the 2019 "*Realidades* Revisited" event of how lucky they feel to have been a part of this idealistic movement for Latina/o authorship and representation on public television. As scholar and film producer Lillian Jiménez noted regarding her time at WNET, "Our lives were difficult, but they were rapturous and they were joyous. There were celebrations, and we loved each other and we took care of each other and we fought with each other. And we learned our values from our parents, who learned them in Puerto Rico and institutionalized them to us."

Local Opportunities Shift, and Professionalization Calls

The network affiliate stations in Los Angeles also produced and aired several Chicana/o-oriented news and culture shows during this period. Like the programs airing on public television, these were funded on a shoestring, in this case by the stations themselves, but only after they were put under the pressure of losing their license through campaigns initiated by Justicia and other advocacy groups, with outside support from individuals and entities such as FCC commissioner Nicholas Johnson and lawyers from Citizens Communications Center, a legal advocacy organization.[60] The resulting programs included *Unidos*, produced by Ruiz, Sylvia Morales, Luis C. Garza, and Jesse Corona; *Reflecciones*, produced by Garza, Susan Racho, David Garcia Jr., and Tony Rodriguez; *Impacto* at KNBC; and *The Siesta Is Over* (later renamed *Bienvenidos*) at KNXT, now KCBS, hosted by Joe Ortiz and produced by Esther G. Renteria and others. Similar to the Latina/o series on public television, they addressed topics of relevance to the Mexican American community through interviews, investigative journalism, and short film segments.[61] Susan Racho, one of the few women to work on an early Latina/o series, recounted this time in her career as exciting, fun, and incredibly busy, as each week they worked day and night to plan, shoot, and edit another episode. She said that she never felt marginalized as the lone Chicana on her production team, as the immense work was a leveler for all of them.

These public affairs series importantly supported the birth of Chicana/o film, as series producers became interested in doing more than was feasible through a local television talk show. As Treviño noted, in comments that were echoed in interviews I conducted with his contemporaries,

> This was the start of a lot of us, that first generation of Latinos in the industry getting a foothold. Because if you were now producing a talk show, at least you had access to the media, at least you could actually hold a camera. This was how we broke in, so to speak. And then because we were smart people, that talk show, pretty soon someone would say, what if we shot some B roll, some additional footage of this or that and then we'd have to edit it in? And so pretty soon the shows became more and more ambitious. And pretty soon, by the end of the first year, we were doing half-hour documentaries. And it was all stuff we were learning. Many of us were learning on the job.[62]

Among their strategies, producers like Treviño used some of their program budget to also produce short films. Among the Chicana/o documentaries and short films that premiered on these shows were *I Am Joaquin* (Luis Valdez, 1969), *Requiem 29* (David Garcia, 1971), *America Tropical* (Jesús Treviño, 1971), *Yo Soy Chicano* (Jesús Treviño, 1972), *The Garment Workers* (Susan Racho, 1975), and *Cinco Vidas* (José Luis Ruiz, 1973). In producing these personal and activist-minded short films, they often had the support of their station. Treviño, who went on to produce and direct other programs and films such as *Seguin* (1982) in collaboration with KCET, cited KCET program manager Chuck Allen as particularly supportive.[63] KNBC also helped to fund and aired Ruiz's documentary films *Cinco Vidas*, which won an Emmy, and *The Unwanted*.[64]

Treviño had to use strong-arm tactics to get KCET to produce a second Chicana/o-focused series after *¡Ahora!* finished its run, however. He did so by getting the Spanish-surnamed staff to sign a petition that they "were all going to resign en masse" if the station didn't support a new series for the Chicana/o community.[65] He ultimately was given the go-ahead to produce *Acción Chicano*, which aired from 1972 to 1974. Trev-iño also exchanged episodes with the New York–based *Realidades* series, initiating the first pan-Latina/o programming. In 1973, José Luis Ruiz, then at KCET, expanded this idea into the formation of a Latino Consor-tium, a programming cooperative of ten public television stations that shared programming they had produced. These included stations in San Diego, San Francisco, Sacramento, San Antonio, Dallas, Tucson, Tempe, Denver, and East Lansing.[66] Tapes were "bicycled" (shipped) around the country so that consortium stations could air them; an originating sta-tion might not get a tape back for two years.[67] Unfortunately, most sta-tions produced only a handful of shows each year, using *Acción Chicano* episodes to fill the rest of their schedule; they apparently were devoting little funding to producing new Latina/o programming. Most impor-tantly, however, this exchange of programming and the communication it involved provided the foundation for a national movement of Latina/o media producers for more presence, agency, and authorship in public television.

This was instrumental to the progress of Latina/o television pro-duction in the coming years, as by this time the Ford Foundation's in-volvement and financial support for Latino public affairs programming had quietly ended. For the most part it withdrew from the strategy of supporting minority communities through television programming, choosing instead to focus on ameliorating racial inequities through support for other social institutions. PBS, which distributes public tele-vision programming nationally and is funded by the CPB, was also now firmly established after taking over from NET in 1970, which may have made it easier for Ford to no longer routinely fund programming.[68] A lack of Chicana/os and other minorities in management positions at the local stations was cited by the foundation as one of the reasons these series did not typically result in long-term employment or pro-gramming changes. Even before this shift, however, the Ford Founda-tion seemed to prefer an assimilationist tone for their Chicana/o and Puerto Rican series, as was mentioned earlier in regard to their feed-back to the producers of *Canción de la Raza*. As Noriega notes, a short-fall in the foundation's support for Chicana/o and Latina/o television was that "Ford identified Chicanos in narrowly socioeconomic terms as a 'targeted audience' consisting of Spanish-speaking families with low incomes, blue-collar employment and below average education."[69] Unfortunately, its view of Mexican Americans apparently did not expand as a result of their short-term experiment with Latina/o programming in the late '60s and early '70s.

The window of opportunity for Latina/o-authored public affairs programs was shifting in other ways as well. Presidents Richard Nixon and Gerald Ford were less supportive of public broadcasting, and the CPB subsequently lost some of its government funding. National sentiment also was turning away from the War on Poverty, while Chicana/o and Puerto Rican civil rights protest-style activism began to diminish as well, in face of the Federal Bureau of Investigation (FBI)'s COIN-TELPRO, which introduced covert infiltrators into and surveillance of several ethnic activist groups and other disruptions that caused many groups to weaken and splinter.[70] Pressure also was lessening on the stations as the FCC began a period of "deregulation" in the mid-1970s and particularly after Ronald Reagan became president in 1981. FCC policies that had encouraged stations to prove their service to local communities and to serve public interest more broadly began to be repealed.[71]

At this juncture the CPB became the primary funding source for Latina/o programming for public television, with the NEA and NEH serving as secondary funders. However, the CPB supported very few Latina/o projects in the 1970s, and in fact its program development chief, Peter Levathes, was not supportive of Chicana/o and Latina/o media, which he deemed too political for PBS programming. Ruiz and Treviño, two of the very few advocates of Latina/o media able to take part in occasional meetings at which CPB funding was discussed, note that he and a few (but not all) of the other CPB staff also saw Latina/os as an unimportant part of the public television audience. Ruiz commented: "If you would talk with them about Chicano programming, they'd be like 'What's a Chicano?'" About Latina/o programming beyond the Southwest, they'd say, "'Where are they?' These were people mainly from the Midwest and educational television. And they didn't know us. If they did, they said, 'Oh, farm workers.' They didn't think of us as urban people; they thought of us as rural workers and very local."[72]

To try to offset Levathes's disregard for proposals focused on Latina/os, Ruiz and Treviño spent a great deal of time and energy in the 1970s getting to know the other CPB personnel and staff at the National Endowment for the Arts and National Endowment for the Humanities, also potential funders. Their aim was to convince them of the importance of Latina- and Latino-helmed media projects and particularly of the importance of adding Latina/o members to the judging panels that decided each year which media project proposals to fund. They noted that this gradually began to have a positive impact on the funding of Latina/o media projects.

Hired as director of the Latino Consortium in 1975, Ruiz convened a national conference of staff from twenty-nine television stations that discussed Latina/o television production and programming. Among other results, it birthed the National Latino Media Coalition, which focused in part on lobbying for federal funding for Latina/o media producers. Humberto Cintrón, other *Realidades* producers, Ruiz, and the Latino Consortium also agreed to develop the first national Latina/o series, a new iteration of *Realidades* (1975–78). As Ruiz later noted,

> it came down to whether we were going to be supportive as Latinos to this Puerto Rican project. And we all agreed to do it, including the Tejanos [who initially were the most resistant], which was a big coup. But we said we've had Chicano projects done, but there's never been a Puerto Rican one other than *Realidades*. And so we're going to go for it. Next time around we'll do a Chicano project.[73]

Ultimately *Realidades* was one of the few Latina/o projects that the CPB funded in these years, however. The CPB provided $60,000 for the series pilot and later a $950,000 budget for two seasons,[74] which aired in twenty-three segments. Cintrón served as executive producer and director; salsa musician Willie Colón was the musical director. The series' premiere in 1975 focused on the National Latino Media Coalition conference, held in San Antonio in April of that year. Also featured was Pedro Pietri, an activist poet considered the founder of the Nuyorican movement, performing a moving tribute to urban New York, "Puerto Rican Obituary." To include the opening stanza: "Here lies Juan / Here lies Miguel / Here lies Milagros / Here lies Olga / Here lies Manuel / who died yesterday today / and will die again tomorrow / Always broke / Always owing / Never knowing / that they are beautiful people / Never knowing / the geography of their complexion."[75] Other episodes included "Who's Afraid of Bilingual Education" and "Your Vote is Powerful." This national version of *Realidades* aired on PBS stations around the country from 1975 through 1977.

In 1978, a Task Force on Minorities in Public Broadcasting, charged with assessing the impact of the Public Broadcasting Act, concluded that the CPB and public television and radio were failing to serve minority audiences. Public television and radio stations and the CPB were not putting adequate funding into programming for communities of color, it found, while 52 percent of public television stations had no minority employees.[76] The task force's recommendations included funding minority programming on a continuous, substantial basis; hiring employees of color; and including people of color in decision-making positions with respect to the dispersal of CPB production funds. In response to these findings, the CPB began to allocate annual funding to African American, Latina/o, Asian American, and American Indian organizations tasked with dispersing CPB funds for media projects that would air on public television.

The Latino Consortium, now renamed the Latino Media Communications Center, began vetting, funding, and syndicating Latina/o media productions for public television with CPB funds, but was stymied in doing so. The CPB was still failing Latina/o audiences, Treviño argued in 1983.[77] It had hired only one employee of Latina/o descent in fourteen years, typically lacked Latina/o representation on its selection panels, and had devoted only 2 percent of its funding to Latina/o programming in the previous three years, he noted. Among the few productions CPB funded in these years were the *Realidades* series, a handful of documentary film projects, including one by Treviño, and *Oye Willie* (1980–81),[78] a drama produced at WNET about a Puerto Rican boy growing up in Spanish Harlem. *Presente!*, an anthology program produced by Consortium members and independent filmmakers, also was produced by the Latino Consortium and KCET in 1979. When the Latino Media Communications Center was found at fault in 1998 by the CPB for mishandling some of its funding, it was shut down as the clearinghouse for independent Latina/o media projects. Latino Public Broadcasting, an organization formed by actor Edward James Olmos and others, was subsequently anointed to fulfill this function, as it continues to do today.

While political-minded public affairs shows were waning, they gave way to Chicana/o-oriented documentaries, narrative feature films, and theatrical performances that occasionally aired in the 1970s and 1980s on public television and network affiliates. Most visible were the theatrical performances of Teatro Campesino, led by their director, Luis Valdez. Teatro Campesino's *Los Vendidos* (*The Sellouts*), a one-act play, was written by Valdez in 1967 and produced for television by José Luis Ruiz at KNBC in Burbank in 1972. Remarkably, in Los Angeles it aired directly after the Super Bowl, bringing it a large, unknowing audience to experience Chicana/o theater for the first time. It and Valdez's earlier work for television prompted a special Emmy award for directing for Valdez in 1973. Teatro Campesino later produced several other productions for public television and network affiliates. These included *Zoot Suit: The Play, The Promise* (1978), produced at KNXT, now KCBS, and *Los Corridos* (1984), produced at KQED in San Francisco.

As the ethos of "by us, for us" shifted to producing Latina/o television programming for a larger, national audience, the issue of what can be lost in such transitions is useful to consider, as this was what Latina/o creative professionals on the verge of making a living in television and film must have grappled with. As Yolanda Broyles-González, who studied Teatro Campesino's adaptations of their theatrical work for television, argues, the political and cultural content of their productions was partially forfeited in the process of what she terms "mainstreaming."[79] For example, she critiqued Teatro Campesino's PBS special *Corridos: Tales of Passion and Revolution* (1987). As she noted, the production was pushed to include mainstream musical artist Linda Ronstadt as its primary performer and singer despite her lack of past connection to the Chicana/o Movement from which Teatro Campesino had sprung, dramatically reducing the political and social impact of the special for viewers. While the early Chicana/o public affairs series did not have to grapple with this problem, given that their audience was narrowly targeted, the price of compromises expected in order to appeal to non-Latina/os became a growing and steady concern of Latina/o producers who wanted to continue to use television to showcase for Latina/o perspectives and narratives.

Conclusions: The Television that Activism Built

While the series discussed in this chapter were for the most part short-lived, they demonstrated the potential of television to provide a forum for Chicana/o and Latina/o perspectives and to serve Latina/o communities, while the Latino and Latina creators and producers who worked on these shows also honed their production skills as they worked in this space. This survey also underscores the importance of individual activist producers such as Jesús Treviño, José Luis Ruiz, Humberto Cintrón, Susan Racho, and Luis C. Garza, who devoted their lives at this juncture to producing Chicana/o and Latina/o television, opening doors for more Latina/os to gain skills as media producers, amplifying the voices of their community members, and making space for Latina/os at local television stations and on media funding boards.

These producers at times faced obstacles to creating the programming that they wished, however. While broadcasting was a promising way to reach Chicana/o and Latina/o communities and to educate others about Chicana/o and Latina/o history and concerns, this meant being subjected to the typically Anglo-centric standards and practices of individual stations or of a funder such as the Ford Foundation. On the other hand, some of the managers and staff of individual stations made a real difference with respect to their support, as in the case of Charles Allen's support of the efforts of Eduardo Moreno and Jesús Treviño at KCET, or if on the other hand they did not support Latina/o programming. And the launch of Latina/o series pitched to national audiences brought about complicated dynamics to navigate as well, with respect to both attempting to appeal to the widely diverse national Latina/o audience and facing the potential pitfalls of mainstreaming.

Chicana/o and Puerto Rican viewers in turn were responsive to shows unabashedly produced for and about them. They made clear in surveys that they wanted shows that reflected their diverse histories and cultural heterogeneity, rather than series that lumped Latina/os under one homogenized umbrella. They also were wise enough to know that one series would not in any way make up for a media system that usually discounted their presence. As Eiselein, who had worked on *Fiesta*, noted in a 1974 study of Mexican Americans' television consumption, they wished "*not* for a single series, but rather for a total programming strategy."[80]

The growth of Chicana/o and Latina/o television required access and individual opportunity to produce local programming, professional training and socialization, consistent and adequate funding, and clearly delineated goals. Latina/o authorship, oversight, and voice were not guaranteed. While funding from the Ford Foundation and Corporation for Public Broadcasting was instrumental in the birth and growth of Chicana/o and Latina/o television, neither entity displayed a deeper, long-term commitment of Latina/o creative authorship or agency in these years. Their ambivalence in this regard and political shifts at the national level meant there was only a brief window of commitment to Latina/o authorship and communities and to the potential of local television stations to foster Latina/o cultural citizenship. Lack of access and cultural capital within the public and commercial television industries were ultimately barriers that Latina/o creatives experienced with respect to national programming; these obstacles were only beginning to be eradicated in the 1970s.

3

1970s

Always the Chico *(and Never the Writer)*

The advent of the first Chicana/o and Latina/o public affairs programs, many of which were led by the first Latina/o television producers in the early 1970s, prompts the question of whether Latina/os were beginning to have an impact in commercial television at the national level. The answer, sadly, was no. While ABC, CBS, and NBC likely felt less beholden to local and ethnic communities than was the case for the public television and network affiliate stations where the first Latina/o series were produced, they were under some pressure from media advocates representing various ethnic groups and the EEOC to demonstrate how they were serving viewers of color. This pressure ultimately had little "teeth" with regard to prime-time network programming, however.

For Latina and Latino actors who wanted to work on network TV shows, this meant they had to scramble—and compete—for a minute number of roles. In the 1970s, this usually meant Mexican American or Mexican guest roles written by non-Latino writers. At best, they might be exploited but dignified migrant workers; at worst, prostitutes, criminals, and gang members. It was a rare prize to audition for a character who was a professional such as a teacher or lawyer, as these roles mostly didn't exist, at least not for Latina/os. To be a Latino or Latina actor was to be considered only for roles conspicuously marked as Latina/o. They couldn't be cast, for instance, as a doctor who was incidentally Mexican. Ethnicity always had to be foregrounded. In contrast, a few starring roles for African Americans began to appear at this time, as cultural diversity began to be imagined on television, but as black and white. The popularity of Bill Cosby and Diahann Carroll in *I Spy* (1965–68) and *Julia* (1968–71), respectively, appears to have been especially influential in convincing network executives that American viewers would watch series with African American leads. Moreover, as writers over the decades ranging from Jack Kerouac to Norman Mailer, and in more recent years Joel Dinerstein and Rebecca Walker, have noted, African Americans have long been viewed as lending an edgy, urban hipness in US popular culture texts.[1] In contrast, Latina/os and particularly Mexican Americans arguably were viewed by television professionals as foreigners, laborers, or belonging only to rural story worlds, which lent to a television industry mindset in which compelling narratives would necessarily have protagonists that were white or black. Chicana/o and Puerto Rican civil rights concerns and activism got far less screen time than the black civil rights movement on national news broadcasts.[2] And while more Latina/os were going to college in the 1970s than ever before, and demands for Chicana/o and Latina/o studies programs were beginning to be heard on college campuses, this appears to have had little to no influence yet on national conceptualizations. In other words, the idea of Latina/o cultural citizenship was just being conceived.

The lack of visibility of and knowledge about Mexican Americans, Puerto Ricans, and other US Latina/os on the part of Anglo television creatives resulted in depictions of Latina/os only as minor characters, typically as vulnerable individuals living in squalid conditions and, at times, in need of rescue. One illustration is a 1963 episode of the ABC series *The Fugitive* (1963–67), "Smoke Screen." The titular white protagonist on the run finds himself in a Mexican farm workers' camp; he ultimately reveals he's a doctor to save the life of a pregnant woman in the camp. And in "Barrio," a 1977 episode of *Lou Grant* (1977–82), about a fictional Los Angeles newspaper, a white female reporter explores a Latina/o neighborhood, but only to learn why a Latina resident was shot by a gang member. The barrio was highlighted as a setting of hardship and danger. Such "special episodes" that showcased Latina/o plight resulted in small guest roles for Latina/o actors; typically, they never resulted in a recurring role. As Bel Hernandez, president and CEO of Latin Heat Media, noted in an interview about her work as an actor in these years, "To get a minor recurring role, that would be a big thing! But that almost never happened." In other interviews with actors, I was told that they met the few other Latina/o actors working in the industry at auditions, as they all were competing for the same few parts.[3]

Chicana/o or Puerto Rican activism was generally not acknowledged in network series narratives, even in these peak years of activism; if it was, it was usually badly misconstrued. An example is a 1971 episode of *The Smith Family* (1971–72), a family drama that starred Henry Fonda as an LAPD sergeant and family man. The episode, apparently written by executive producer Don Fedderson, in fact is titled "Chicano." In this episode, Sergeant Smith has to arrest Ramon, who is a Chicano activist—which, according to the episode, entails nihilistically making and setting bombs and spending time with other ne'er-do-well young militants, as well as neglecting his young sister in his charge. She later is removed from their home, with her brother's secret agreement, by child welfare services. Sergeant Smith is shown as justified in viewing Ramon primarily as a young criminal and unfit guardian.

Chicana/o and Latina/o advocacy groups, which now included the Mexican American Legal Defense and Education Fund (MALDEF), the League of United Latin American Citizens (LULAC), the National Council of La Raza (NCLR), and the media-specific groups Justicia (Justice), the National Mexican American Anti-Defamation Committee (NMAADC), and the Imagen Foundation, actively protested against these sorts of common characterizations of Latina/os on network television. Founded in 1971, Justicia gained particular traction with the networks in its efforts, after representatives established a working relationship with ABC.[4] They had the network's agreement—albeit one that was unenforceable—that they could review scripts featuring Mexican American characters. Their demands to all three networks included that they set aside $10 million to create new shows "with Chicanos in significant roles" as compensation for decades of demeaning portrayals.[5] As I described in chapter 2, activist-minded community members had begun to challenge station license renewals to put pressure on their local stations in Los Angeles and other cities to push for Latina/o employment and programming; they took up these efforts with the networks as well. Given the expense of fighting bad press and license renewal challenges, network executives tried to keep advocacy groups appeased in part through showing efforts to develop a series or two that might be considered for broadcast.[6] Meanwhile, the EEOC hearings, discussed in chapter 2, had put pressure on the networks to at least pay lip service to improving ethnic and racial diversity in their employment and programming. Some white writers and producers, many of whom were Jewish, were also personally motivated to tell the stories of Chicana/os and other

Latina/os because of an affinity they felt for the Chicana/o and Puerto Rican civil rights movements. Meanwhile, Chicana/o and Latina/o actors were often sharply divided on whether working in Hollywood films and in network television was a valid career objective or "selling out" the goals of the Mexican American community and Chicana/o activism.[7]

In the midst of these social shifts and negotiations, Latina/os were still largely on the outside when it came to creative authorship. Television writers and producers, and importantly, network executives were almost exclusively white men, and it was typically not possible for others to gain the training and experience needed to join their ranks. One exception I came across in my research was the late William Douglas Lansford (1922–2013), known to his friends as Bill Lansford, a writer of Mexican, English, and Scots Irish descent. His widow, Ruth Lansford, talked with me about her husband's remarkable career. Lansford was a television, film, and non-fiction book writer whose work in television stretched from 1956, when he wrote a script for the anthology drama *Four Star Playhouse* (1952–56), through *Star Trek: The Next Generation* (1987–94) in 1991. Throughout his long career he wrote for a wide variety of popular series, including *Bonanza* (1959–73), *The Rookies* (1971–76), *Ironside* (1967–75), *Starsky and Hutch* (1975–79), and *CHiPs* (1977–83). Lansford may have received more opportunities because his last name did not signal his Mexican heritage to his colleagues, but he didn't shy away from writing about Mexicans and Mexican Americans.[8] His work included several TV movies and feature films focused on Mexican American and Mexican characters and historical figures. These included *Villa Rides* (1968), based on his book about Mexican revolutionary hero Pancho Villa; the television movie *The Deadly Tower* (1975), based on a real-life mass shooting at the University of Texas by an unhinged sniper who was stopped by a Mexican American police officer (played by Richard Yniguez); and *Who Will Sing the Songs?* (1990), about a middle-aged man who creates family turmoil when he decides to become a mariachi musician, which starred popular musical artists Freddy Fender and Vikki Carr. Lansford was the exception rather than the rule as a Latino writer in a position of creative autonomy, however, and he often had to contend with showrunners who resisted his inclusion of Latina/o characters in episode scripts, particularly in the 1970s and 1980s.[9]

Because of these industry dynamics, I set out in this chapter to illuminate some of the rare moments when Latina/o-focused series and pilots were included in the commercial networks' prime-time lineups in this period. In addition to exploring this decade of programming broadly, I examine two series in depth, one now viewed as a failed experiment, *Viva Valdez* (1976), and one that was deemed a hit, *Chico and the Man* (1974–78). *Viva Valdez*, which aired on ABC from May through September 1976, centered on a Mexican American family in East Los Angeles, and starred film actors Rodolfo Hoyos Jr. and Carmen Zapata. While it had the distinction of being the first commercial network series about a Mexican American family, it was badly written, poorly promoted, and failed to draw a large audience. Most of the other Latina/o-focused series in this decade suffered the same fate. In contrast, *Chico and the Man*, the one successful series of the decade by network standards, centered on the culture clash that ensues when a carefree young Chicano, Francisco "Chico" Rodriguez (Freddie Prinze), pushes his way into the life of a crotchety and bigoted white auto shop owner, Ed Brown (Jack Albertson). Chico endures Ed's barbs with good cheer, and eventually they come to appreciate each other and become almost like father and son. Some viewers clearly enjoyed the chemistry between Prinze and Albertson and were able to overlook the far-fetched premise; despite protests from other viewers that the series portrayed Mexican Americans in a demeaning light, it became a hit, finishing as one of the top-five shows of the 1974–75 season. It also made Prinze a national star before he tragically died by suicide in 1977. In addition to interrogating how each series imagined and constructed notions of Mexican American, Chicana/o (in the case of *Chico and the Man)* and Latina/o identity and culture, I examine how they were produced, envisioned their audiences, and were promoted, with an eye to the industry climate for Latina/o storytelling in this era without Latina/o storytellers.

Latina/os and '70s Network TV

The Big Three networks and individual producers in this era, for the first time, began on a small scale to try to develop a few Latina/o-focused series. Within and as a result of Chicana/o activist agitation and national pressure, a handful of Latina/o-focused series were imagined, greenlit, and produced as pilots and a few series. *Chico and the Man*, notably, is the only series of this era that is well remembered today. With all of its flaws and critics, which I discuss later in this chapter, it was buoyed, at least initially, by the talent and charm of its star, Freddie Prinze, a young comedian of Puerto Rican and Hungarian descent. Meanwhile, all other Latina/o series that were attempted never made it to broadcast or were canceled after airing a few episodes or a season. I define a Latina/o series as one that has at least one Latina or Latino protagonist and acknowledges Latina/o cultural identity at some point in the narrative.[10] In the 1970s, these series included, in addition to *Chico and the Man*, the drama *The Man and the City* (ABC, 1971–72), starring film actor Anthony Quinn as the mayor of a Southwestern city; *Hernandez, Houston PD* (NBC, 1973), a series pilot that ultimately aired as a television movie and starred Henry Darrow, of *High Chaparral* (1967–71) fame, as a Houston police detective with a complicated home life;[11] *On the Rocks* (ABC, 1975–76), an improbable sitcom about the hijinks of and camaraderie among a group of inmates and sympathetic guards at a prison; and *Popi* (CBS, 1975), a dramedy about a Puerto Rican widower with two unruly sons, based on a recent film of the same name.

How did the networks view these series and their possibilities? Not with a great deal of seriousness, I would argue. Likely they were greenlit because demonstrating an interest in a Latina/o series could keep advocacy groups off their backs and lend to their appeal to the younger and more socially aware audience beginning to influence programming as advertisers pushed to capture this desired subset of viewers.[12] This Baby Boomer audience played a decisive role in the success of such politically aware comedy and drama series as *All in the Family* (1971–79), *Good Times* (1974–79), *M*A*S*H* (1972–83), and *Barney Miller* (1975–82).[13] The writers and producers of these series, such as Norman Lear and Hal Kanter, were largely Jewish American and progressive minded, and aimed for their programming to help promote a less racist, more compassionate society while also drawing in a large audience of American viewers. However, even while *Good Times* and several other series focused on African American families, and series such as *All in the Family* regularly focused on black–white relations, Latina/o characters were seldom included in these series' story worlds, despite that fact that Chicana/os and Puerto Ricans had been publicly fighting similar social and political battles.

Figure 3.1. Anthony Quinn, star of *The Man and the City*, and guest star Janice Rule, in a 1971 episode of the series, "A Hundred Black Pages."

One of the few Latina/o "sightings" that I came across in this cycle of programs was a recurring character in *Sanford and Son*, about a cantankerous African American junk dealer and his adult son in South Central Los Angeles. In "The Puerto Ricans are Coming!" which aired November 10, 1972, Fred Sanford gets a new next-door neighbor, Julio Fuentes, played by Puerto Rican actor Gregory Sierra, and is upset to learn that he is Puerto Rican and opening a junk business of his own.[14] Fred initially is completely rejecting, making fun of Julio's name and describing Puerto Ricans as destroying neighborhoods with their "Puerto Rican cockroaches" and "Puerto Rican rats," but his son Lamont, the voice of reason on the show, has befriended Julio and defends him. For his part, Julio is confident and capable, in every way Fred Sanford's match. However, his underdeveloped character comes across as a social misfit as well. He lives alone and has no connection with other Latina/os. While he has cleaned up his property, he also keeps a goat (to eat his trash), which wanders into Fred's living room twice. The recurring sight gag and implications of rural backwardness are hard to disassociate from his character, despite his later character development as simply a neutral friend of the Sanfords.

All in the Family's approach to Latina/o guest stars also hewed close to industry norms that typically forgot to include Latina/o characters and cultures. Norman Lear and Bud Yorkin's hit comedy focused on Archie Bunker, a bigoted white World War II veteran, and his clashes with his more progressive son-in-law and daughter, Michael and Gloria, over Archie's racist, sexist, and homophobic ideologies. Michael's friend Lionel, who was African American, became a recurring character whose own family became the subject of a spin-off, *The Jeffersons* (1975–85). However, Latina/o characters were seldom seen. In "The Elevator Story," written by Alan J. Levitt and Lear and broadcast January 1, 1972, Archie gets on an elevator with three strangers: the Mendozas, a working-class Puerto Rican couple played by Hector Elizondo and Edith Diaz; a wealthy African American man; and a seemingly wealthy white woman. When the elevator gets stuck between floors for several hours, everyone's true feelings are revealed. Archie is rude to the Puerto Rican couple, particularly upon finding the wife is pregnant, and is surprised that the African American man has similar thoughts. Carlos Mendoza, who reveals that he is the janitor of the building, is able to ably defend himself from Archie's barbs, proving his intelligence and compassion in how he treats Archie despite his bigotry. As the group's wait for rescue is prolonged, the couple's baby is eventually born on the elevator, and Archie finally is touched by the humanity of the birth and by the couple as new parents. He has shifted from hostility to tolerance and perhaps even a sense of kinship, although he is loath to admit it. The husband and wife were not brought back as recurring characters on the series, however, unlike Lamont Jefferson and his parents, George and Louise.

There additionally were occasional Latina/o characters in ensemble-cast shows who were fantastical in their absurdity in this television era. A case example is Juan Luis Pedro Felipo de Huevos Epstein (yes, de Huevos, "of Eggs" in Spanish), a Puerto Rican and Jewish student who was part of Mr. Kotter's "Sweathogs" class in *Welcome Back, Kotter* (1975–79). Played by the late Robert Hegyes, who was Hungarian and Italian American, Juan was chosen by his peers as the student "Most Likely to Take a Life," but was more wise guy than tough guy; he made money selling absurd excuses from parents for missing homework assignments.

In addition, the few series that directly aimed to relate the stories of Latina/o lead characters were problematic and hampered in a variety of ways, whether through writing teams misunderstanding their own characters or through mishandling the production and promotion of a series. As Todd Gitlin notes in his 1983 study of the television industry, network executives' decisions about greenlighting new series in the 1970s and early '80s were (and, I argue, still are) based on reducing the risk of failure, given how difficult it is to predict whether a new series will appeal to a large enough audience.[15] In line with the patterns described by Gitlin, Latina/o-oriented series used the same strategies. Executives tried to reduce risk by casting already popular stars in lead roles, by greenlighting "pre-sold" properties (such as a popular movie), and/or by repeating popular story formulas. Two of ABC's efforts, *The Man and the City* and *On the Rocks*, and CBS's *Popi* illustrate several of these strategies. As was noted earlier, *The Man and the City* starred Anthony Quinn as a mayor of a Southwestern city.[16] ABC's promotion of the series focused heavily on Quinn's celebrity and critical acclaim.[17] Despite this, it failed to pull in more viewers than the other series in its time slot, CBS's detective series *Mannix* and NBC's *Night Gallery*, a Rod Serling anthology drama series.[18] It ran for fifteen episodes, from

Figure 3.2. The cast of *On the Rocks*. Standing, from the left: Leonard Stone, Hal Williams, Rick Hurst, Jay Gerber, Bobby Sandler. Seated: José Pérez.

September 1971 through January 1972, after which it was canceled. *On the Rocks* (1975–76), in contrast, was a sitcom with an improbable premise—it was set in a prison. This remake of the hit British series *Porridge* (1974–77), created by *Porridge* producers Dick Clement and Ian La Frenais, overlooked the harsh realities of incarceration, stressing instead lighthearted banter and regular laughs.[19] The series starred Puerto Rican actor José Pérez as Hector Fuentes, a charming Puerto Rican small-time thief returning to Alameda Minimum Security Prison after some time outside.[20] Perhaps because of its subject matter, it struggled to be continuously funny over 23 episodes.[21] It aired Monday nights, where it lost to CBS's *Rhoda*.[22]

Finally, CBS's *Popi* (1975) was an example of banking on a "pre-sold property," as it was adapted from a popular 1969 comedic film about a Puerto Rican widower learning to parent two rambunctious sons on his own. The television version retained the film's writers, Tina and Lester Pine, and producer Herbert Leonard. It chose to cast Hector Elizondo, of Puerto Rican and Basque descent, in the lead role, while the film had cast a Jewish actor, Alan Arkin. Puerto Rican actress Edith Diaz played Abraham's girlfriend, depicted in the film by Rita Moreno.[23] Elizondo, in a 2015 interview for the Archive of American Television, describes it as "an idea before its time" that thus didn't succeed.[24] *Popi* aired and quickly languished opposite ABC's wildly successful *Happy Days*. After eleven episodes that aired from January through August 1975, it was canceled.

Among the failed Latina/o series of the decade was also a third effort by ABC, the family comedy *Viva Valdez*. *Viva Valdez* had the distinction of being the first nationally broadcast series about a Mexican American family. However, by many measures it also was the most spectacular failure of this decade of Latina/o programming. The creators and writing team included no Latina/os, and conflicts apparently rose between the writers and actors as a result. While only a few of the episodes are accessible at this time, the original pilot script and few episodes that are archived are strong illustrations of how a Mexican American series can lack a Mexican American perspective. It aired a short series of twelve episodes before it was canceled by ABC. In the following section, I explore the making of the series, the narrative, and the response that it received from television critics and viewers.

The First Mexican American Family Sitcom: *Viva Valdez*

Viva Valdez, which aired on ABC in 1976, provides a vivid illustration of Mexican Americans' outsider status to the commercial television networks at the national level in this decade. An adaptation of *The Plouffe Family*, a popular Canadian radio and television series about a plumber and his family, by Jack Wohl, Bernard Rothman, and Stan Jacobson, *Viva Valdez* aired at 8 p.m. Mondays, beginning May 31, 1976.[25] It centered on the Valdez family in East Los Angeles, with Rodolfo Hoyos Jr. and Carmen Zapata leading the cast as Luis and Sophia Valdez. Its positioning as a summer replacement series (then the "dead time" in the programming year) signals that ABC wasn't expecting it to be a major draw, however.

As could be expected in this time period, the series was written by a team of non-Latino writers, in addition to creators Wohl, Rothman, and Jacobson and producers Phil Mishkin and Alan Rafkin. Asked prior to the series premiere about how he felt *Viva Valdez* would do, considering the recent failure of *Popi* and other ethnic family sitcoms, Wohl stressed to journalist Paul Henninger that he was optimistic that the series had universal appeal. "[*Viva Valdez*] has Mexican American color, but one of the things you notice right away is that they're no different from anybody else. They have their problems, too."[26] Despite what were likely good intentions, Wohl's quick glossing of the Valdezes as just another American family with "Mexican American color" lends a dismissive tone that in retrospect is hard to miss. It comes as no surprise in an era of television characterized by very few portrayals of Latina/o families, however.

Notably, negativity and dysfunction were the dominant family traits I observed in the original pilot script for *Viva Valdez* by Elias Smith and Frank Shaw, which later aired as the series' fifth episode.[27] The family members largely fight and show little regard for one another. Luis doesn't want to make his son, Victor, a partner in the plumbing business that he started but that Victor now actively works in. Sophia tells their teen daughter, Connie, to make the most of a blind date, saying she'll soon be too old to get married. These scenarios are meant to be funny, but aren't. Luis and Sophia bicker throughout the episode. These stories run counter in particular to traditional Mexican American values, which typically privilege family commitments over work and emphasize young women's virginity before marriage. Finally, Sophia's full day of cooking results only in . . . bean burritos and mole sauce. Any self-respecting Mexican American mother in the 1970s would have included meat in a meal for her hungry family. In other words, the writers apparently didn't have a clue about Mexican American families and culture.

Figure 3.3. The Valdez family in the 1976 series *Viva Valdez*. The cast consisted of, from left, standing: Nelson D. Cuevas, Claudio Martinez, and Lisa Mordente; seated: Rodolfo Hoyos Jr., Carmen Zapata, and James Victor. The white line in the photograph is an alteration related to its publication in a newspaper or magazine.

The series was retooled in production, however. For instance, the credit sequence, promotional ads, and publicity photos for *Viva Valdez* stressed the closeness and happiness of the Valdez family, which included Sophia and Luis's three sons Victor, Ernesto, and Pepe, daughter Connie (played by Lisa Mordente, the daughter of Broadway actress/dancer Chita Rivera, of Puerto Rican, Scottish, and Italian descent), and Luis's cousin, Jerry. The promos present the Valdezes as happy, easygoing Americans in an introductory montage. Sophia happily cooks in her kitchen, giving Luis a bite of food to taste, and they embrace; Luis and Victor show frustration but comfort with one another as they work together; Jerry ogles pretty coeds on a college campus; Connie perkily does a cheer with her fellow cheerleaders; and Victor and Pepe play baseball. The happy-go-lucky musical score and a few disparate cultural markers (Sophia cooking tortillas on the stove, and baseball) are meant to signal that this cheerful family is Latino.

One of the few episodes accessible to researchers today was the fourth to air. "Nervous Breakup," written by Howard Albrecht and Sol Weinstein, aired on June 21, 1976. It focuses on the family's goofy interloper, cousin Jerry (Mexican actor Jorge Cervera Jr.). Jerry, naïve and simpleminded, is set up as the comic foil of the series. His catch phrase, "Hello, everybody!!" (which calls to mind Jimmie "J.J." Walker's "Dy-no-mite!"on *Good Times* [1974–80], also airing in these years on CBS), appears meant to reinforce that he's a funny, idiosyncratic newcomer to American culture. However, Cervera portrays Jerry with a knowing wink, and his mestizo appearance and accent do lend warmth to his character and credence to the Valdez family as Mexican American.

In the episode, the family learns that Jerry has been acting strangely around his girlfriend, Inez (Maria O'Brien). He's been very distant and sleepwalking at night at their house. (This implies that they're living together out of wedlock, somewhat surprising for prime-time content in this time period, but nothing is made of it.) When the Valdezes realize Jerry's sleepwalking is rooted in wanting to propose to Inez and fear that she'll reject him, each family member tries to coach him in how to propose, with their distinct personalities, age, gender, and experience with love (or, in the case of his nephews and niece, lack of experience) coloring their advice. When Jerry decides he'll take a chance and propose, he's so nervous about what to say that Connie writes their ideas on index cards and hides them through the living room. As Jerry gets tongue-tied, he reads them verbatim, in a patchwork, nonsensical proposal. At first confused, Inez is touched by how hard it was for him to ask her and by his feelings for her. She says no—exactly what he feared—but adds that she has strong feelings about him, too, and just wants to wait, in what ends up being a happy conclusion. The Valdezes are kind and warm with each other throughout the episode, in contrast to how they were depicted in the screenplay draft for the pilot. However, jokes are often made at Jerry's expense. For example, in response to Inez saying she was worried about Jerry acting strange, Luis says, "Jerry, strange; with him how can you tell?" The laugh track that follows emphasizes that not only that this is this funny, but that Jerry is meant to be laughed at. The show also often makes fun of Jerry's accent. For instance, he says to Ernesto, "tell me how to say something sentimentimental" in his proposal to Inez. In describing his job working at a car manufacturing plant, he also says earnestly that he works in the "glove department" (rather than the glove box department). These errors are treated as comical and Jerry thus as comical as well. Nods to the family's Mexican American identity are featured in the episode only in the form of stereotypical, flat references. For example, Luis has purchased a cologne called "Mucho Macho" from Inez, who is a seller for an Avon-like company. Ernesto also teases his brother Victor for presuming he's a marriage expert, calling him "Abigail Van *Burrito*."

Another episode, "Papa's Legacy," aired as the series' eighth episode on August 18, 1976. It was written by Earl Barret, a white writer from Ohio, who wrote several episodes of the series. Again, the narrative might be considered universal to any American family, with no clear link to Mexican American experience. After the family goes to the funeral of a contemporary of Luis and Sophia, Luis decides that he must write down his wishes before he unexpectedly passes away and begins to draft his will. He initially he chooses to make his children's and wife's inheritance contingent on them making particular choices about their lives. When they all rebel against being told how to live their lives, he realizes his mistake. He drops his ideas about the will in favor of enjoying life with his family in the present.

The episode includes some idiosyncratic behavior on the part of several family members that is included simply to add humor. For instance, Ernesto goes to the funeral in a flamboyant ruffled shirt and considers it an opportune time to hit on women, and Luis obsesses on the fact there is makeup on the deceased man, which he finds emasculating. In contrast to Luis's wish to put his final wishes in writing, Sophia is superstitious and scared about him doing this, feeling it is flirting with death. For her part, their daughter Connie is relaxed. For instance, she asks seemingly endless questions about how he wants his will formatted as she takes shorthand for him, a skill she is learning in school. And Jerry again is positioned as a kind-hearted but naïve interloper. When Luis is about to tell the family his last wishes, Jerry interrupts: "In Mexico people do not usually read their own wills. They can't. They are dead. They just lie there. You know . . . quiet." In this episode, the only elements that characterize the family members as identifiably Mexican American are clichés such as these that position the Valdez family as especially emotional, superstitious, lacking in seriousness, or naïve.

The lack of Latina/o writers appears to be at the root of many of the weaknesses of the series. Howard Albrecht, a Jewish American writer who cowrote a few episodes of *Chico and the Man* before becoming a story editor and writer for *Viva Valdez*, is an illuminating case in point. Albrecht notes that the he and Sol Weinstein felt they could successfully write scripts for the Valdez family without including Latina/o writers by writing as if the Valdezes were Jewish.

> I don't know about the others, but Sol and I wrote stories about a Jewish family. That we did know. The minute our all-Hispanic cast uttered our words and put in a couple of "Oy Dios" [*sic*], they turned what we wrote into something that sounded like it came straight from south of the border. If you haven't realized it yet, all families be they Italian, German, Irish, Jewish or Latino basically have the same problems and the same joys. It's just the food, the accents and the dirty words that make them different.[28]

Not everyone on the set felt the same way, however. Representatives from Justicia and Nosotros raised complaints to the production team.[29] And producer Phil Mishkin reported that the shoot was difficult because the actors were often unhappy with the scripts, even while some of the writers took their lack of knowledge too lightly.

> One of the problems was that we used a cast of Latino actors constantly at odds with us over authenticity. It was one of the great us-against-them fights that I was ever involved in. . . . It's always, "Those writers are giving us bullshit we can't say." "Those damned actors can't say our bullshit." But in this case, it was also ethnic mix. It seemed to give them the right to say, "You Jewish writers don't know what the hell you're talking about." I think we weren't all Jewish, but I remember somebody said to me, "Write it Jewish and their accents will make it funny and Latin." That was a kind of ethnic divisiveness that I didn't hold with. . . . The audience just didn't buy into that confusion.[30]

Carmen Zapata, in contrast, remembered these struggles from the actors' perspective when asked what had gone wrong. She told Wesley Hyatt, author of *Short-Lived Television Series, 1948–1978*, "We had writers coming out of the Catskills of New York. I definitely think there were missed opportunities and the writing was not what was needed."[31] Meanwhile, Jack Wohl invoked Zapata as the series' "in-house consultant" on Mexican American culture when the production team needed to stanch criticism about whether they could present Mexican Americans with respect and authenticity.[32] It appears that the creative team struggled to do so. In discussing what he saw as the weaknesses of the series, Mishkin claimed that they tried to hire Latina/o writers but there were none to be found. Of the few Latina/o writing apprentices they hired, he noted, "They never worked out. . . . They hadn't come up from the start. Still and all, we were trying to do a comedy. And they were not the people [to write comedy]."[33] It appears that he felt these writers, and the Chicano advocacy groups, had an agenda of uplift of Latina/os that was antithetical to television comedy—at least as he viewed it.

Chicanismo, Network TV-Style: *Chico and the Man*

In this same time period, one NBC series about a Latino main character, *Chico and the Man*, attracted a sizable audience and made its star a household name, despite complaints by some Latina/o viewers that it was a demeaning characterization. Like the other '70s series, it was conceived of and written without input from a Latino or Latina writer or other creative professional. The star, Freddie Prinze, did have significant creative impact on the series, however, after it proved a success for the network. What helped *Chico and the Man* succeed where other series with Latina/o protagonists failed, particularly in light of its problematic story premise?

In research that I published on Prinze and the series in 2009 and updated in this study, I found that *Chico and the Man*'s creator, James Komack, had primary control over how the narrative and characters were imagined, developed, and later modified in response to viewers' complaints.[34] The writer and producer, of Jewish descent, was well ensconced within the circle of working executive producers at the time the series was pitched. Komack had been a successful stand-up comedian before shifting to television as a writer and later executive producer on a number of successful series, including *My Favorite Martian* (1963–66), *Get Smart* (1965–70), and *The Courtship of Eddie's Father*

(1969–72). Komack maintained that *Chico and the Man* was his attempt to do something about the lack of Mexican American representation on television; he meant to introduce a Chicano character who was a positive role model. However, he had grown up in New York, with no connection to a Mexican American neighborhood or community, and it appears that his knowledge of Mexican American individuals and culture came later in life. Komack's original script for the pilot, "Now Chico!" (later revised and retitled "The Man Meets Chico"), showcased this lack of cultural knowledge.[35] Many of its problematic elements were removed in the revised pilot script, credited also to Don Nicholl, Michael Ross, and Bernie West. For instance, in the original script Chico understands the mechanics of cars, a skill he wants to use at Ed's garage, because "he's been stripping-them-down and ripping-them-off for years." Other elements that were not changed included that Chico has no job and spends his days wandering around the neighborhood. Perhaps most problematic, Chico has no family ties or friends and needs to live in Ed's garage, highly improbable for a charming young man in a vibrant Mexican American community where he had lived his whole life, aside from time spent serving in the Vietnam War. Families in a 1970s Mexican American community simply would never leave a young man without a place to sleep, something that the writers apparently didn't know. Ironically, this was during the years when young Chicana/os like those that worked on the public affairs series were most likely to be connecting with and helping others in their communities.

That the script was considered promising by NBC is indicative of the industry's misunderstanding of Mexican American culture and families, as well as perhaps the network's simple desire to get Chicana/o media advocates off their backs. As was noted earlier, Justicia had convinced the network to include a Chicana/o-led television series in their lineup. The network greenlit the pilot and a full season of episodes. When the time came to cast Chico, the casting call was shared widely, including with the advocacy groups. Reportedly over forty Latino actors auditioned; Freddie Prinze ultimately won the role opposite Jack Albertson. Among other actors, he beat out Mexican American actor Isaac Ruiz, who was cast as Chico's best friend, Mando.[36] The hiring of Prinze prompted criticism, however, as not hiring a Mexican American actor was seen as a major affront by Chicana/os in Los Angeles and around the country.

As was the case for the other Latina/o series of this decade, *Chico and the Man* was created and written by non-Latino writers. Fairly quickly, James Komack had to answer to critics questioning the series' cultural authenticity. Chicana/o media advocacy groups had a particularly loud voice and willingness to protest in various ways in this era, as I detail in chapter 2; Komack in turn attempted to pacify unhappy viewers. Among other strategies, Komack did interviews in which he described his deep ties to the Mexican American community. As a UPI newswire story noted on June 30, 1974, Komack was "deeply involved with the Hispanic culture and lifestyle" and had "talked to hundreds of Chicanos" before working on the series.[37] He was quoted as wanting to rectify the invisibility of Mexican Americans on television. He added, "They are a proud and beautiful part of the American scene, and I think viewers will take them to heart."[38] He claimed that he based Chico on two acquaintances, actor Cheech Marin, then a stand-up comedian, and a lesser-known actor, Ray Andrade.[39] Andrade, an actor and part-time military technical adviser on film shoots, perhaps not uncoincidentally was a past president of Justicia.[40] Before the series debuted, Justicia had lent its support. In a press release dated January 30, 1974, the organization stated that it and other groups approved of the pilot and felt the series would support "harmony between such various opposing factors as the young and the aged, Latin and Anglo, fear and confidence, love and respect."[41] When the series began to take heat, Andrade was also hired as a consultant to the production. His title was initially associate to the producer, and later changed to associate producer. If the hiring was meant to quiet complaints, the strategy soon backfired, however, as before long Andrade also spoke out against the series, as detailed further below.

Chico and the Man debuted on September 13, 1974, capitalizing on ethnic humor. Ed, who initially says he can't stand Mexicans, is driving business away with his crotchety demeanor; Chico cleans up the garage, helps Ed end his constant drinking, and soon brings business in with his good cheer and craftiness. In other words, Ed is a bigot who ultimately grows because he allows Chico into his life and learns from him. However, Chico's growth was never a focus in the first season.

Culture clash drove the early episodes; the jokes are especially barbed in the pilot and second episode. An example is the dialogue that ensues

Figure 3.4. Promotional materials for *Chico and the Man*, like this image from its pilot episode, emphasized the comedic clash and chemistry between its two protagonists, played by (from left) Freddie Prinze and Jack Albertson.

when Chico rides his bicycle into Ed's garage and meets Ed in the pilot episode.

ED: What are you doing in here?

CHICO: Who me?

ED: Yeah, you. Do you see anybody else in the garage?

CHICO: Garage? It looks to me like un basurero.

ED: What's that supposed to mean?

CHICO: Basurero. It means junk yard.

ED: Get out of here! And take your flies with you.

CHICO: What flies?

ED: Your Flies. You people got flies all around you. And while you're standing here your flies are getting together with my flies and making more flies!

CHICO: (somewhat sarcastically) You're a nice man.

ED: Would you get out here and get back to your neighborhood?

CHICO: This is my neighborhood. I grew up watching this garage run down! . . . You need me.

ED: For what?

CHICO: I'm Super Mex!

ED: Who's Super Mex?

CHICO: Super Mexicanic! Ask anybody about Chico Rodriguez . . .

As I noted in 2009, even while Ed adds that Chico's flies are now mating with his flies, his reframing doesn't completely absorb the sting of the ethnic slur.[42] The episode got strong ratings, however, which likely speaks both to the small percentage of the audience that was likely Latina/o at that time and also to Freddie Prinze's charisma and comedic chops. It earned the number three spot in the ratings, and critics were generally positive as well. As I shared in 2009, Lee Winfrey of *Philadelphia Inquirer* called it a "remarkably good show," and said Freddie Prinze "may be the best new comic who has developed anywhere in this country during this decade so far."[43] *Time*, similarly, called Prinze the "hottest new property on prime-time TV," while critic Cecil Smith described him as "one of the most gifted young comedians to come along in years."[44] Such praise ushered in Freddie Prinze's rise to stardom; the young actor was only twenty at the time. It was just a year prior that he had been noticed by Komack while performing on *The Tonight Show Starring Johnny Carson* and invited to audition for the role of Chico.

Freddie Prinze was born Frederick Karl Pruetzel on June 22, 1954, in New York City to a Puerto Rican mother and a Hungarian father of German descent. In his comedy act Prinze made fun of his multicultural, "Hungarican" heritage, which lent to his appeal as an American rising star but complicated his casting in a Mexican American role. Prinze grew up in Washington Heights, a working-class and multiethnic upper Manhattan neighborhood, and often used his supposed inner-city upbringing as fodder for his comedy. For instance, he cracked that his neighborhood was such a slum that "even the birds were junkies."[45]

With the debut of *Chico and the Man*, Freddie Prinze and his humor, tempered for television, made their way to prime time. Unsurprisingly, after he was cast, Chico was developed with Prinze's brash and topical stand-up comedy in mind. However, the comedy bits that were mined for inclusion were typically not politically challenging to stereotypical views of Puerto Ricans, Mexican Americans, or other Latina/os. Jokes included in *Chico* episodes (without credit to Prinze until an episode in the second season) included "Eez not my job," a line that Prinze in his stand-up act put in the mouth of his former apartment building super-intendent. When some viewers complained it supported notions of lazy Latina/os, this was replaced with Prinze's drawn out "Looking good!" The actor, then just twenty years old, was promoted in a manner in tune with the social consciousness and edgy aesthetic of the times. Magazines such as *Rolling Stone* and *Playboy* and teen-oriented *Tiger Beat* ran feature stories on Prinze as an urban man of the times, while *Chico and the Man* was spoofed in the satirical *MAD* magazine.[46] Prinze's stardom was further complicated by playing a Mexican American role. This became contentious, as Prinze was criticized for imbuing the role with his own cultural and comedy style.

After the pilot aired, protesters picketed NBC's Burbank studios and wrote letters protesting the casting of Prinze and the series' demeaning characterizations. Letter writers, both Latina/o and non-Latina/o, complained to the newspapers in Los Angeles and to the producers and NBC. They charged that the series premise of a Mexican American young man who wishes to work for a bigoted older white man only reinforced stereotypes and notions of Mexican American inferiority. For example, educators at the Los Angeles Hispanic Urban Center wrote in the *Los Angeles Times* that the series, through Chico, presented Chicano youth in a manner that "reinforces or elicits racist Anglo-American feelings of superiority over Chicanos by ridiculing the character of Chico."[47] Ray Andrade also chose to speak out publicly in October 1974. He charged that "the show does indeed lack authenticity. . . . And it's the result of non-Chicano writers. . . . There are good Chicano writers, but they won't hire them, now. They'll wait until the show is a solid hit before taking a chance on them."[48] The Chicano Coalition filed a petition to the FCC to deny the renewal of the NBC affiliate KNBC's license, stating in their affidavit that *Chico and the Man* was "detrimental to the self-image of Chicano children who watch it."[49] They also threatened boycotts of the series and its advertisers. Other critics, in contrast, felt that if changes were made and Chicanos were employed behind the scenes, the series could be salvaged.[50]

In response, the show's producers made broad changes to appease critics. Ed Brown's racist tendencies were softened, while Chico's Latino identity became more fluid. Chico was revealed to be half Puerto Rican and raised in New York, and even to have a grandmother who could "speak a little Hungarian."[51] Employment was also used as a public relations strategy. In this period when few Latina/os had training in media production or screenwriting and the experience to be hired as a writer for a television series, *Chico*'s all-white creative team hired a few Latina/o production assistants.[52] As Andrade alleged, Latina/o writers were not hired, however, even while they were now submitting unsolicited scripts. A $10,000 fund was created by NBC to assist in the development of *Chico and the Man* scripts by promising Chicana/o writers and other writers of color.[53] I found in my research, however, that the mentoring program never got off the ground, as there were disagreements over which of the series writers would mentor the writing apprentices.[54] Prinze, with his usual irreverent humor, defended his right to portray Chico. For instance, he was quoted as saying, "If I can't play a Chicano because I'm Puerto Rican, then God's really gonna be mad when he finds out Charlton Heston played Moses." He also questioned whether the politically correct portrayal of a Mexican American that protesters demanded was a realistic goal.

Chico as portrayed by Prinze did challenge previous patterns of depicting Latino and particularly Mexican American characters with respect to initially attempting to portray him as proudly Chicano. As I noted in 2009, his

> *Chicanismo* is made central as early as the pilot. In the episode storyline, Chico has decided to sneak back into Ed's garage and clean it up and move in, despite Ed's refusal to give him a job the day before. Some police officers come by and want to arrest him on suspicion of some thefts in the area, even though they have no proof he was involved. They ask if he has papers to prove he's legal, and this is his response: "Why; you got papers to prove where you were born? I'm a Chicano, man; I was born in this country. And what's more, we had it first! *Una pregunta chota* [Chicana/o

slang for "a cop question"] . . . And you people are the outsiders." He finishes, "I *hablo* your English; why can't you *habla* a little Español?" The reaction from the studio audience was one of laughter and applause, contributing to a prime-time first, an expression and celebration of Chicano identity.[55]

This was a monumental first, a moment of Chicana/o subjectivity and resistance on network television. The show in moments such as this provided a showcase for Chicana/o cultural citizenship. This symbolic rupture soon was forfeited, however. When Ed later provides an alibi for Chico to the cops, he glibly responds "Viva la Raza!" The series never followed through on constructing Chico as a nuanced Chicano character in the later episodes, moreover. Instead of clarifying the significance of "Chicano" as a label, the struggles and goals of Chicana/o activism, or the unique struggles of Mexican American Vietnam veterans, it filled these narrative gaps with props such as a "Chicano power" badge sewn to Chico's jacket and *serapes* used as décor in Chico's van.

While failing to persist in presenting a clearly Chicano point of view in the narrative, later episodes did offer other moments of ideological rupture, when whiteness was made strange and decentered through humor and language. While Chico was often established as subservient to Ed, as portrayed by Prinze he also was a cocky "Super Mex," an effective motivator, businessman, and lighthearted rebel. And given Prinze's considerable talent, his performances often spilled beyond the bounds of his character, for example in his constant mix of accents and ethnic impersonations, which hinted that his accent as Chico was also a performance. Spanish was also occasionally used in a manner that privileged bilingual viewers, as when Chico made comments to himself in Spanish that demonstrated his true frustration with Ed, or in scenes in which English-speaking characters misunderstand the Spanish spoken around them. Through moments such as these, a Latino if not Chicano sensibility drives the series, albeit briefly.

Prinze's performances in the last episodes that he acted in, and particularly the very last, "Ed Talks to God," are noticeably different from his sunnier performances in the first episodes of season one, however. He's wan, thin, and often looks ill at ease. In this episode, Prinze tries to trick Ed into thinking he's talking to God to convince him to accept a birthday party thrown in his honor by his friends. To deal with Ed's ire after he discovers the truth, Chico puts a knife to his own throat, in a supposed joke regarding what Ed wishes he could do to Chico. Because of Prinze's gaunt frame and serious demeanor, the humor doesn't really come through. Ed instead "gives" Chico a piece of cake—in the face. When Chico/Prinze laughs in this final moment along with the rest of the cast and the studio audience, it's a joyful moment reminiscent of his lighthearted performances in season one.

The shifts in Prinze's appearance and performance style were the result of depression and drug use, I learned from interviews that former members of the production team did with the Television Academy Foundation and other sources in recent years. Those who cared about the now twenty-two-year-old Prinze unfortunately were not able to stop him from getting in his own way through substance abuse, which occurred simultaneously to his being offered more creative agency. As writer Ron Friedman noted, it resulted in the production team having to adapt to a chaotic set and unpredictable star.[56] While Prinze now had a voice in episode development and could push for particular writers to be hired during the second season, this agency was for naught. When negotiations between the series producers and Chicana/os critiquing the series broke down because "each wanted something quite different for Chicanos within episodic television,"[57] Prinze, sadly, took his own creative vision out of these negotiations. From the outside, it appeared that all was well, however. Prinze told reporters not long before his death that one of his dreams was to produce and star in a series of his own making. *Chico and the Man* was nominated for a Golden Globe for Best Television Series—Comedy or Musical in 1976, while Jack Albertson was nominated for an Emmy for Best Lead Actor for his work on the series in 1975, 1976, and 1977, and won the award in 1976. Prinze was also nominated for a Best Actor Golden Globe prior to his death in 1977. Reportedly in fall 1976, he had signed a contract with NBC that provided over $6 million for five seasons of work. He also performed at President Jimmy Carter's inauguration celebration shortly before his death.

Freddie Prinze's death was a clear crisis for NBC. Hoping to bank on *Chico and the Man*'s prior success, they renewed it for another season, with Chico's character written off. A young Mexican American actor, Gabriel Melgar, was cast as a Raul Garcia, a Mexican boy who comes into Ed Brown's life after Chico Rodriguez has moved to New York. Ed, inexplicably, chooses to call Raul "Chico." The series never achieved the ratings of its first season, however, and was canceled in 1978. Despite this, the show's first two seasons had shown that casting talented Latina/os in roles in which their charms could shine through could be a recipe for a hit series. Encouraging Latina/o TV stardom became one of the network's overriding strategies for Latina/o TV from this point on.

Conclusions

These 1970s series provide telling illustrations of an industry mindset in network television that meant Latina/o creative professionals were not given opportunities to forge careers in the industry. Even while experiencing pressure from advocacy groups to increase and improve Latina/o and particularly Mexican American representation, and beginning to hear complaints in substantial numbers from Latina/o viewers for the first time, the networks believed there were no Latino or Latina writers or producers with enough experience to be included on production teams in other than nominal positions. Freddie Prinze's success in *Chico and the Man*, meanwhile, offered a reminder of the creative potential of (and potential profits to be made from) identifying and providing roles for Latina/o performers who would appeal to and attract American audiences.

Chico and the Man, Viva Valdez, and other 1970s series are evidence of an industry that was only beginning to imagine television narratives about Latina/o characters and headlined by Latina/o stars. Arguably, the networks' efforts were halfhearted and thus destined to not likely succeed, however. In this decade in which Mexican Americans lived mostly in the Southwest and Puerto Ricans in New York and New Jersey, the television industry conceived of cultural diversity primarily as black and white, to the neglect of its Latina/o audience. The system of social apartness that characterized cities like Los Angeles, with Latina/o communities typically segregated from white communities, further contributed to a lack of awareness by television writers and producers of the compelling stories that weren't getting told. Meanwhile, hiring, training, and mentoring Latina/o writers was an idea beyond the pale, even while Chicano media advocacy groups such as Justicia were making their presence felt and arguing for just that. While a handful of series featured Latina/o main characters, these depictions revealed a common tension regarding where Latinos and Latinas fit, both inside and outside the boundaries of television story worlds.

4

1980s–90s

"What Works for TV": Series that Tried, and Failed

I think that I shall never see
any Chicanos on TV
It seems as though we don't exist
and we're not even missed
and yet we buy and buy their wares
but no Chicanos anywhere.

We need more color on TV
'cause black and white is all you see.
I'd like to see a shade of brown,
in real life we're all around.
All kinds of TV shows abound,
but no Chicanos can be found.

There are Chicanos in real life,
Doctors, lawyers, husbands, wives.
But all they show us on TV
are illegal aliens as they flee
Or some poor cholo that they bust,
flat on his face, he's eating dust.

Script writers never write for us.
I think it's time we raised a fuss!
Casting directors never call,
they never think of us at all.
Edward James Olmos and Montalbán
that's all we've got, son of a gun!

Don't buy the product if you see
no Chicanos on TV
Huggies has its three babies
White and black and Japanese

Chicano babies also pee,
but they don't show them on TV.
"No Chicanos on TV," 1986 song by the late Chicano musician and songwriter Lalo Guerrero[1]

Paul Rodriguez's play *The Pitch: Or, How to Pitch a Latino Sitcom that Will Never Air*, presented at the Los Angeles Theater Center in September 2017, included Lalo Guerrero's comedic and poignant "No Chicanos on TV" as part of its opening. It was perhaps the play's most lighthearted moment. *The Pitch* depicted the challenges of pitching a series about Latina/o characters and weathering the reception from network executives of flattery, stalling, and ultimate rejection. As Rodriguez said in an interview after I watched the production, it aimed to expose and skewer the absurdity and injustice of this unproductive, soul-crushing cycle. Rodriguez and his costars, Mike Gomez and John Lopez, playing Mike Perez, a fellow actor, and his real-life son, Paul Rodriguez Jr.,[2] respectively, reenact the many pitch meetings he had attended at the Big Four networks since the 1990s. The trio is left endlessly sitting in network waiting rooms as receptionists and entry-level staff offer them beverages and make lame excuses for their boss's delays (and in some cases, actual absence from the building or the city). The audience also witnesses development meetings in which cultural misinformation about Latina/os on the part of the executives results in insulting suggestions and in which Rodriguez and his team are presumed incapable of taking the lead in writing and producing the series they've created. In the end, as Guerrero's song intimates, nothing results from the meetings, and there still are no Chicanos (or Latina/os) on TV. This was despite the charm of the "sizzle reel" of Rodriguez's early 2010s pitch that bookended the play, of a comedy that would feature him, his son, and Edward James Olmos as three generations of a loving family that often locks horns.

The Pitch was able to offer a glimpse into programming development at the networks that few Latina/os could know. Thirty-three years earlier, Rodriguez, then an up-and-coming comedian, had been promoted as the next Freddie Prinze when he was cast as the lead of the ABC sitcom *a.k.a. Pablo* (1984). It was Norman Lear's first Latina/o-focused series to make it to broadcast. Because of this pedigree, *a.k.a. Pablo* got more promotion than most series with Latina/o stars, but it wasn't renewed after its truncated, six-episode season. When two other series in which Rodriguez later costarred, *Trial and Error* (1988) and *Grand Slam* (1990), both on CBS, were also short-lived, he turned to stand-up comedy and a steady career in smaller roles in films and television. Rodriguez's experience was representative of missteps that were commonly made in the 1980s and 1990s when networks made attempts at Latina/o-centric programming. In these years of post-network television, about a dozen series with a Latino or Latina lead character progressed from the nebulous stage of development to air as a pilot, partial, or full season of episodes. The networks' Latina/o-focused series in the 1980s included ABC's *Condo* (1983), *a.k.a. Pablo* (1984), and *I Married Dora* (1987–88), NBC's *One of the Boys* (1989), CBS's *Trial and Error* (1988), and the cable USA Network's *Sanchez of Bel Air* (1986). In the 1990s, network attempts at Latina/o series included ABC's *Common Law* (1996), NBC's *Union Square* (1997–98), CBS's *Four Corners* (1998) and *Frannie's Turn* (1992), FOX's comedy sketch series *Culture Clash* (1993–96) and *House of Buggin'* (1995), and fledgling network The WB's *First Time Out* (1995). Very few Latino or Latina professionals were involved in their conception and production, and none in leadership roles. Latina/os still were outsiders to the industry with respect to television writing and producing.

Notably, all of these series were situation comedies. In these decades this meant a half-hour series, shot affordably on a set. For a production company and network, this translated to a lower budget and low commitment. With respect to connections to be found between the various series produced and aired in these two decades, I was surprised to find very few links between series; they were the work of disparate, non-Latina/o-led production companies and almost exclusively Anglo writers and producers. It appears that a great many production companies attempted to develop a Latina/o-focused series in this period. The dramatic growth of Latina/os as part of the US audience between 1980 and 2000 was likely one motivation, as Latina/os grew from 6.5 to 12.5 percent of Americans in these decades.[3] On the other hand, one of the factors in the ultimate failure of these series was the dearth of Latina/os on their writing teams. Latino and Latina writers were scarcely employed;

they composed only 1.7 percent of television writers in the 2001–02 season.[4] Even while the National Hispanic Media Coalition, Imagen, the National Hispanic Foundation for the Arts, the National Council of La Raza, and a new group, the Hispanic Academy of Media Arts and Sciences, or HAMAS, acted as television watchdogs in these decades, they had less sway than groups such as Justicia in the 1970s and certainly less than the NAACP (the National Association for the Advancement of Colored People, which advocates for African Americans), with regard to influencing the still white- and male-dominated networks.

Several of these series were star vehicles. After 1970s audiences responded so well to Freddie Prinze and *Chico and the Man*, the thought of a Latina/o star vehicle, built around the perceived charms of a particular performer, was no longer unthinkable. Maria Conchita Alonso, a Cuban-born Venezuelan actress who had appeared in several Hollywood films, was given a chance to star in *One of the Boys* (1989),[5] while Edward James Olmos was able to negotiate for a nonexclusive contract and creative control over his character on the uber popular NBC series *Miami Vice* (1984–90) after successes in theater and film. Latina/o comedians in addition to Rodriguez who were given opportunities to star in sitcoms included Jackie Guerra in *First Time Out* and the late Greg Giraldo in *Common Law*.[6]

Despite the charms of these talented performers, their shows and the other Latina/o shows of the '80s and '90s didn't draw large enough audiences to convince their networks to keep them on the air. And in truth, most of the series are flawed in various ways as well. Even so, there are still reasons to study them, as *how* they were "bad" is informative with regard to how Latina/o authorship and perspectives continued to be stymied. As Judine Mayerle also argues, failed programming "pushes back the layers" of the collaborative process of television development, and can reveal a great deal about how programs are conceived by the television industry.[7] Considering that these series were the primary attempts at creating Latina/o narratives and protagonists for television in these decades, peeling back these layers helps us understand the common assumptions that were being made in the industry about Latina/o cultures, appeal, creatives, and audiences.

With this social and industrial history in mind, I examine how a number of these series were produced, aired, and promoted in a manner that undercut their potential for showcasing Latina and Latino voices and stories and how Latina/o actors and writers navigated their participation in their making. To do so, I searched for and studied whatever traces could be found of these series and their productions, including episodes, promotional videos and print ads, production memos, published or videotaped interviews with members of the production teams, and reviews by television critics. When possible, I conducted interviews with professionals involved in the productions. For each series, archived materials were almost nonexistent, an illustration of the lack of attention to preserving and archiving artifacts related to the cultural history of Latina/o Americans. Some series episodes were found at the Library of Congress, UCLA Film and Television Archive, and the Paley Center for Media's television collection. Just as often, only extratextual traces, such as a print advertisement that had run in *TV Guide*, could be found archived in Google Images or for sale on eBay. Based on these artifacts, previously published writing on failed series and pilots, and interviews with media industry professionals, I initially worked to construct a chronology of shows and pilots greenlit, produced, and broadcast with major Latina/o characters in these decades. While it can be presumed that some pilots may have been inadvertently left off the list, it offered a preliminary overview of the networks' approaches to representing Latina/o lives in their prime-time programming in the 1980s and 1990s. I then delved more deeply to explore how these series creators imagined their Latina/o characters and narratives and the impact these series might have had at the time and on future programming.

I also homed in on a case study in each decade to investigate in relation to the industry contexts in which it was developed and produced, with an eye to what got in the way of creating more compelling narratives and characters. This of course means having to gloss over a great many television series that I hope will be the subject of future studies. As a case study of the 1980s, I turned to *a.k.a. Pablo* (1984), the Paul Rodriguez sitcom and star vehicle described above, as the strongest effort by a network series in that era to create a nuanced portrait of a Mexican American family for television. In my examination of 1990s series, I chose to home in on *First Time Out* (The WB, 1995), the first series centered around a Latina protagonist (Mexican American actress Jackie Guerra) who was not a housewife and the second Latina/o-focused series to air on a cable network.

In the case of both *a.k.a. Pablo* and *First Time Out*, their productions included both well-meaning efforts and a privileging of proven writers, which ultimately was a reiteration of the industry's status quo. In particular, insiders' supposed knowledge of "what works for TV" was privileged over the insights of Latina consultants to the *a.k.a. Pablo* production and those of the Latina star of *First Time Out*. Latina and Latino voices also were at times undermined in other ways. Given the complete lack of Latina/o executive producers and network executives and the ultimate failure of all Latina/o series aside from *Chico and the Man* in previous decades, these dynamics were silencing.

The 1980s, *a.k.a. Pablo*, and How Industry Lore Trumped Latina/o Input

The 1980s brought some optimism but ultimately few changes for Latina/os in television. This is somewhat surprising, as Latina/os were becoming more visible in other realms of popular culture, especially film. A number of Latino-directed feature films, including *Zoot Suit* (Luis Valdez, 1981), *El Norte* (Gregory Nava, 1983), and *Born in East L.A.* (Cheech Marin, 1987), debuted to critical acclaim at film festivals and found national distributors, reaching a broad US audience for the first time. Some of these films had in fact premiered on television, on PBS's *American Playhouse* (1982–93).[8] There were no Latina-led feature films among these 1980s films, however. While Latina filmmakers were actively producing and directing films in these years, they tended to work in documentary and experimental forms and to produce shorter films in this decade, which received less attention in these years, as Rosa Linda Fregoso aptly argues.[9] Meanwhile, African American family sitcom *The Cosby Show* (1984–92) was a major hit for NBC. These developments encouraged some television writers to pitch new series built around Latina or Latino performers who showed promise to appeal to a national audience. Latina/o writers were still typically not invited to contribute to these productions or to create their own series, however. Partly as a result of this limitation, almost all of the networks' efforts were unimpressive.

The story lines of these series were different from one another, but often rooted in a grab bag of "universal" comedy ideas rather than in

Figure 4.1. From left, Daniel Hugh Kelley, Jason Horst, Juliette Lewis, and Elizabeth Peña, the cast of *I Married Dora*, a 1987–88 ABC sitcom. It featured a widower and his Salvadoran nanny who marry so she won't be deported but also harbor romantic feelings for each other.

Mexican American or other Latina/o cultural histories or contemporary experiences. ABC's *Condo* (1983) cast Cuban American actor Luis Ávalos as the patriarch of a middle-class Mexican American family that clashes with a stuffy white upper-class couple in the condo next door. Comedy ensues, especially when their daughter marries the other family's son.[10] *I Married Dora* starred Elizabeth Peña as a doctor and refugee

Figure 4.2. Maria Conchita Alonso and Robert Clohessy in character as Maria Conchita Alonso and Mike Lukowski, coworkers and later newlyweds in *One of the Boys* (1982).

from El Salvador working as a nanny who marries her employer to avoid deportation; afterward she continues her work as the family nanny and they pretend to ignore their mutual attraction.[11]

CBS's *Fort Figueroa* (1988), about a white Midwestern farm family that moves to a working-class Los Angeles neighborhood when the father inherits an apartment building there, was an East LA–focused *Beverly Hillbillies*.[12] They're forced to question their cultural assumptions as they get to know their neighbors, Latina/o and Vietnamese families.[13] And NBC's *One of the Boys*, a star vehicle for Maria Conchita Alonso, was likewise a culture-clash romantic comedy about a Cuban-Venezuelan free spirit who gets a job as a secretary for a construction company, only to fall in love with the owner, a white widower with three adult sons.[14] It was bland and promoted largely with emphasis on Alonso's beauty and clichés of an opposites-attract romance. Finally, the first Latina/o series to air on a cable network, *Sanchez of Bel Air* (1986–87), must have been envisioned as a Latina/o *Jeffersons*; it was a comedy about a Mexican American family that has "moved on up" from East Los Angeles to the tony neighborhood of Bel Air.[15] While it likely pleased some Latina/o viewers who wanted to see more images of Latina/o professionals, it had a generic feel and featured mostly uncompelling characters.[16] The series was poorly promoted and not renewed after its season of thirteen episodes ended.

It was within this era of misguided attempts at launching a series with Latino protagonists that *a.k.a. Pablo* premiered on ABC, illuminating new possibilities for Latina/o subjectivity in English-language television but still falling short of fully incorporating Latina/o voices and perspectives. Notably, it included the first narrative episode script to be credited to a Latino writer in this era. A comedy about Paul Rivera, a stand-up comedian who lives with his large and colorful extended Mexican American family, it was centered around stand-up comedian Paul Rodriguez, who was beginning to reach a level of success similar to his television character's. Lear, for his part, approached the creation of a series about a Mexican American family with more cultural sensitivity than previous non-Latina/o showrunners. He assembled a creative team that included Puerto Rican writer José Rivera and hired two Latina consultants, who were given an opportunity to provide some input in the development phase of the production.[17] The team took pains to conduct research on and to immerse themselves in Mexican American life in Los Angeles, as Mayerle documented.[18]

Figure 4.3. The cast of *Sanchez of Bel Air* (1986) included, from left, standing: S. Marc Jordan as Bernie Cohen, Alitzah, and Richard Coca as Gina and Miguel Sanchez, and Bobby Sherman as the Sanchezes' neighbor, Frankie Rondell; seated, Marcia del Mar, Reni Santoni, and Alma Beltran as Rita and Ricardo Sanchez and Ricardo's mother, Teresa.

As Rodriguez describes in a 2007 interview with Bill Dana and Jenni Matz for the American Comedy Archives, his first encounter with Norman Lear was after a stand-up set that he gave at The Comedy Store in LA.[19] Lear had attended at the behest of Eve Brandstein, head of casting for his production company, Embassy Television, who had noticed

Rodriguez doing audience warm-up for another Embassy series. Also impressed, Lear invited him in for a meeting. At the time, Lear had a six-episode deal with ABC to try out a new series; he had been planning to remake *Qué Pasa, USA?* (*What's Up, USA?*) (1977–1980), a Cuban American family series produced by Miami public television station WPBT, and he was thinking of casting Rodriguez as one of the family members.[20] Rodriguez declined, telling Lear that he was Mexican, not Cuban.[21] They talked further about Rodriguez's family and Mexican American cultural quirks, the fodder of much of his comedy at the time, and Rodriguez invited him to dinner at his parents' house in Compton to see for himself. Lear went, and decided then to base his new series on Rodriguez's family, with Rodriguez as star. Working with Rick Mitz, Lear created *a.k.a. Pablo*. It changed Rodriguez's life dramatically. As he stated in the American Comedy Archives interview, "it was a true story—as true as it could possibly be—about my family, how so many of us lived at home. And, I went from 'Nobody knew who the hell you were,' to, within a period of six months, 'My face was on the cover of *TV Guide*.'"[22]

Aside from Rodriguez, several Latina/o actors, but few of Mexican descent, were cast as Paul Rivera's family members. They cast Italian American actor Joe Santos and Mexican film actress Katy Jurado as his parents, while Hector Elizondo, of Basque and Puerto Rican heritage, played his agent, José Sanchez/Joe Shapiro. Alma Cuervo, Martha Veléz, Arnaldo Santana, Maria Richwine, Bert Rosario, Mike Binder, Claudia Gonzáles, Marta Yolanda González, Mario Lopez (now a well-known actor and star), Beto Lovato, and Edie Marie Rubio played his siblings, nieces, and nephews; of these actors, only Santana and Lopez can be confirmed as being of Mexican descent. José Rivera, now known for *The Motorcycle Diaries* (2004) and *On the Road* (2012), was hired as one of the writers. Actor Hector Elizondo also directed three of the six episodes. Although material from Rodriguez's stand-up comedy was at times included in the script, he strangely was not given credit as a writer. He also did not have executive producer status on the series, as we sometimes see for Latina/o television stars today.[23]

In a first for network television, there were attempts on the part of Lear and Mitz to draw input from members of the cast and crew, including the two Latina consultants mentioned earlier, to comment on

Figure 4.4. Paul Rodriguez as Paul/Pablo Rivera, with the cast that portrayed his large family in *a.k.a. Pablo* (1984). From left, seated in front: Hector Elizondo, Beto Lovato, Joe Santos, Rodriguez, Katy Jurado, Antonio Torres, and Alma Cuervo; standing in back: Bert Rosario, Mario Lopez, Maria Richwine, Martha Veléz, and Arnaldo Santana; the three children in standing front of Richwine and Veléz are Edie Marie Rubio, Marta Yolanda González, and Claudia Gonzáles.

the story lines of the six episodes. Mayerle notes that Embassy Television was known for a collaborative creative process in the preproduction phase; this had been the case for *The Jeffersons* and the original *One Day at a Time*. Despite this, the production's original vision about representing the perspectives of all of the members of a large and loving Mexican American family disintegrated during this stage, with the eventual episodes focusing primarily on Paul/Pablo and his stand-up career (and thus, jokes about the foibles of Mexican American culture). This shift was due largely to the writers' ideas of what would "work" in television comedy and appeal to the audience. More aware of the burden of representation that Mexican American characters carried in 1984, the consultants tried to voice their concerns about some narrative elements that bothered them, such as characterizing Paul's parents as foolish and out of step with society. However, they ultimately had to accept that they would not change the minds of the writers and that they "were never going to get it 100% right," as one of the consultants, Dolores Sanchez, indicated. "It was a compromise that I didn't willingly accept, but that I realize had to be made. I know how we [Hispanics] think, but it isn't always funny. I'd have writers telling me, 'well you know, we have to do such and such thing, because it will work on television.' I couldn't very well dispute that."[24]

ABC and Embassy Television appear to have put considerable money into their promos for the first episodes of the new series; they emphasize the colorful, chaotic excesses of Pablo's family, Pablo's sometimes-rude comedy about Mexican American culture on the stand-up stage, and the family members' love and care for one another. Lear, in an appearance on *Good Morning America* on the day of the show's debut, March 6, 1984, described the series as representative of many Americans' experiences. "This is about a large Mexican family, a Mexican American family, at a time when 240 million Americans are desperate for some feeling of connection and belonging," he noted. "And here's a family with sixteen people who would fight the world for each other, who love each other and who belong to each other. It is a mirror of that new, fresh immigrant experience in our culture."[25]

The pilot introduces Paul/Pablo and his large and passionate family, with whom he lives in East Los Angeles.[26] The original credit sequence emphasizes the size and excitability of the family and moments from Rodriguez/Rivera's work as a comedian (particularly a joke about the "Mexican express card," which amounts to putting a knife in his mouth as if he's a stereotypical undocumented immigrant, wading through a river). Shots of Rodriguez as Paul in East LA outside are interspersed with random shots of Latina/os in the city. We see Latino men stacking bags of oranges and playing baseball in the park, a young Latina holding a baby, and city residents walking past a Chicana/o mural in Monterey Park that pays tribute to Argentine revolutionary Che Guevara, emblazoned with "We Are Not a Minority." The credit sequence that opened later episodes is dramatically different, however. It focuses on Paul as a successful comedian. Rodriguez-as-Rivera confidently performs stand-up for a mostly white comedy club audience, including "the Mexican Express card" and other jokes and physical comedy, as the credits roll.

He's vibrant, youthful, and a hit with his audience, shown laughing hard at his jokes. The final moments of the credit sequence are close-ups of Rodriguez as the theme song ends.

In the pilot, because Paul's a comedian who works late into the night at comedy clubs, he sleeps late in the day. Paul's mother and father argue; his mother wants to let Paul sleep, while his father feels he's not working while his job is "making fun of Mexicans" on the comedy stage. This discussion and the rest of the episode includes quite a bit of unsubtitled Spanish. Soon other family members, including multiple siblings, in-laws, and a niece and nephew, come in noisily and have to be reminded to let Paul sleep. To the extent of cliché, all are manual laborers. The father is a gardener, Pablo's brother works as a bricklayer and goes to night school, one sister cleans houses in Beverly Hills, another works at Kmart, and his brother-in-law works at a gas station. We see that the family is at odds over Paul's comedy—one sister excitedly imitates it, which doesn't go over well with their father. Such an approach matched the complicated and conflictual family dynamics that livened other Lear family comedies such as *All in the Family* (1971–79), *Good Times* (1974–79), and the original *One Day at a Time* (1975–84). Once Paul is awake, the family eagerly turns on the TV to see his latest television appearance. He is described by *Entertainment Tonight* as "a new young Mexican comedian," and a segment of his stand-up show is aired. On stage in front of a receptive audience, he performs parts of a comedy set, first showing the many uses of a tortilla for Mexican Americans, including as a 30-day deodorant. He does his "Mexican Express card" joke, much to his family's chagrin but making the audience laugh.[27]

Soon Paul's new agent (Elizondo) arrives, and Paul introduces him around the family. Paul teasingly describes them as "the Aristocrats" and notes the gendered traditions that they hold onto. Women in the family serve the men, he explains, and his mother is part of a crazy cult called "the Sock Ironers!" José shares his good news: Pablo has been given money to create his own television show. The family celebrates with him, especially when they learn that he wants to spend the money on them, but his father is still unhappy: he doesn't like Paul making fun of Mexicans. They argue about whether his father is treated with respect in his own job as a gardener. The episode ends with a poignant reconciliation, however. Paul learns that his father's reluctance for his son to be a comedian is because of Freddie Prinze's death at such a young age. He doesn't want his son to have a life of hardship as a comedian and particularly not to die young. Finally understanding, Paul tells his father in Spanish that he loves him dearly, and they hug. When Paul later trips and falls face first into a plate of food, his father and the rest of the family laugh. "Now that's funny!" his father says as the episode concludes. The self-reflexivity of the final joke conveys a clear affection for its Mexican American characters.

Similar humor and family dynamics guide the other five episodes. In "The Big Mouth," Pablo has to contend with having embarrassed his family with jokes that make fun of their quirks. In "My Son the Gringo," Paul's agent, José, sets up a meeting for him with Pearl Wallace (Bea Arthur, who played the title character in *Maude* [1972–78]), the best press agent in town. When she suggests that he change his name to Paul Rivers, he invites her to his house for dinner to show her why he doesn't want to. When Pearl mentions the name change idea to his family, they're shocked, especially after also learning Paul's nephew, Tomás, has flunked Spanish. Finally, Pablo is stirred to tell off Pearl and to say how proud he is to dress and act like he does, that he's Mexican. The episode ends with affirmation of the importance of Paul's family and cultural identity, unique for Latina/o televisual representation at the time: his final words are "We've got what billions in the people in the world wish they had. We've got each other." Clearly the series was meant to emphasize the strengths of Mexican American families more than the jokes that Paul Rivera made about them, but this wasn't always the perception of Latina/o viewers, some of whom complained, Rodriguez noted in interviews.

The fourth episode is the only one that I found to be credited to José Rivera.[28] In "The Presidential Joke Teller," Paul struggles with how to present himself when he has the opportunity to perform for US President Reagan. His sister Sylvia convinces him, against his father's wishes, to dress in his regular clothes rather than a tuxedo, to show that he's proud of where he comes from. Unfortunately, Paul and his agent end up getting pulled over on their way to the performance; they're jailed for speeding when the police don't believe that he's supposed to perform for the president, and because his mother had tampered with his performer's pass, inserting a childhood picture where his professional

Figure 4.5. Paul Rivera (Paul Rodriguez)'s agent and family admire how he looks in his tuxedo as he prepares to perform for President Reagan in *a.k.a. Pablo*'s "The Presidential Joke Teller," which aired March 27, 1984.

photo had been. His mother and the rest of his family—and eventually his stern father—all come to the station to bail him out. The episode includes a few moments of commentary from a distinctly Latina/o point of view, such as when family members argue about whether Reagan, or any president, has done anything to help Hispanics (the term, popular in this era, by which the family self-identifies), and another moment when his brother-in-law Hector says that he knows after a night in jail that Mexicans aren't treated well there. And the episode's premise includes a deeper critique—its emphasis on no one believing that Paul, a Mexican American, would be asked to perform for the president. It's slipped into jokes, as when Paul tells the police as he's being put in jail: "There's a room of very important people waiting for us! They're Caucasians!" It's hard to imagine a white writer coming up with the narrative, with its spot-on understanding of the outsider identity that Latina/os typically might experience in stand-up comedy and other popular culture arenas in these years.

Even more complex and pointed about Latina/o social issues was the next episode, "The Whole Enchilada," which skewered both television portrayals of Latina/os *and* Latina/o media advocates who serve as cultural watchdogs. Credited to Seth Greenland, the episode is set within the backdrop of the family getting ready for Paul's niece's quinceañera, which needs to impress their nosy neighbor Señora Alvarez (played by the late, great Mexican American actress Lupe Ontiveros in a showy guest role). Meanwhile, Paul is offered a television series, but it's not at all he had hoped for. This is because Paul is expected to play an undocumented immigrant named Pedro Enchilada, who lives in the back seat of his car—perhaps making fun of the flimsy premise of *Chico and the Man*. He and his parents and sister Sylvia are all crushed. In addition, the family is besieged by two members of a Chicano media advocacy group (played by Carmen Zapata and Danny Mora), who say the series would be a disgrace to Mexican Americans. They are humorless and unresponsive to Paul's quips about it. Sylvia, in contrast, says he should do the series, adding, "You've got to get in on the inside to change things, and I know you will." Setting the decision aside, Paul sets up a family photo during the quinceañera, only to be interrupted by the media advocates. When the woman calls Paul a "poor foolish menso" (a fool) for considering the series, Domingo, Paul's father, takes a stand. He shows them the door and slams it behind them, garnering a cheer from the live audience. The family goes back to the photo, reveling in their posh appearance—and earning shock and awe from Señora Alvarez. This prompts the first smile from Paul's mother, Rosa. The episode ends before the audience learns how Paul navigated the series offer. As a whole, the narrative is remarkable for the complexity of its commentary and humor. It addresses cultural nuances and divisions among Latina/os as well as ironies inherent in networks' attempts at Latina/o narratives, and manages to do so with sincerity and affection. But by the date it aired, ABC had already decided not to renew the series.

As a whole, I found that despite some clumsy character development and an overemphasis on Paul's jokes about Mexicans, the series included the most intelligent and nuanced commentary of the 1980s series on

Latina/o life. It stumbled in several respects, however. The series misses out at times when it depicts the Riveras from a distance that implies a white-centric narrator and white target audience. The fact that the production's Latina consultants were not taken seriously when they voiced discomfort with something in an episode because they didn't know "what will work on television" is telling regarding how television professionals were unable to give up their sense of creative and cultural authority, even regarding how to accurately depict Mexican American experiences and perspective.

The lore about the series is that it was canceled because of its ratings. The pilot got an overnight share of 28, an impressive number, but also a weekly rating of 14.9, with a 22 percent share, which in 1984 wasn't enough to sustain a network series.[29] That was likely just one of the factors that ABC considered. Rodriguez said in interviews that while Mexican Americans and other Latina/os watched it, some viewers complained who were unhappy with his Mexican Express card joke and other humor they didn't like. "It got cancelled because of the complaints that they received from Mexican Americans, from Latinos everywhere," he noted.[30] Criticism by some viewers may have made a difference to the protest-shy network. Despite a letter-writing campaign by other Latina/o fans who attempted to save the show, ABC chose not to renew it. Nevertheless, *a.k.a. Pablo* stands out in retrospect for its attempts to understand and reflect Mexican American realities and to include Latina/o input in its developments. It had tremendous potential and, in my personal estimation, often hit the mark in relating a second-generation Mexican American perspective with wit and good humor.

The importance of network executives' tastes in these decisions is illustrated in a 1988 industry executive panel on networks' consideration of fan campaigns to save series. Perry Simon, Senior Vice President for Series Programming for NBC, noted, "I saw *a.k.a. Pablo* and I didn't think it was very good. My guess is that they [NBC executives] cancelled it because they didn't think it was very good in spite of all of those very legitimate factors [raised by fans arguing for its merits]."[31] The importance of diversity among network executives is underscored here. A homogeneous group of white male executives will more likely share a sense of cultural taste, which becomes codified as "good TV"; when

Latina/os are excluded from executive ranks, it's less likely that a series like *a.k.a. Pablo* will be valued and given a chance to develop and draw a larger audience.

The 1990s and *First Time Out*

The 1990s witnessed the rapid growth of the Latina/o population in the US and a seemingly linked rise of legislation proposed at state and local levels that aimed to deny services and rights to Latina/o undocumented immigrants. In turn, Latina/os and their allies took to the streets in public demonstrations for immigrant rights. The most visible of these battles took place in California in 1994, when Proposition 187 became a ballot initiative. It proposed denying education, health, and other services to undocumented youth and families and would mandate that teachers, health professionals, and other state workers report undocumented individuals to the authorities. In response, demonstrations were organized around the state to protest Prop. 187. Latina/o high school students, teachers, and social service professionals walked out of classes, clinics, and social service agencies to demonstrate against the measure; 70,000 protesters gathered in Los Angeles alone.[32] The measure still passed, but it was halted by a lawsuit and found unconstitutional days later. Even so, Latina/o voting in California increased in response to Proposition 187 and other anti-Latino measures in the state, while it was increasing nationwide for similar reasons, a claiming of cultural citizenship key to Latina/os gaining a greater voice in the political process.[33]

This social and political history underscores that the rising participation of Latina/os in the public sphere in the 1990s was met with mixed responses and at times with clear resistance. With this in mind, it's not surprising that while more television series featuring Latina/o characters and stars were made, true progress for Latina/os in the media industries often seemed fleeting. A number of Latina/o filmmakers continued to have success in film, which likely encouraged some of the professionals working in television. Films such as *El Mariachi* (1992), *Desperado* (1995), *My Family/Mi Familia* (1995), and *Selena* (1997) illustrated that compelling Latina/o storytelling and narratives could draw national audiences and make money for production companies and distributors. The rise of such stars as Selena (especially her posthumous stardom),

Jennifer Lopez, Ricky Martin, and Benicio del Toro also demonstrated that Latina/o celebrity performers could appeal to non-Latina/o audiences. This encouraged the greenlighting of only a few Latina/o-focused television series, however. 1990s series featuring Latina/o lead characters included ABC's *Common Law* (1996), NBC's *Union Square* (1997–98), CBS's *Frannie's Turn* (1992) and *Four Corners* (1998), and The WB's *First Time Out* (1995). Reflecting increasing appeals to female viewers and more female writers and producers entering the industry in the 1980s and 1990s, several series featured Latina protagonists for the first time.[34] Frannie Esocobar, a Cuban American housewife (played by a non-Latina, Miriam Margolyes) was the central figure in *Frannie's Turn*, while Mexican American comedian Jackie Guerra and the late Cuban American actor Elizabeth Peña starred in *First Time Out* and *I Married Dora*, respectively.

Latina/o advocacy groups were still making their presence felt, but much of the direct impact felt in the 1970s had been nullified in relation to deregulation of the media industries by the FCC and government oversight groups such as the EEOC. Citizens' options to challenge television stations that didn't meet their communities' needs had been largely dismantled. However, Latina/o groups were working together in a more cooperative fashion, in order to increase their efficacy and news coverage of the problems of Latina/o misrepresentation and exclusion from the creative and executive realms of film and television. In the 1990s, groups that included the National Hispanic Media Coalition (NHMC), Nosotros, and the Imagen Foundation in Los Angeles, and the National Council of La Raza (NCLR) and the National Hispanic Foundation for the Arts in Washington, DC, still acted as media watchdogs, but now primarily through media consumer–focused campaigns, as Scott Wible has aptly documented. In 1996, many of these organizations had protested the lack of lead characters of color in all of the major networks' new series with a "Brownout" to publicize the networks' lackluster efforts to represent the country's diversity.[35] A few years later, in 1999, twelve Latina/o groups joined efforts to gain a louder voice in the industry as the National Latino Media Council (NLMC), with the NHMC serving as the council's administrators. The NLMC also joined the NAACP, the Asian Pacific American Media Coalition, and American Indians in Film and Television in 2000 in forming the Multi-Ethnic Media Coalition, which works to pressure the networks for greater ethnic and racial diversity and inclusion in casting and employment behind the scenes. It was able get a great deal more press coverage for their efforts than had been the case for individual Latina/o organizations.[36]

This was prompted in part by a decade in which Latina/os gained little visibility in prime-time programming or traction toward creative agency for Latina/o storytellers. ABC produced and aired only one series for a full season with a Latina/o lead, the workplace sitcom *Common Law* (1996). Created by Rob LaZebnik, the series starred Columbian and Spanish American comedian Greg Giraldo as a smart but unconventional Latino lawyer secretly dating his coworker, who is also the daughter of the head of the firm.[37] Nine episodes were produced, but the series was pulled after five aired. NBC, CBS, and FOX, in turn, each aired one or a few Latina/o-led series that floundered. NBC's *Union Square* cast Constance Marie as part of an ensemble of disparate New York City professionals who all spend time at a neighborhood diner and talk about their lives.[38] The revised series was canceled after a thirteen-episode season. For its part, CBS's attempts at a Latina/o series were hampered by misperceptions about how to appeal to both non-Latina/o and Latina/o viewers. *Frannie's Turn* was centered on a Cuban American seamstress and housewife and her family, but Cuban American cultural elements were rarely part of the narrative. Frannie Escobar was played by Miriam Margolyes, a British actress of Scottish, Polish, and Belarusian descent.[39] It was not renewed after its six episodes aired. CBS's prime-time soap *Four Corners* was more ambitious and was even promoted as the first TV drama simulcast in Spanish and in English.[40] It focused on Amanda Wyatt, the matriarch of a white ranching family (played by film star Ann-Margret), and her adult son and daughter. Brazilian American actress Sônia Braga played Amanda's friend Carlotta, who organized migrant workers; Carlotta's son, Tomás, has a complicated romance with Amanda's daughter. When the ratings and share for its two-hour premiere were dismal, it was canceled after one more episode aired.[41] Meanwhile, FOX offered a brief space for Latina/o self-representation through sketch comedy. In the same years that the Afrocentric *In Living Color* (1990–94) was a hit for the network, it tried out two Latina/o-centric series, *Culture Clash* (1993–96), named after the Latina/o comedy troupe that performed in it,[42] and *House of Buggin'* (1995), led by

John Leguizamo, of Colombian, Puerto Rican, Italian, and Lebanese descent. Both were remarkable as showcases for unfiltered Chicana/o and Latina/o creativity and cultural production in sketch comedy format.[43] However, they failed to capture a large enough audience to convince FOX to keep them on the air after their seasons ended.

The industry itself was undergoing major shifts in these years of post-network television. Fledgling cable networks, some following a concerted strategy of outreach to underserved viewers as they tried to become established, had an increasing impact. It was within this television landscape that newly established cable network The WB created the first series to feature a Latina comedian, *First Time Out* (1995). The series, which starred thirty-year-old Mexican American comedian Jackie Guerra, attempted to capitalize on the vogue for young adult–oriented programming after the success of *Friends* (1994–2004) a year prior. *First Time Out* featured Guerra, best known for portraying Tejano singer Selena's sister Suzette in the film *Selena* (1997), as a young professional navigating adult life alongside her roommates and her coworkers at the hair salon where she works as a receptionist. Described incorrectly as a "Latina *Living Single*,"[44] given that Guerra is the only Latina with top billing, at its best it was unique in its depiction of a modern-minded Latina who was informed but not confined by her cultural identity as Mexican American and who challenged Hollywood norms of beauty. The sitcom ultimately bombed, however, because the narrative was predictable and lackluster, and perhaps because the network failed to promote Guerra as a television star. Airing September 10 through December 17, 1995, it was canceled after twelve of its sixteen episodes aired. Only a few of those episodes are now accessible: the pilot, "Tradition," of which only an excerpt still exists, "The Sale Show," and the never-aired "Psyched Out."

First Time Out was the result of Guerra, a self-described "Mexican American valley girl" stand-up comedian and former community organizer, being offered a development deal by Columbia TriStar Television and The WB.[45] That is to say, she was offered a chance to star in a sitcom on The WB if it made it through development to be picked up as a series. This ultimately came about, after "a lot of miracles," Guerra notes in her autobiography.[46] Notably, Warner Bros. Entertainment and Tribune Broadcasting had just launched The WB in 1995, initially with just two nights of prime-time programming each week. The network

Figure 4.6. Jackie Guerra, the star of The WB's *First Time Out*, is featured with the supporting cast in this promotional photo that telegraphs the series' focus on young, single professionals. From left, standing: Mia Cottet, Guerra, and Leah Remini; seated: Tracy Vilar, Craig Anton, and Roxanne Beckford.

took a page from what had worked for the nascent FOX a decade prior through programming series that might appeal to African American viewers or other underserved audiences. The network's lack of established programming or a sense of who their audience might prove to be created a unique opening to try out a show centered around a Latina comedian; even so, *First Time Out* was the network's only attempt at a Latina/o-led series. Two white female writers, Shawn Schepps and Diane Wilk, created the series with Guerra attached as star; it was initially executive produced by Marc Sotkin.[47] The WB had not prioritized finding Latina/o creatives to work on the production, but they demonstrated some openness to this when pushed later by Guerra. The WB programmed it on Sunday nights between *Cleghorne!* (1995), a series featuring African American comedian Ellen Cleghorne, and the sitcom *Simon* (1995), about two white American brothers of different temperaments who are forced to live together. There it faced off, poorly, against FOX's more popular *Married . . . with Children* (1987–97).

Guerra notes that she fought for more Latina/o hires, but that the situation felt very pressured. As she put it, "As the first Latina to star in a network sitcom, I became an unwitting role model for my community. I was an actress, activist, organizer—and scared."[48] She didn't hesitate to push the network, however. As a result of her advocacy, a few Latino professionals were hired to the production team. Marco Bario was hired as an associate producer and John "Jellybean" Benitez as music producer, while Bill Torres was one of the Latina/o writers hired; Guerra was credited as executive consultant. Guerra also had to wrangle with the producers over casting. She fought for Tracy Vilar, an Afro-Puerto Rican actor, to play Rosa, her best friend and coworker. She noted that Vilar clearly had the best audition, but the producers balked, insisting she was African American rather than Latina. Guerra, realizing that they didn't understand that Latinas could be of various races and were not all of Mexican heritage, earnestly tried to educate them. Vilar was eventually hired, but the episodes that I was able to view relegated her character to a comic side note as Jackie's coworker while beefing up the white roommates' (Leah Remini and Mia Cottet) roles as Guerra's quirky and neurotic best friends. For instance, many of the promotional photos include only Guerra, Remini, and Cottet. While a greater emphasis on Jackie and Rosa's friendship would have lent veracity to The WB's "Latina *Living Single*" description, this did not happen, revealing what seems to be network discomfort and disagreement regarding how many Latina/os could be included in a narrative without alienating a presumed white audience. Guerra's character also lost professional status in the execution of the series. While initially written as an ambitious Yale University graduate who owns and works in a salon while attending law school at night, the focus becomes her job as a salon receptionist who only applies to law school in the season's last, unaired episode.

Another, more gendered element of the series' lackluster development and promotion was linked to how the network perceived Jackie Guerra's appearance. Guerra was heavy; the title of her autobiography, *Under Construction: How I've Gained and Lost Millions of Dollars and Hundreds of Pounds*, speaks to the impact of her weight on her career in an industry that values female—and especially Latina—performers primarily when they fit Hollywood beauty ideals as thin, fair-skinned, and traditionally feminine in appearance. If a Latina star didn't meet this physical ideal, was she seen as offering any value at all? Guerra's weight clearly was viewed as an obstacle to her potential stardom. She notes, for instance, that an unnamed female executive producer who came late to the project expressed great disdain for her as a series lead.

A lack of optimism about Guerra's potential appeal also can be discerned in the series' forty-second opening credit sequence. It opens on the title in a colorful graphic of a sun. The sequence then cuts to images of the cast interacting with animated backdrops meant to whimsically evoke Southern California and Los Angeles highways and buildings. It begins with Guerra in a park setting, behind and perhaps watching an African American man playing basketball. She is sitting on a park bench, but curiously, with only her back showing—for several long seconds on screen. Then a side view is shown; Guerra looks blankly at nothing. Finally, Guerra has turned around and faces the front, smiling. The park bench obscures most of her body through this multi-second sequence. It can only be assumed that the producers of the sequence were given directions to hide Guerra's body as much as possible. Guerra's white costars are then introduced. Both Cottet and Remini are depicted with side and front views and in a manner that relates their characters' vibrant personalities and, in Remini's case, lithe body. Craig Anton is introduced with a long-shot photo of his whole body. The name of Tracy Vilar then appears, but no photo accompanies it—only a graphic of what may or may not be her back, as a female roller skater crosses the screen in the distance. From this sequence, it appears that WB executives had little hope that *First Time Out* would attract an audience or that Latinas could become television stars, particularly if they were not body beautiful by Hollywood standards.

The episodes of *First Time Out* are often not distinguishable from other young (and white) professional female buddy comedies of the 1990s. The pilot, which aired September 10, 1995, and particularly Guerra have some appeal, but it's a rambling and underwhelming narrative. In it, Jackie (Jackie Guerra) is waiting in a restaurant for a date, looking beautiful, plump, and stylish. She surreptitiously grabs and eats a dinner roll, tossing it slyly under the table when he shows up. The date, a white American man, turns out to be a boring dud. She salvages her evening by using her bilingual language abilities; she speaks in subtitled Spanish to the waiter, asking him to come back and say she has an emergency phone call. "Your mother had a heart attack? Your dog got hit by a car?" He suggests. She approves this last idea, before picking up another roll and eating it with abandon. Jackie also is struggling because she's not over her ex-boyfriend, Mario, who was handsome and good in bed, but domineering. He shows up at a bar where Jackie is spending time with her friends; it's revealed later that she spent the night with him and has decided to get back together with him. But it becomes clear that Mario is as controlling as ever. He gives her a dress too small for her to wear as a gift, and at dinner orders her meal for her—a salad with no dressing. Jackie instead tells Mario she's going to lose "175 pounds, immediately," and dumps him. She and her roommates make plans for the fun they'll now have, because they don't need men, but are quickly lured into forgetting that when they hear a party in the apartment above.

Two subsequent episodes, "Tradition" and "The Sale Show," both offer blandly generic moments that could be part of any white female friendship series. In "The Sale Show," the three roommates wait in line to get into and then go wild at a sale at one of their favorite clothing boutiques. It also offers a few moments that are more culturally distinct. Much of the episode focuses on Jackie auditioning for a second job where Rosa already works, translating and dubbing old American television shows for Spanish-speaking viewers. While these scenes are brief, they highlight the naturalism of Jackie's bilingualism, the warm friendship between Jackie and Rosa, and the humor of sloppily dubbed Spanish slapped on top of English-language television (a practice that

Spanish-speaking viewers of the 1980s would readily know). There's even a manager at the dubbing studio who indicates he'd really rather be making progressive films for Latina/os, in an aside that makes a nod to Latina/o independent film.

It's with the never-aired season finale, "Psyched Out," that the potential of the series to showcase its effervescent and wacky star is especially evident. It notably focuses on Jackie finally pursuing her professional dream as she interviews for admittance into a law school. Nervous, she thinks she's blown the interview with the older white male dean, leading to a comic scene when Rosa invites a psychic to meet with Jackie and her friends to tell Jackie whether she got in or not. When Jackie later discovers she was in fact rejected she won't take no for answer; she follows the dean into the men's room to argue for her right to be admitted. In her frustration, she proves she was truthful about her cheerleading past that she had listed on her application, which leads to her acceptance. Doing a balls-out cheer in her own defense, Jackie has achieved her goal (but is told she might want to quickly get up from the men's room floor, where she has done the splits). It's unfortunate that this episode that showcased Guerra's comedic chops and appeal never aired. Guerra notes in her autobiography that she knew the end for the series was near when another episode script called for her character to go to Tijuana to have a tooth pulled cheaply by a stereotypical Mexican dentist. Feeling it reinforced negative stereotypes, she appealed to the executive in charge to make changes, but was given no support and had to go through with it as written.[49] The series had not found a large enough audience to please The WB, and it was soon canceled.[50]

It's clear from Guerra's experience with *First Time Out* that for some in the industry, and for Latinas in particular, they were still imagined and deemed palatable for US audiences only in certain packages and modes. Funny. Sexy. Exotic. Agreeable. Not making waves. Jackie Guerra came out of this experience not cowed and still vocal about the importance of fighting for Latina/o employment in television, however. In Guerra's words,

> I'm very proud to say that I was able to get writers into the Writers Guild who are Latino, who had their first shot at working on a sitcom [and] on a network show because I wanted to make sure that whether the show

lasted or not, people would continue to work. And that no longer could any executive look another Latina in the face and say well, there are no Latino producers; there are no Latino writers; there are no Latino wardrobe people. It's ridiculous. Of course there are. And of course we're out there.[51]

She further commented on what still, twenty years later, needs to be done to improve Latina/o television narratives and to ensure that Latinas and Latinos are telling their own stories. "Know what's important to us by speaking with *us*. By inviting us to the party and then letting us get out on the dance floor and let our freak flag fly."[52] Her words continue to be extremely relevant with respect to Latina/o struggles to enter the realm of television storytellers.

Conclusions: Making and Marketing TV Latina/os

The most obvious takeaway after exploring *a.k.a. Pablo* and *First Time Out*'s production histories is that while both hired at least one Latina/o writer, this was generally not considered a necessity for Latina/o-focused programming in the 1980s and 1990s. Similarly, even top-billed Latina/o television stars had only tenuous status or agency with respect to the narrative content of their series. Even while the Latina/o population in the US was growing dramatically and would surpass African Americans in the early 2000s as the largest non-white ethnic group, the perception of a mostly white audience, or of a white and black audience, still held sway. Meanwhile, if networks wanted to appear modern-minded and politically correct, they might greenlight and back one series with a Latina or Latino lead, but with little thought to what it meant to do so without opening doors to Latina/o writers or creators.

It was a time of very little network confidence in Latina/o creatives or consultants knowing "what would work" in television comedy, the genre to which Latina/o characters were confined. As I discuss in more detail in chapter 5, the first Latina/o creatives to eventually become showrunners, among them Rick Najera, Gregory Nava, Dennis Leoni, and Silvio Horta, had begun to get opportunities to pitch projects and pilot scripts in these decades, while other Latina/os began to be employed as staff writers. However, the networks were wary of greenlighting their shows or of offering Latina/o actors leading roles. As Najera writes, "I'd write a pilot, or a show [in the 1980s and 1990s], and producers would tell me, 'Oh, we love this script but we don't have any Latino stars to be in it.'"[53] It was clearly a Catch-22 with respect to Latina/os not being given a chance to prove their potential and executives declaring they could only launch a Latina/o-focused series with an already proven star. In addition, talent agents were almost exclusively white and uneducated about Latina/o cultures in these years. Agents typically didn't want to represent Latina/o writers or actors, or if they did, typically did little to advocate for Latina/o writers' projects or for color-blind auditions or casting, I was told in several interviews. Particularly clear is the distinct lack of knowledge of the benefits to be gleaned from creating avenues for Latina/o creative professionals' and career advancement growth in their subfields.

While this was the period in which the ascent of "quality" television and greater cultural openness on the part of American viewers was beginning to be felt in many popular prime-time series, Latina/o series were handicapped by networks' assumptions. *a.k.a. Pablo* and particularly *First Time Out* ultimately reflected the perspectives of their non-Latina/o creators, including their notions of universal storytelling and comedy, which centered whiteness and resulted in oddly constructed or bland Latina/o protagonists. Relatedly, the national audience was presumed to be largely white and unfamiliar with Latina/o cultures. The networks also enacted marketing campaigns that built on stereotypical associations, of Latinas as hypersexual beauties, as in *One of the Boys'* promotional materials featuring Maria Conchita Alonso, and of Latino and Latina comedians as always colorful and quirky, as was the case for Paul Rodriguez's, Greg Giraldo's, and Jackie Guerra's series. The assumptions that undergirded these constructions were indicative of the marginalization and ambivalent cultural citizenship that Latina/os faced in US social life in this period.

Along these same lines, the few Latina/o creative professionals able to enter this arena in these decades had to accept the industry's emphasis in these years on "mainstreaming" Latina/o narratives, to borrow a term Yolanda Broyles-González used to describe the compromised cultural impact of Chicana/o theater company Teatro Campesino when it adapted some of its theatrical productions as public television specials.

A corollary would be Latina/o "crossover" stardom, a term used in the 1990s news media when Latina/o performers became national stars.[54] As Broyles-González implies, when Latina/o performances prioritized non-Latina/o audiences, this could entail a loss of cultural meaning and political significance. The additional exclusion of Latina/o creative professionals and executives and lack of knowledge of Latina/o cultures in the television industry as a whole made it generally impossible to resolve these tensions in favor of storytelling that privileged Latina/o perspectives. The industry ethos of Latina/o mainstreaming began to shift in the 2000s, however, as my focus in the next chapter on the first Latina/o showrunners makes clear.

5

2000s

By Us, For Everyone: Latino Storytellers
Enter TV's Mainstream

In June 2000, I attended the television version of a film premiere for
the Showtime series *Resurrection Blvd.* (2000–02) on the Paramount
Pictures lot. Watching Tony Plana, Michael DeLorenzo, Elizabeth
Peña, and newcomers Nick Gonzalez, Ruth Livier, Mauricio Mendoza
and Mirasol Nichols walk the red carpet took my breath away, and
the one-hour pilot was stylish, dramatic, and emotionally satisfying. I
hadn't anticipated how exhilarating it would be to see an all-Latina/o
cast at a premiere. It was *our* story, populated with our stars. It felt like
we had moved at last into the spotlight, where our beauty and complexity could be seen for the first time.

My experience was one finally made possible in the early 2000s.
In these years we witnessed the first national programming *by* Latino
(that is, mostly male) creators *about* Latino and Latina lead characters. The writer-producers and, in one case, performer who achieved
these feats—Dennis Leoni, Jeff Valdez, Peter Murrieta, Gregory Nava,
Silvio Horta, and George Lopez—made their way into the industry
from a variety of paths. Some, like Dennis Leoni and Jeff Valdez,
worked their way in after years in other roles in the industry, while
George Lopez came in as an executive producer and writer after success writing and performing stand-up comedy. Maria Perez-Brown,
Gibby Cevallos, and Mike Cevallos also began as executive producers
of children's series, a division of the industry that opened earlier than
others to Latina and Latino showrunners. Regardless, all ran a production team and achieved the audience numbers to keep their series
afloat. And all fought to represent Latina/os with nuance and dignity
while appealing to a broader audience, within an industry that didn't
prioritize these goals.

From the 1970s through the 1990s, with only a few exceptions, selling new series about Latina/o protagonists was next to impossible for writers who tried to pitch them, as many executives were unconvinced that American viewers would watch. From the ABC family sitcom *Viva Valdez* (1976) through The WB's one Latina-centric series, *First Time Out* (1995), these series failed to garner enough viewers to convince their networks to keep them; all but *Chico and the Man* (1974–78) were canceled after a season or less. It was in the late 1990s that the tenor of these pitch meetings began to shift, as networks became more open to programming about Latina/o characters. Among the reasons was the awareness that Latina/os were growing in numbers and becoming a substantial subset of the English-language television audience. More executives realized there were profits to be made from Latina and Latino stars, characters, and narratives, especially after Tejano singer Selena died tragically in 1995 and sales of her music soared.[1] Jennifer Lopez, Ricky Martin, and Cristina Aguilera were marketed to non-Latina/os as part of an exciting and sexy "Latin Boom." Pitches for series featuring Latina/o leads thus got more purchase, and stars such as Edward James Olmos, Elizabeth Peña, Constance Marie, Martin Sheen (of partial Latino descent), and Benjamin Bratt could be included as selling points. Latina/o writers began to be employed, on a small scale.[2]

Meanwhile, the networks needed to brand themselves, at the very least, as concerned about diverse programming in an increasingly multicultural United States. Studies of racial and ethnic representation on television were consistently finding Latina/os the most dramatically underrepresented group, adding pressure in this regard.[3] By the early 2000s, Latina/o media advocacy targeting ABC, NBC, CBS, and FOX was carried out most visibly through the National Hispanic Media Coalition and the Multi-Ethnic Media Coalition, which brought the four major ethnic advocacy groups together to pressure the networks for greater diversity and inclusion in programming and employment.[4] Among other strategies, the Multi-Ethnic Media Coalition issued public "report cards" annually on network progress toward more inclusive practices and programming. At the behest of the Coalition, the Big Four networks created executive positions in 2000 with the job of encouraging improvements at their network on these issues.[5]

It was within this industrial landscape that we witnessed the first commercial television series *by* Latina/o creators *about* Latina and Latino lead characters. The first Latino-led prime-time series to air was *Resurrection Blvd.*, produced by Dennis Leoni, of Mexican and Italian descent, for Showtime. A drama about a Mexican American family in East Los Angeles with a multi-generational focus on boxing, it was touted as the first series with an all-Latina/o cast and crew. It was followed by a "wave" (of three!) series that premiered in 2002. These shows included *Greetings from Tucson* (2002–04), a family comedy created and co–executive produced by Peter Murrieta for The WB;[6] the eponymous *George Lopez* (2002–07), a family sitcom that Lopez helped write and executive produce for ABC; and Gregory Nava's family drama *American Family* (2002–04), initially produced for CBS but broadcast by PBS.[7] Cable networks had also greenlit a few series by Latina/o creators that further proved that Latina/o series could appeal to national audiences. These included the Maria Perez-Brown–helmed *Taina* (2001–02), about a Puerto Rican teenager at a performing arts high school in Manhattan, and Jeff Valdez, Gibby Cevallos, and Mike Cevallos' *The Brothers Garcia* (2000–03), a teen sitcom about three brothers and their sister in San Antonio, both on the children's network Nickelodeon. Several less successful prime-time series launched on FOX and CBS as well.[8]

Given this new cycle of programming, it must have felt like the breakthrough that Latina/o creatives had been dreaming of. Television critics in turn described these new series as part of a revolution in programming. Howard Rosenberg, writing about *Resurrection Blvd.* and *American Family* for the *Los Angeles Times*, pointed to how they challenged the depiction of Latina/os as "invisible minorities" and typecast as "[the] Frito Bandito, vanloads of illegal immigrants and gangbanger stereotypes."[9] Mireya Navarro, for *The New York Times*, similarly underscored how *George Lopez* was "a television rarity as much for its all-Latina/o cast as for its occasionally heart-wrenching bite."[10] When the series became a solid hit for ABC in 2002, it did in fact mark a turning point for Latina/o television representation, as I elaborate on below.

That doesn't mean that getting these series greenlit and produced was easy, however. Latina/o writer-producers had to get past the industry's hegemonic notions about Latina/os as uninteresting and unworthy of a narrative spotlight. Additionally, the rarity of Latina/o-focused series meant they carried a heavy burden of representation and could face harsh scrutiny from viewers. In this chapter, I illuminate how creators navigated this uncertain terrain, with focus on their series' development, production, and promotion, the kinds of stories that they told about Latina/os, and how they responded to critics and fans. To do so, I examine three series, each of which took up a distinct narrative or production strategy. The first is *Resurrection Blvd.*, which embodied the network strategy of elevating a Latina/o narrative as a prestige drama. My second case study, *George Lopez,* I examine in part as an example of the star-driven sitcom. While this was a broadcast network strategy that can be traced back to Jackie Gleason's *The Honeymooners* (1955–56) and that had been attempted with previous Latina/o series, it was the first time the star was also a writer and executive producer (Desi Arnaz had been executive producer, but not a writer, on *I Love Lucy)*. Finally, I explore the network strategy of telenovela adaptation in my exploration of the dramedy *Ugly Betty* (2006–10). Inspired by the popular Colombian telenovela *Yo soy Betty, la fea* (1999–2002), *Ugly Betty* was created by the late writer–executive producer Silvio Horta and also championed by film star Salma Hayek, who served as one of the executive producers.

Aside from Sandra Bullock and Salma Hayek, non-writer showrunners for *George Lopez* and *Ugly Betty*, the executive producers and most of the staff writers of these series were men. This reflects the overwhelming dominance of male writers and especially executive producers in the 2000s, while women had been employed sporadically as television writers since the 1950s. While a gender imbalance would still exist in the 2010s, a number of Latinas would join the ranks of executive producers, especially in the latter half of the decade.[11] I focus on their contributions in chapter 6.

How Latino (and Some Latina) Writers Got in the Room, and a Few Got a Show

While a handful of Latina/o writers began to break into television as early as the 1980s, this was not without difficulty. They had to navigate their precarious positions in relation to the industry from which they previously had been shut out. The dynamic was similar to Chicana and Chicano artists' complicated relationship with museum culture in the 1980s, as scholar Alicia Gaspar de Alba illuminates.[12] In this case, Latino and Latina writers working during these years describe having to develop thick skins and learn to overlook cultural slights to survive in the industry and build their careers.[13] For writers who later became executive producers and showrunners, their goals were often different from those of the Chicano and Puerto Rican producers who had worked on the 1970s activist-oriented series. While the producers of public affairs series thought of their local Latina/o community, or in later years the national pan-Latina/o community, as their target audience, Latina/o writers working in 2000s commercial television typically targeted a multi-ethnic national audience. For the most part, they aimed to gain entrée into and legitimacy within the industry and to have the chance to create and share their stories via television.

Breaking in as a television writer was close to miraculous and a testimony to the resilience and determination of these creative professionals. These writers typically garnered their first opportunity to write for a prime-time series because of writing success in another creative arena, such as theater. A few got their start through forming and performing in theatrical collectives, as was the case for Rick Najera and Luisa Leschin, writer-performers who formed Latins Anonymous with Diane Rodriguez and Armando Molina in 1987. As Leschin and Najera relayed in separate interviews, they formed Latins Anonymous after meeting in rehearsals of an actors' repertory company. Wanting to address the frustrations that they and other Latino and Latina actors felt with respect to limited casting opportunities and roles in theater, film, and television, they came together to begin writing and performing their own material.

As Leschin stated, "The impetus for Latins Anonymous really came from feeling typecast and feeling frustrated. And knowing that none of that could change from being on the [typical film or television] set."[14] She shared stories from the 1980s, when she worked as an actress in television and films. Leschin would land guest star roles on well-respected television series, only to find that her character was going to be costumed and made up in a fashion that was not only inaccurate to the role, but demeaning. For example, on the stylish detective series *Hart to Hart* (1979–84), playing a mule for a drug dealer, Leschin was made up with purple eye shadow up to her eyebrows. When she tried to protest, she was told by the makeup artist, "Latinas always wear purple eye shadow."

She found the broadcast footage later too embarrassing to add to her demo reel. On an episode of the medical mystery drama *Quincy, M.E.* (1976–83), in which she played a hard-working, working-class young Latina, she was costumed in a dirty sweater with holes in it. Leschin's recollections were eerily similar to those relayed to me by other Latina and Latino actors with long careers in television and film.[15]

Latins Anonymous performed at the Latino Theater Center and other California theatrical spaces in 1989 and 1990, and later toured with their show, *The LA LA Awards*. Television writer-producers Barry Blaustein and David Chipperfield, former *Saturday Night Live* writers who had a deal with Imagine Television, were impressed with the show and extended an offer to the group to write a pilot.[16] Their pilot, *Add Love*—a copy of which, sadly, no longer exists—was a workplace comedy about the Latina/o wing of an advertising agency. While it was not picked up by a network, it got them into the writers' guild. Agency representation soon followed. In a highly unusual turn, they began to be able to take meetings with the networks and pitch series ideas. Leschin notes, "The four of us did it all backwards." While the broadcast networks had occasionally cast Latino and Latina performers in protagonist roles in pilots, this is the earliest mention that I heard of Latina/o writers being invited to pitch series ideas. But these writers' lack of experience as television creators and showrunners and the lack of Latina/o stars to play lead characters (at least, in the eyes of executives) were seen as reasons not to greenlight their pitches. As Leschin put it, "In retrospect, it was like the network gets to tick off the box: We saw, we heard from some diverse writers. So it was wide open. But we didn't have show-running experience. We didn't have that kind of experience that you really need to be given a show." Leschin eventually wrote a *Seinfeld* episode that earned her acceptance into the Walt Disney Television Writing Program,[17] meant to launch the careers of writers from underrepresented groups, and this was the beginning of a television writing and producing career that has spanned three decades.[18]

Other opportunities to become staff writers, the first of the three tiers of employment and status in television writing, began to occasionally open up in the 1990s. Rick Najera, Peter Murrieta (later to lead *Wizards of Waverly Place* [2007–12]), and Dennis Leoni began as staff writers for a variety of programs in this period. Murrieta worked on *Ask Harriet* (1998) and *Jesse* (1998–2000); Najera from 1992 to 1993 on *In Living Color* (1990–94), *Townsend Television* (1993), and on the 2005 season of *MADtv* (1995–2009); and Leoni on the 1994 season of *The Commish* (1991–96) and on *Covington Cross* (1992), and *McKenna* (1994–95). As Murrieta and Najera noted, their first jobs were on African American sitcoms and sketch comedy series because there were no Latina/o series and it was thought that they were best suited to write for characters of color. They and their Latina/o peers in the writers' guild were a very small consortium in the 1990s. I note in chapter 4 that when Jackie Guerra, the star of The WB series *First Time Out* (1995), urged her show's producers to hire some Latina/o writers, she was told there were none. By the 1990s and 2000s, that was simply not true. Series pitches centered around Latino and Latina protagonists still were typically rejected, however, at times with the excuse that there were no stars to play them, both Najera and Leschin told me. Leschin remembered thinking at the time, "Who's out there who can carry off this fantastic lead role? And at that point, all there was . . . there weren't that many people [with the recognized stardom or acting experience]."

The tide began to turn for Latina/o creators by the end of the decade. In 2000, the same year that *Taina* and *Brothers Garcia* began airing on Nickelodeon, *Resurrection Blvd.* debuted, followed by *Greetings from Tucson*, *George Lopez*, and *American Family*, with a number of Latino and Latina writers on staff.[19] Meanwhile, a few industry interventions such as the Walt Disney Television Writing Program were helping to level the playing field for a few writers. Individuals accepted into this competitive writers' program are given training in television writing and the industry and the opportunity to write for an ABC or Disney series. Peter Murrieta, Dailyn Rodriguez, Cynthia Cidre, and Tanya Saracho are among the writers who went through the program. These individuals clearly didn't need to learn to write, but they benefited from an orientation to writing for television and from gaining access to vital gatekeepers and professional networks through it.

As this historical summary makes evident, it was an eventful decade in which Latina/o cultural production was beginning to flourish. In the following sections, I examine how several Latino showrunners worked to navigate the challenges of pleasing their network while also maintaining their show's appeal for Latina/o and non-Latina/o viewers. Notably, compromises had to be made in the 2000s that are less often expected today.

The Prestige Drama: *Resurrection Blvd.*

Occasionally a television series or film dramatically showcases progress for a social group with respect to multidimensional and empowered self-representation. Such was the case of *Resurrection Blvd.* The series, touted as the first with an all-Latina/o cast and crew, aired on Showtime, a premium cable network. A family drama about the Santiago family in East Los Angeles, it also included a focus on the uber-masculine sport of boxing. The men in the family were or had been boxers, and the sport was central in the lives of the sisters and aunt in the family as well. Perhaps most importantly, it had a budget much higher than that for a half-hour comedy, and this showed, particularly in its glossy pilot episode. Even so, however, it didn't come close to the budget of some of the other premium cable series at the time. While episodes of HBO's *The Sopranos* (1999–2007) cost $2 million in its first season and rose to $6.5 million in its last, *Resurrection Blvd.*'s episodes had budgets of only $1.1 million, and faced a reduced budget in the show's last year.[20]

A number of television industry and social developments were catalysts in Showtime's decision to air the series. The music and media industries' marketing of the Latina/o media "boom" in the late 1990s set the stage for more Latina/o-centric programming on broadcasting and cable networks. In addition, *The Sopranos* had debuted in 1999 on HBO, the first premium cable channel known for innovative and cinematic original programming. It was a critical and popular hit, proving that series with complex narratives and aesthetics could be lucrative and enhance a network brand. Showtime was clearly chasing the HBO market when it greenlit *Resurrection Blvd.*, one of several new series meant to appeal underrepresented communities and especially to brand the network as embodying a compassionate, indie ethos. In 2000 as *Resurrection Blvd.* premiered, Showtime also launched *Soul Food* (2000–04), an African American friendship drama, and *Queer as Folk* (2000–05), a drama about a group of white gay men. All were promoted in a splashy

"No Limits" promotional campaign. Showtime also aimed to build on its current audience, in particular its audience for televised boxing matches. In illustration, one October 2000 *Resurrection Blvd.* promo, showcasing the dramatic and romantic surprises in an upcoming episode, appeared after an ad for an upcoming Mike Tyson–Andrew Golota boxing match and before a promo for *Soul Food*. The network was clearly targeting boxing fans and viewers of color as *Resurrection Blvd.*'s potential audience.

Given the invisibility of Latina/os in premium dramas before this time, *Resurrection Blvd.*, which debuted on June, 26, 2000, was an important milestone in a number of respects. It employed a record number of Latina/os in front of and behind the camera and demonstrated the universal appeal of a Latina/o-centric drama. At the center of the narrative were the Santiagos, a family of three sons and two daughters led by widower Roberto (Tony Plana). Roberto had been a boxer in his youth and had later trained his sons as boxers. The eldest, Miguel (Mauricio Mendoza), was working as a boxing promoter, and middle son Carlos (Michael DeLorenzo) was moving into the championship ring, while the youngest son, Alex (Nick Gonzalez), was in college and more interested in his pre-med training. Yolanda (Ruth Livier), in turn, worked for a law firm, while the youngest sibling, Victoria (Marisol Nichols), was a high school student. When Carlos's chance at the championship is dashed by an attack by a neighborhood gang member that leaves him with a serious injury, Alex forgoes his studies to carry on the family dream, setting in motion the events of the first season. Over the fifty-three episodes of the show's three seasons, the Santiagos face challenges, some typical and some not so typical to their East Los Angeles community, begin and end relationships, celebrate successes, and reaffirm their commitment to family.

Given its unique prestige as an hour-long drama on a premium cable network, *Resurrection Blvd.*'s premiere was treated as a major event by the LA and national Latina/o audience. In fact, two premieres were held for news media professionals and industry insiders that week to generate buzz and news stories about the show; it was one of these premieres that I was able to attend while a doctoral student. It was much loved by its Latina/o viewers. Across its three seasons, the series and its actors garnered several awards from the National Council of La Raza and other Latina/o advocacy organizations, and demonstrated that nuanced Latina/o narratives can attract a wide variety of viewers. Countless members of the cast and crew were able to join an industry professional guild and further their careers.

Leoni credits Jerry Offsay, Showtime's head of programming from 1994 through 2003, for creating an opening for *Resurrection Blvd.* As reported by *USA Today* journalist Gary Levin in 2001, Offsay decided to seek out a Latina/o series after noticing that films about people of color drew in Showtime's largest audiences.[21] As Pancho Mansfield, then senior vice president of original programming, noted in interviews, they wanted to develop Latino projects and showrunners, given that there had been none up to that point. Showtime also was aiming for edgy projects that "pushed the limits" of television. A number of writers were invited to pitch projects. After submitting a script for a family drama that Offsay liked but said wasn't right for the network, Leoni added boxing as a major story element. With that, *Resurrection Blvd.* was born as a successful pitch.[22] When Showtime greenlit the series, Leoni brought on Jesús Treviño, longtime television director, filmmaker, and producer of two Chicana/o public affairs series in the 1970s, highlighted in chapter 2, as a co-producer and director.

A number of challenges arose in preproduction, however. Despite Showtime's support for the series, network representatives were, at first, not on board with Leoni and Treviño's push to hire as many Latina/os on their production team as possible. The network executives initially said they wanted "more qualified" professionals. Treviño noted that they had to threaten to leave the project before they were given the go-ahead to make the hires they wanted. As he described it,

> I said, well, you know, I think you may have something there. You may be correct. But if that's the case, then I think what should happen, I know there are directors much more qualified than me, and there are writers more qualified than Dennis. So I think we should be out of the running. I think you should just go ahead and hire all of these non-Latino directors and actors and everything else, and then you can have the first Latino show on American television, bilingual—with no Latinos involved at all. That makes sense. Dead silence. And Dennis and I are just beaming at each other. And then the producer says, Okay, let's look at the resumes.

And that's how we got our people on the series. . . . Because no one trusted that we had the quality people to produce a quality show.[23]

Ultimately Latino and Latina professionals were hired in almost every job category.[24]

In developing the narrative across three seasons, Leoni and the other writer-producers worked to balance their vision with Showtime's expectations and assumptions about Latina/os, and also with their audience's interests and wishes. In this juggling act, what Latina/o viewers might most want to see at times had to be dropped. While Showtime's executives wanted *Resurrection Blvd.* to appeal to Latina/o viewers (and they would in fact be valuable new subscribers), even more they didn't want the show to repel the network's bread and butter, its current white subscribers. As Scott Wible notes, to succeed, the series had to instead "'create curiosity' and offer the network's white, upper-middle class viewers a comforting glimpse into a middle-class, Mexican American home," which discouraged the show's producers from telling a Latina/o narrative with what might be viewed as too much cultural or political specificity.[25] "Universal" storytelling at this time translated to a pan-ethnic rather than Mexican American framework for greater appeal to non-Latina/o viewers and Latina/os of all national origin groups, of which Leoni took heed. He and Treviño at times disagreed on whether this was the best approach. While Treviño was able to add more Mexican American specificity in the show's "bumpers" that offered glimpses of daily life in the Mexican American neighborhood of Boyle Heights, some viewers complained that they implied that all Latina/os were working class.

Another negotiation that Leoni faced was regarding casting. While hiring only Mexican American actors would be the most culturally authentic casting possible, Leoni chose to cast Latina/o actors of diverse national origin groups, in the hope that this would increase the show's broad appeal. This also allowed the production to cast more experienced and proven actors. The small group of working actors in Los Angeles who regularly play Latina/o roles is quite diverse with respect to national origin group; pan-Latina/o casting of Mexican American roles has been commonplace in films such as *La Bamba* (1987), *Selena* (1997), and *Stand and Deliver* (1988) and in television since *Viva Valdez. Resurrection Blvd.*, after being touted as the first all-Latina/o series, was under

Figure 5.1. The cast of *Resurrection Blvd.* in a publicity photo. From left, standing: Elizabeth Peña, Mauricio Mendoza, Tony Plana, Nicholas Gonzalez, and Daniel Zacapa; seated: Ruth Livier, Michael DeLorenzo, and Marisol Nichols.

particular scrutiny, however. Some viewers complained about the casting and the resulting mixed accents, arguing that it hurt the believability of the narrative. Leoni told me in February 2018 that he would likely cast for more specificity today.[26] Throughout its three seasons, however, the show employed more than 600 Latina/o actors, a distinction that likely no other series of that era can match. Rita Moreno, Paul Rodriguez, Edward James Olmos, Jackie Guerra, Seidy López, Esai Morales, Cheech Marin, Nestor Carbonell, Rubén Blades, and Lupe Ontiveros were among the actors cast in the show's three seasons.

While aiming to present the Santiagos in a universal fashion to which Americans of all backgrounds could relate, *Resurrection Blvd.* focused on social issues that particularly impacted Mexican Americans in East

Los Angeles. Cultural identity differences across generations, gang violence, the plight of undocumented workers, and racial profiling by the
police were addressed. While it received only one nomination for an
award from the television industry (a nomination from the Writers
Guild of America for Robert Eisele's script, "Niño del Polvo" ("Child of
Dust"), the drama received numerous nominations and awards from the
National Council of La Raza, Nosotros, and the Imagen Foundation for
its positive portrayals of Latina/os and excellence in production, acting,
writing, and directing. GLAAD (the Gay and Lesbian Alliance Against
Defamation) also recognized the series for its sensitive portrayal of ho-
mosexuality in Latina/o families.

Above all, *Resurrection Blvd.* meant a lot to its fans. While Leoni
noted that complaints from Latina/o viewers were always hard for him
to shake, I found far more evidence of viewers who found the series
importantly affirming. The Dennis E. Leoni *Resurrection Blvd.* Papers
at UCLA's Chicano Studies Research Center include dozens of emails
and letters from Latina/o viewers praising the production and asking
Showtime to renew the series. For example:

> I've recently gotten Showtime added to our cable service in order to
> watch Resurrection Blvd. Finally there's a well-crafted series on Latinos
> in America. I hope you keep it around a long time.

> Please renew the series. I can't believe there's any question of whether to
> renew it. It's the ONLY Latino drama on TV. I watch it (and tape it) each
> week. Then, I pass the tape along to my friends and family who do not
> have cable. They also enjoy it. Don't cancel the only show that reflects the
> Mexican American community. It's a strong family-oriented program and
> we need more of these—not less.

> I just wanted to write in to compliment Showtime on its new series
> Resurrection BLVD. I started watching it and then I introduced it to
> my parents and now we all watch it FAITHFULLY!! We love the show
> because it portrays the true life of a Latino family living in the U.S.
> It shows the good and the bad things that Latinos deal with! It's very
> realistic. We watch it and we can see parts of our family in the series.
> We appreciate even the smallest details like switching back and forth

between English and Spanish in conversations and from the crosses and other Catholic items hanging through the house. There is a market for shows like this and we just wanted to thank you for creating this show! We are faithful fans and will continue to spring the word to the rest of our family and friends!!

I want to commend and congratulate Showtime for its original program Resurrection Blvd. Thank you for giving Latinos an opportunity for depicting ourselves as mainstream people. Too often film and television have typically depicted our people as shallow blue collar workers, ex-cons, bandits, drug users, street walkers, uninterested in bettering ourselves through an education and simply interested in having a good time by partying too much. Your program is the first Latino program to depict Latinos as part of the mainstream in which we have been historically ignored.

For countless Latina/o viewers, *Resurrection Blvd.* was the first time they saw themselves and their families in English-language television.

Despite these effusive responses from its fans, the production struggled to get the kind of promotion that might draw in more Latina/o viewers and others interested in nuanced portrayals of Latina/o family. Showtime's lack of experience promoting a series with Latina/o leads or content led to some misguided decisions. I was told by Luis Reyes, one of the publicists for the series, and others who worked on the production that the network initially wanted to promote the show primarily through Spanish-language media outlets, such as radio stations in the Los Angeles area. Members of the production team had to argue that this meant missing the viewers who would most likely watch the show. Showtime's decision to heavily target African American viewers through tie-ins with *Soul Food* in the last year of *Resurrection Blvd.*'s run also was not successful enough to prevent the show's cancellation.

That the series was on a premium cable network was an obstacle, as courting the Latina/o audience meant convincing them to subscribe to and pay for Showtime. "That was the hardest thing," Leoni said. Media advocacy in this instance meant introducing Latina/o viewers to the series and organizing Showtime sign-up campaigns. Advocacy groups such as NCLR, Imagen Foundation, and the National Organization of

Hispanic Journalists took on this challenge and organized fans to send letters to Showtime in support of renewing *Resurrection Blvd.* for a second and third season. This work entailed encouraging Latina/o viewers to think of themselves as what Wible describes as a "citizen-consumer." As he notes, Latina/o fans were mobilized in these campaigns "as 'audiences'" and media consumers, rather than as "'publics' or as 'citizens,'" as activism to support Latina/o television now was linked to telegraphing media consumption practices and linked purchases.[27]

The audience that ultimately found the series was quite multi-ethnic; about 85 percent of viewers in 2002 were non-Latina/o. The series was later syndicated in twenty-three Latin American countries, with either full pickups or pay-per-view options, according to Leoni. While Latina/o subscriptions to Showtime did go up from 10 to 12 percent of all subscribers while the show was on the air, this was not seen by the network as enough.[28] They cut the episode budgets in the last season, and finally chose not to renew the series. As Leoni noted, "The problem was that Jerry [Offsay] was on his way out [as president of programming at Showtime]. So we lost our *patrón.*"

The Sitcom that Made Latina/os
Americans: *George Lopez*

Meanwhile, the broadcast networks were making minor attempts to showcase Latina/o characters and series in their prime-time programming of the early 2000s. ABC, CBS, NBC, and FOX occasionally cast a Latino or Latina actor in a (white-centric) ensemble series and greenlit a handful of Latina/o-led comedies and telenovela adaptations, programming strategies meant to calm Latina/o media advocates and please Latina/o viewers. *George Lopez* was one of three Latina/o-led sitcoms that ABC developed and aired in these years. ABC also later aired *Ugly Betty* (2006–10) and *Freddie* (2005–06). *Freddie* was a historic first as a series with a star, Freddie Prinze Jr., whose father, Freddie Prinze, had starred on television, in *Chico and the Man* (1974–78) three decades prior.[29]

George Lopez was particularly important as the first series to offer its Mexican American star executive producer status. Notably, Lopez's then-wife, Ann Serrano Lopez, was his manager at the time. She and the rest of his management team can be credited for Lopez's deal with the network. The eponymous series star came on as an executive producer and writer of the series, which afforded him substantial creative control over the series. He was joined by three other executive producers, including writer-producers Bruce Helford and Robert Borden, along with Sandra Bullock, who championed the series with the network and served as an occasional guest star. Fortis Films, Bullock's production company, ABC, and Warner Bros. produced the show.

Details about the deal ABC forged for *George Lopez* illuminate network doubts in the mid-2000s, however; the producers had to work hard over an extended period of time to convince ABC to fully embrace it. The sitcom initially received just a pilot commitment. Later, it was given an abbreviated first season of only four episodes, before it got a partial and eventually a full second season of twenty-two episodes. Several of the actors also had to undergo multiple auditions before the network signed on to their casting. Mexican American actor Constance Marie, who plays George Lopez's wife, reported she had to go through seven auditions, and wasn't the initial pick, before getting the part.[30] The hiring of Helford and Borden, two white male television veterans who ultimately were stalwart supporters of the series, also can be considered an insurance policy in the eyes of the network.[31] Later, a few Latina and Latino writers were added after the first, truncated season. The writers' table eventually included Luisa Leschin and Dailyn Rodriguez, while the late Michele Serros, Valentina Garza, Ann Serrano Lopez, Danielle Sanchez-Witzel, and Victor Gonzalez wrote for the show for shorter periods.

Among the show's appeals were its naturalistic comedy and emotional authenticity that drew from George Lopez's actual, not rosy childhood, also the subject of his stand-up comedy. Lopez has shared in his comedy and in other writing that television was an important source of entertainment and comfort in his childhood; Freddie Prinze's television performances inspired him to become a comedian, he noted in 2003.[32] Reportedly it was Lopez's stand-up comedy that led to his discovery by Bullock and Jonathan Komack Martin—son of James Komack, creator and producer of *Chico and the Man* thirty years earlier—at a comedy club in Austin, Texas.[33] They were excited by his performance and later decided to build a series around his childhood memories.

Writers who worked on the series emphasize the natural feel of the Lopez family as Latina/o *Americans* as one of the key appeals of *George*

Lopez. Luisa Leschin noted that one of the smart choices the writers made at the behest of Lopez was to approach his character's ethnic identity with subtlety. "George had a very strong vision and goes, 'I live in the Valley, I eat hamburgers,'" she stated. "I actually thought that it was smart to do that to try to minimize the otherness. And of course, some producer said, 'Well, do we have enough Mexican touches in the kitchen?' George goes, 'I'm in the kitchen. That's enough.' That's a quote of his. And it was true. And it worked." Lopez similarly reports in the documentary *Brown is the New Green: George Lopez and the American Dream* (2007) that he quipped, "You don't need a tortilla maker in the kitchen. In my house, my grandmother was the tortilla maker!" As Lopez and the other head writers noted in a seminar on the series at the Paley Center for Media in March 2003, they wanted to bring his memories of everyday family struggles and find the humor in them. Helford added that Latina/o identity came naturally into story lines in this way, rather than as an overwrought first concern. As a strong illustration of *George Lopez*'s universal approach, the credit sequence doesn't try to broadcast that this is a Latina/o sitcom. Instead, it features its cast dressed in casual but polished clothes, buoyantly appearing and disappearing from the screen as they jump from what presumably was a trampoline, with "Lowrider" by the funk band War playing in the background. They look happy, serene, and vibrant, with beautiful skies in the background. As Lopez might say, it is a Latina/o show, because there are Latina/os in it.[34]

Peaceful optimism was only occasionally the tone of the show, however. In drawing on his childhood for episode ideas, Lopez was pulling from memories that were often strained or downright sad, rather than a childhood that was picture perfect in any way. In creating the fictional story of the Lopezes for television, he included George's mother, who is more likely to razz and laugh at her son than praise him, and in later episodes a deadbeat father that he has to track down. These characters and other elements make it clear George has personal demons with which he contends because of his childhood, realistically complicating the narrative. This lends the series an inner pathos and complexity, increasing its relatability and appeal.

In the pilot, "Prototype," co-written by Helford, Lopez, and Borden, George adjusts to a new job as the floor manager at the airplane parts factory where he has worked for over a decade. He's given an ultimatum

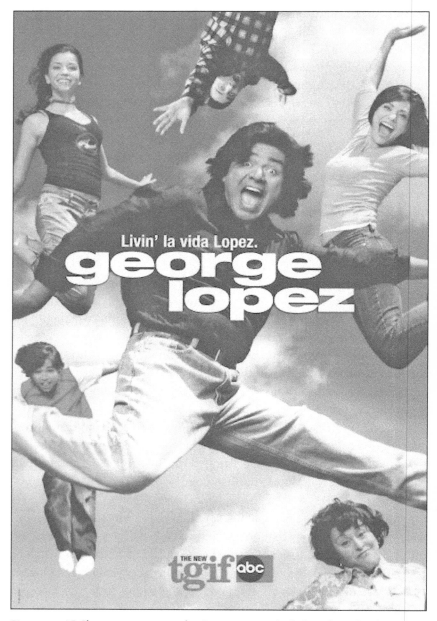

Figure 5.2. ABC's season one poster for *George Lopez*, which drew from the show's credit sequence that featured its cast bouncing in the air, apparently from a trampoline.

by his supervisor: he needs to fire several coworkers, which means firing either his best friend, Ernie—or his mother, Benny. He ultimately decides to fire his mother, with whom he has an often-antagonistic relationship, despite the fact that this will mean she'll have to come live with him and his family. But soon he finds out, to his consternation, that the firing won't need to happen. As a result, he and his mother have a meaningful conversation ("You've got balls!" she admits, after teasing him mercilessly for not being tough enough to fire his own mother). Meanwhile, George and his wife, Angie, cope with their daughter's new teen struggles (George jokes "You've got jungle pits!" when his daughter gathers the courage to show him her underarms and ask for permission to shave her body hair) and with parenting their pre-teen son, Max. Other episodes focus more on George and Angie's parenting as Carmen begins to want to date and Max wants to walk to school by himself. The audience also witnesses George learning to let go of childhood trauma and enjoy things like birthdays, dealing with further challenges in his new job, and deciding to look for his father. Throughout, the warmth, rewards, and common frustrations of family life are conveyed, often through comedy and subtle quips.

This approach of personal storytelling marked a sea change for Latina/o televisual representation; it made the story that of an American family, and one that is admirable but imperfect. This approach and its success both enacted and telegraphed American Latina/o cultural citizenship. At the same time, the narrative subtly reminds viewers this is not just an American family, but a Mexican and Cuban American family. This comes in the form of funny and affectionate asides that George or other cast members make. In "Prototype," Carmen calls out to her son, who is late getting ready for school, "Hey Rico Suave, we got to go!" In "Who's Your Daddy," episode six, George jokes about lying to one's kids and the lying he endured from his mother as a kid, "Who knows what else she lied to me about? Maybe Santa Claus does like Mexican kids." And George and Ernie have occasional moments at work when, from across the factory floor, they affect the pachuco-style "lean," proudly jutting their chins out and leaning back on their heels as if with hands in pockets of their zoot suits, to make each other laugh. These are fluid moments that quickly pass, simply part of the cultural hybridity of the family, a narrative approach that feels affectionate and real.

Figure 5.3. George Lopez poses in 2006 with his *George Lopez* television family as he receives a star on Hollywood's Walk of Fame. From left: Masiela Lusha, Belita Moreno, Luis Armand Garcia, Lopez, and Constance Marie.

The series was a minor hit with American viewers, and would go on to perform even better in syndication. It won its time slot when its initial season aired as a mid-season replacement, with nine million viewers, and in its second season, with ten million viewers. After five seasons, ABC canceled the series, however. Disappointed, Lopez noted that it had been moved around the prime-time schedule four times in five years, and that the show that replaced it, *Cavemen* (2007), was far less successful. *George Lopez* was the first Latina/o series to go into syndication, however. Distributed by Warner Bros., it aired in syndication from 2007 to 2011, becoming more successful in its second run.[35] It aired on The CW, FOX affiliate stations, Nick at Nite, MTV3rs, ION Television, and TV Land networks through 2016. The show's success in syndication, and the star on Hollywood's Walk of Fame that George Lopez received in 2006 with his entire television family present, made it clear that he and his series about a Mexican and Cuban American family were firmly part of US popular culture.

A Beautiful Dramedy Before Its Time: *Ugly Betty*

Another Latina/o series hit soon followed, this time with a focus on a female protagonist, Betty Suarez, an ambitious and fashion-impaired young Mexican American woman from Queens, New York, who dreams of being a magazine writer and ultimately a magazine owner. She takes a job as the executive assistant to the editor-in-chief of a fashion magazine, which kicks off the complicated and often daffy story line. ABC's *Ugly Betty* was an adaptation of *Yo soy Betty, la fea*, a Colombian telenovela that had been remade in dozens of countries; the show's success in the hands of the late Silvio Horta broke the pattern of producers' fumbling attempts to adapt popular Spanish-language telenovelas for US audiences.[36] In the hands of Horta, a young Cuban American writer-producer whose imagined and produced media projects had resisted the typical genre formulas of 2000s and 2010s television prior to his tragic death in 2020,[37] the series was a creative curiosity that caught ABC by surprise. In particular it was a decidedly genre-busting narrative with a Latina lead character for the first time on network television.

The idea of adapting *Betty, la fea* was initially championed by William Morris Agency vice president Raul Mateu, who happened to be of Venezuelan heritage, and producer Ben Silverman, then head of International Package Division for William Morris. Silverman shepherded a *Betty, la fea* adaptation comedy pilot for NBC and later a dramedy pilot for ABC; both failed to garner interest.[38] Juan Piñon describes Silverman's attunement to the promise of narrative formats still untried in the US as "cosmopolitan."[39] Silverman later added Salma Hayek to the development team; she ultimately played an important role in garnering support for the project and bringing on Horta, remembered as a wunderkind. As his agent at William Morris Endeavor, Paul Haas, put it, "He burst onto the scene like a bright, shining star . . . the first five scripts he wrote as TV pilots went straight to series."[40] They were typically offbeat narratives appealing to young performers. Horta noted in an interview with Nancy Harrison for the Television Academy Foundation in 2013 that he had heard about the failed *Betty* pilots and was interested in trying his hand at an adaptation because his mother had enjoyed the original series.[41]

As Piñon documents, the first, unproduced ABC pilot, titled *Betty, the Ugly*, included no Latino or Latina creatives.[42] According to Horta, it was not particularly appealing and never aired. He wanted to take a different approach. "I just tried to make it my own," he noted in the Television Academy Foundation interview. Initially he pitched Betty Suarez as an undercover spy, but this gained no traction with the network. Then he made it a workplace dramedy set at a New York fashion magazine, which allowed for commentary on constructed norms of beauty in relation to Betty's ugly duckling story and tale of determination. He also chose to not be confined to tradition in his blend of realism and surreal narrative elements and the show's colorful and visually striking aesthetic, from the set design of *Mode* offices to Betty's idiosyncratic and character-defining outfits.

The development and eventual pickup of the series was aided greatly by Hayek as an executive producer. While she was involved as a celebrity showrunner rather than as a writer, she was very hands-on. Among other things, she fought for the story to remain centered on a Latina protagonist and family. "Salma Hayek was very insistent that the lead remain Latina, and she wanted to tell an immigrant story as well," Horta noted, which was also important to him.[43] Hayek also advocated for the actors they wanted to cast. There apparently was hesitation from ABC about casting America Ferrera as Betty Suarez in particular. The executives weren't familiar with Ferrera's film roles, which included *Real Women Have Curves* (2002) and *The Sisterhood of the Traveling Pants* (2005), and initially expressed ambivalence. "Salma just fought tooth and nail and make sure she got cast," Horta noted.

> They weren't sure if: Was she was too pretty, was she not pretty? Nobody knew . . . everybody was looking at the original version, where a supermodel had glasses on and braces, and then she has this very dramatic makeover. . . . America personified someone that was not a 6-foot-2 Glamazon who we just put fake braces on. We never wanted that; we wanted someone that felt more real.[44]

Another challenge had to do with the genre blend and unique tone of the series. The dramedy included narrative moments that lent a quirky tinge of surrealism to its otherwise realistic story line. "Tonally it was something very different and unique," Horta stated. "And it was hard to put a box."[45] ABC put the show in a not-great time slot of Friday nights. Additionally, they pushed back against some episodes, especially as the narrative began to include a prominent character who was transgender, and as sexual orientation became a common subject of story lines.

The network's support shifted dramatically after the first season of *Ugly Betty* was warmly received by the Television Critics Association, however; it was nominated for both Outstanding New Program and Outstanding Achievement in Comedy. As Horta put it, "I think the reception at the TCAs were what led them to move the show from Friday night to Thursday night."[46] America Ferrera then won Best Leading Actress in a Comedy Series, while the series won Best Comedy Series in the Golden Globe Awards in January 2007. By the show's second season, it was a critical darling and, in its new time slot, a ratings success. That year at the upfronts, the networks' annual presentations of potential programming to advertisers, ABC made the series central to its branding, culminating in an *Ugly Betty* musical number performed by Ferrera, the rest of the cast, and a chorus line of Bettys played by the Rockettes. The season launched with a new theme, "Brighter. Bolder. Bettyer," and a splashy music video, set to Mika's "Hey Betty (You are Beautiful)," featuring the cast.

Despite *Ugly Betty*'s popularity, ABC continued to express discomfort with the content of episodes, Horta noted. They liked the premise he had envisioned. As Isabel Molina-Guzmán notes in her cogent study of the series, Betty's story in many ways is a Latina version of the American Dream, long a popular subject of prime-time programming.[47] Horta shared in interviews that he drew in part on his own experiences in the Hollywood writing world. Horta's personal inflection of Betty's story arguably brought her identity as a second-generation Latina to life with greater nuance. For example, in the series' sixth episode, "The Lyin', the Watch, and the Wardrobe," Betty has to take on a loathsome task for her lothario boss: She has to talk to each of the women he slept with the week before to track down where he has left his watch. She's viewed as an outsider at *Mode* and looks like one, less because she's the only Latina than because she lacks the fashion sense of her couture-worshipping coworkers. This takes a unique form in this episode. Betty, tricked by her coworkers into dressing up for Halloween, arrives in a

Figure 5.4. America Ferrera, the star of *Ugly Betty*, and the rest of the cast in a promotional image for their second season. The network promoted the series with more confidence after it won major awards from the Television Critics Association.

charming butterfly costume, only to find no else has dressed up. The undeniable charm of Ferrera as Betty in the costume interjects a surreal and beautiful element in the otherwise melodramatic and somber story line. Now stuck in the outfit all day, Betty has to walk the Manhattan streets in costume to carry out her boss's request.[48] However, what comes through in the episode is Betty's strength of spirit and inner beauty.

Meanwhile the ensemble's gay, questioning, and transgender characters are given equal nuance and heart in Horta's storytelling. In its inclusion of Betty's sexually questioning young nephew, a transgender character, and gay coworkers at *Mode*, the series was particularly forward leaning.[49] Also part of the series' unique tone was a critique of *Mode* and the fashion world, for judging Betty's fashion sense and thus cultural capital as a Latina from Queens. The many melodramatic narrative arcs delved into devious plans and subterfuge on the part of Betty's coworkers, Betty maturing as a young woman and professional, romantic possibilities and disappointments, and unjust immigration policies as experienced by Betty's father Ignacio.

Figure 5.5. America Ferrera as Betty Suarez on Halloween in *Ugly Betty*, "The Lyin', the Watch, and the Wardrobe" (2006).

It's important to note that Betty's Mexican American identity is only occasionally addressed in the narrative; the family's identity is marked more as working-class in relation to their neighborhood in Queens. There are only occasional moments in which Mexican or Latina identity is a central focus. In the first season, Betty and her sister Hilda learn that their father has been living in the US without papers for decades. In "A Tree Grows in Guadalajara," they travel to his home in Guadalajara, Mexico, to try to obtain a visa for him. There, Betty ends up meeting their maternal grandmother. Ignacio's family members, played by Rita Moreno and Justina Machado, are depicted as urbane, but the rural area outside the city, where Betty grandmother lives, is desolate and mysterious. An aesthetic of magical realism is used to suggest a magical and serendipitous encounter between Betty and her abuela.[50] Notably, and in keeping with Horta's creative vision, the most magical element—Betty's delusions of her estranged (white) boyfriend Henry riding a moped alongside her rickety bus—are not native to Mexico. In following her delusions of Henry, she finally finds her grandmother's house. Betty ends up gaining a lost connection to her and thus to her Mexican heritage in the episode, which is formative to her growing confidence and adult identity.[51] A later episode, "When Betty Met YETI" (2008), which aired as episode nine of season three, takes a radically different turn in its narrative of Betty turning down an internship when she learns that the offer was based solely on her Mexican American heritage. It was well in line with the post-racial (and, I would add, neoliberal) discourses that were circulating in this period, in the years after Barack Obama was elected US president.[52] It also reflected the pan-Latina/o and post-racial orientation that was encouraged in network programming in this decade.

Arguably, *Ugly Betty* succeeded because of narrative qualities and creative strategies of the series that were before their time. It was a fantasy-tinged ugly duckling tale about a Latina striving in a hostile landscape, a queer-friendly dramedy that transcended ethnic and race relations, and an auteur-driven narrative before these were common, all of which ran against ABC's favored strategies in this era. Given the need to capture and maintain a massive audience, falling ratings were ultimately its downfall. *Ugly Betty* garnered strong ratings, particularly its second and third seasons. But its viewership dropped by half to about five million viewers in its fourth season, when it was canceled.

At an *Ugly Betty* reunion event at the ATX Television Festival in Austin, Texas, in June 2016, the cast and Silvio Horta discussed their memories of the show. It was a festive occasion that highlighted the cast's strong sense of community and the supportive messages that the series had conveyed to fans. As Betty, America Ferrera became a Latina role model and star, while gay fans found affirmation and role models in Marc and Justin and the actors who played them. Michael Urie, who played Marc, noted receiving countless messages from fans, especially after an episode in which Marc came out to his mother. "And we all got lots of messages like that," Urie told the crowd. "The show really touched people. And really spoke to truths. They [the writers] never took the easy way out." Horta, asked about whether things were getting better for writers of color who wanted to work in television, said there were still few opportunities—but also not enough writers of color seeking them. He didn't mention his own struggles to get a new series off the ground since the show's cancellation. Led by Ferrera, the cast half-joked that Hulu should spring for an *Ugly Betty* reboot or movie. Despite the hashtag Ferrera made up on the spot, #HuluBringBackUglyBetty, the reboot never materialized.[53]

It turns out that this may have been a very difficult time in Horta's life. He had been going through other struggles aside from the difficulty selling a new series after *Ugly Betty* ended. He also reportedly struggled with depression and addiction, and had left Los Angeles to live with family. In January 2020, Horta passed away at the age of forty-five. It's difficult to know whether Horta's lack of career traction after *Ugly Betty*'s cancellation was due primarily to the impact of his personal demons, or to an industry climate that was still less open to Latina/o creatives. Regardless, it's a shame that we won't get to watch the next boundary-pushing series sprung from Silvio Horta's imagination.

Conclusions

These first instances of Latina/o television storytelling on the broadcast networks highlight the precarious position held by Latino showrunners in the 2000s. In addition to pitching a series, these writer-producers had to sell themselves, countering industry logic that insisted on hiring proven, and thus non-Latina/o showrunners.

As Paul Rodriguez noted in *The Pitch*, when a network was interested in his series pitch, they wanted to put its development in the hands of more experienced, non-Latina/o writers. Teaming with professionals with more status in the industry, whether writers or actors with a level of celebrity, was one strategy that could help circumvent this obstacle. Sandra Bullock and Salma Hayek each notably had their own production company and helped produce *George Lopez* and *Ugly Betty*, respectively.[54] In an important step forward, George Lopez was the first Latino performer to sign on as an executive producer and writer of his own series. The necessity of supportive talent management and legal representation to secure an advantageous deal is highlighted in this accomplishment.

Convincing network executives that a narrative about ordinary Latino and Latina characters could draw in non-Latina/o viewers was also a feat. As I was reminded in interviews, the lack of Latina/o network executives with the status to greenlight projects contributed to a lack of receptiveness to Latina/o stories.[55] Programmers also might be overly cautious in avoiding narratives that depicted Latina/os as working class, or interested only in stories of noble, striving immigrants and bland model citizens.[56] Otherwise, networks would have to be convinced that a series idea included *value added* in addition to a universally appealing narrative. For *Resurrection Blvd.*, it was boxing. For *George Lopez*, it was Lopez's successful stand-up comedy and Sandra Bullock's popularity and guest starring role. For *Ugly Betty*, it was the international success of *Betty la fea* and, similarly, Salma Hayek's celebrity and guest role in the series' first season.

For writer-producers lucky enough to get a season pickup of their series, the negotiations were just beginning. Such things as time slot, promotional strategy, and the overall production budget were in the hands of the networks, with the showrunners at a distinct disadvantage. They might have to fight to hire the writers and production team that they wanted, or the actors they wished to cast. All three series did eventually bring in Latino and Latina creatives into a variety of positions, many of whom have since moved up in their fields. On *George Lopez*, for instance, Lopez agreed to the hiring of Helford and Borden for the pilot and abbreviated first season, but added Latino and Latina writers in subsequent seasons.

Appealing to a large enough audience and their network while also staying true to their own vision was another challenge. Horta's work on *Ugly Betty* illustrates that, while an idiosyncratic Latina-centered narrative appealed to viewers and critics, it made ABC executives nervous. Narrowcasting, or programming meant to appeal to a smaller, targeted audience, had begun as an industrial strategy, but it was presumed that solely targeting Latina/o viewers would alienate others. Showrunners thus had to appeal to white viewers first, and Latina/os second; the way they threaded this needle was through "universal" story lines, acculturated Latina/o protagonists, and very sporadic inclusion of Spanish. In *Resurrection Blvd.*, this translates to a boxing championship, which epitomizes success for the Santiagos, while in *George Lopez* and *Ugly Betty*, it's about workplace success and balancing work, family, and romance. However, the success of these three series involved a more brilliant alchemy. The creators and writers of each series were also able to tell stories from a unique personal perspective and to create (somewhat) culturally nuanced Latina/o protagonists, and this is why they worked where previous series failed. They often did so through drawing on their own memories and cultural experience, which offered points of connection for both Latina/o and non-Latina/o viewers.

Resurrection Blvd., *George Lopez*, and *Ugly Betty* illustrate one of my main arguments: that Latina/os telling their own stories on television matters, above all else. As these narratives began to appear on broadcast and cable networks, they provided validation and inspiration to countless viewers, as the letters from *Resurrection Blvd.* fans to its production company and Showtime, and fans' reactions to the cast and creator of *Ugly Betty* years after the show had ended, make evident. We want and need to see our identities reflected on television, and sharing our stories and art is part of our empowerment and cultural citizenship.

While Latina/os were entering screenwriting and film schools in large numbers for the first time in these years, Latino and Latina television writers still faced resistance to furthering their careers. For one thing, the industry positioned them to work against one another. Because of a lack of network support for expanded Latina/o programming or authorship, writers had to fight for the one spot a network might offer to a writer-producer for a pilot or new potential series each year. They thus had to view one other as competition. As I was told in interviews, through the 2000s, Latina/o writers were almost never offered overall development deals, multi-year contracts with a network or studio to produce projects. Without this sort of long-term support, it was hard for the Latina/o writing community to operate in a mutually supportive manner and for individual writers to rise. This began to shift by the 2010s, as a handful of Latina writers gained the status to lead popular series, the subject of chapter 6.

6

2010s

The Latina Wave and Other Trends

As I worked on this book over the last few years, a number of new series fed my soul. The story of the fun and loving Alvarez family, led by a badass single mom, in the rebooted *One Day at a Time* (2017–20). The hilarious love letter to a band of creative misfits who create horror-themed experiences for their clients in *Los Espookys* (2019–). And the raw and fiercely sympathetic story of two estranged sisters whose mother's death brings them back to their East LA neighborhood in *Vida* (2018–20). These series of the late 2010s are part of a new turn in Latina/o cultural production in television, as intimate storytelling that unapologetically puts Latina/o/x audiences first is becoming the norm rather than the exception.

I heard echoes of my reactions to the new wave of what has been called "Latinx television" in my interviews with television professionals.[1] I often ended these interviews by asking my sources what gave them hope. The answer that I got most often was the rise of Latina writers and showrunners in the industry. And in fact, the first Latina executive producers in US television history are responsible for or helped write and produce many of the new, richly imagined series on the scene in recent years. These professionals include Cristela Alonzo, the first Latina to cowrite, co–executive produce, and star in her own series, *Cristela* (2014–15); Gloria Calderón Kellett, the cocreator of the critical hit *One Day at a Time*; and Tanya Saracho, creator of the critically acclaimed *Vida*. Additionally, actors America Ferrera, Jennifer Lopez, Eva Longoria, and Gina Rodriguez have been active constituents of the small group of Latina executive producers in the late 2010s, alongside writer-producers such as Natalie Chaidez, Cynthia Cidre, Danielle Sanchez-Witzel, Dailyn Rodriguez, and Luisa Leschin. Latinas have been front and center among the authors of the most exciting Latina/o programming of the 2010s and early 2020s.

It's been an exciting decade for Latina/o representation as well. Latina/o characters who've made it worthwhile to watch in this "peak TV" era (defined by a boom of programming and more diverse protagonists than ever before) include Penelope, Elena, and Alex Alvarez of *One Day at a Time*; Emma and Lyn Hernandez of *Vida*; Jane, Xiomara, and Alba of *Jane the Virgin* (2014–19), Ruby, Monse, Cesar, and Jasmin of *On My Block* (2018–), and *primos* Ana, Chris, and Erik, and their grandfather, Casimiro, of *Gentefied* (2020–). All are complicated and intriguing characters.

These developments are directly linked to the evolution of television audiences, and of media more broadly, in the 2010s. Just as important as earlier activism that prompted the first Chicana/o and Puerto Rican producers to begin using the first portable video cameras to document their communities, the advancement and affordability of digital video production and exhibition in the late 2000s and early 2010s has been a major catalyst of this shift in opportunities and authorship. Additionally, the fragmentation and growth of broadcast, cable, and digital television outlets has had a tremendous impact, as networks and streaming platforms have been able to target and profit from smaller and more narrowly defined audiences. Programming can survive with niche audiences, particularly if they include young adult viewers. This youthful audience of Millennials and Generation Z viewers is more diverse, politically progressive, and interested in nontraditional stories and protagonists than previous generations. The youth of the Latina/o population in recent years also is an important factor. Almost one-fourth of Millennials are Latina/o, while they are only 11 percent of Baby Boomers.[2] Unsurprisingly then, Latina/os are finally part of the imagined audience of peak TV programming, as US national identity itself is shifting. This evolution, alongside the growth of the Latina/o population, has resulted in a desire for contemporary Latina/o narratives, particularly on the part of digital television outlets such as Netflix, Hulu, and Amazon Prime. Examples from the 2010s include the teen drama *East Los High* (2013–17), which aired on Hulu, and *One Day at a Time*, *On My Block*, and *Gentefied* on Netflix.

Even with these signs of progress, Latinas and Latinos still are dramatically underrepresented in television, I should reiterate.[3] It is thus all the more important to understand how a handful of Latina creators are succeeding in recent years, at the same time that many Latinos and Latinas are not. In this chapter I aim to answer that question as I explore the entrance of three of the first Latina showrunners in the industry and the impact of Latina creative production from the mid-2010s through 2020.

What does it mean that women have finally broken in to the industry and are leading Latina/o series creation in recent years? To better understand this new era of Latina/o storytelling and other recent trends, I explore case studies that bookend and illuminate this recent era of programming: the ABC comedy *Cristela* and its star, writer, and co–executive producer, Cristela Alonzo; *One Day at a Time* and its cocreator Gloria Calderón Kellett; and the Starz drama *Vida* and its creator and co–executive producer, Tanya Saracho. In doing so, I explore these new showrunners' entrances into and rise in the industry, and the production history and narrative and political strategies of their series. I was fortunate to be able to interview all three as part of my research. In addition, I engage in textual analysis of representative scenes and episodes of each series, and explore how television critics and audiences responded to them. Notably, all three series epitomize Anzaldúa's concept of *haciendo caras*, or the vital importance of honest and personal storytelling, discussed in the introduction to this book. They draw closely from their makers' and writing teams' experiences and perspectives, including moments of pain, anger, pride, and oppositional consciousness as Latina/o/xs in the United States.

It did not always seem that this would be possible. While a handful of series in the 2000s proved the potential profitability of shows with Latina and Latino leads, the early 2010s was a fallow period for Latina/o television, even while Latina/os had grown to 16.3 percent of the population in 2010, surpassing African Americans as the largest non-white ethnic group in the US. *George Lopez* and *Ugly Betty* were canceled by ABC in 2007 and 2010, respectively, and there were few Latina/o characters on screen or creative professionals employed on series. Meanwhile, ethnic and racial ambiguity had increasing cachet in film, television, and popular culture. In 2009, Barack Obama became president, which ushered in a focus in the news media on the country's supposed "post-racial" status, in which race no longer mattered because problems of racism had been resolved. While this was quickly proven to be empty rhetoric, it reinforced a vogue that had begun in 1990s film and television for casting

ethnically ambiguous performers and for narratives featuring multicultural ensemble casts but no sustained focus on racial or ethnic identity,
such as the *Fast and Furious* film franchise and the television series *Glee*
(2009–15).[4] Latina/os typically appeared only as afterthoughts in these
ensemble casts and story worlds. Narratives that focused on characters
and families of color ("ethnic shows," in industry parlance) in fact had
fallen out of favor at the broadcast networks. A network executive whose
position was focused on diversity and inclusion confirmed this in a 2011
phone interview; advertisers at the upfronts were now making it clear
that they thought multicultural casts and only superficial attention to
the lived experiences of ethnic minorities were the only way to acknowledge diversity, period. Latina/o writers and other writers of color were
struggling as well. Kimberly Myers, then Director of Inclusion and Eq-
uity for the Writers Guild of America West, lamented to me in a 2011
interview that there were no more than five employed showrunners of
color at that time.[5]

The tide began to turn around 2013, as Shonda Rhimes's *Scandal*
(2012–18), featuring African American actress Kerry Washington as a
Washington "fixer," became a smash hit. ABC subsequently launched a
slate of programming with leads of color, including *Fresh Off the Boat*
(2015–20), *Black-ish* (2014–), *Cristela* (2014–15), and the Rhimes legal
drama *How to Get Away with Murder* (2014–20). Another catalyst that I
believe encouraged Latina/o programming and writing was the success
of independent, Latina/o-helmed web series in the early 2010s. Dozens
of series about Latina/o protagonists, produced on a shoestring, often
by first-time writers and producers, debuted on personal websites and
YouTube, especially in the last years of the 2000s and the early 2010s.
They garnered buzz and were shared, especially by young viewers looking for something new and fresh. As Vittoria Rodriguez and I found
in a 2016 study of Latina/o web series such as *East Los High* (2013–17),
East WillyB (2011–13), *Ylse* (2008–10), and *Undocumented and Awkward*
(2011–15), these narratives about contemporary Latina/o protagonists
had compelling appeal. Many starred and were produced by women.[6]
I later learned from Ruth Livier Nuñez, creator and star of *Ylse* (and a
former cast member of *Resurrection Blvd.*), and Katie Elmore Mota, one
of the executive producers of *East Los High*, that the much lower costs
of digital television production and exhibition allowed them to take on

more radical (and from a viewer's perspective, more culturally authentic, feminist, and funny) material than would ever be possible with a broadcast network. While all were ultimately impossible to sustain financially and only *East Los High* found a home on a network or streaming outlet, they showcased the creativity and talent of their Latina and Latino makers and made clear how smart, funny, and entertaining Latina/o television could be, with no holds barred.

Meanwhile, networks and streaming platforms were under pressure to better represent the diversity of Americans and increase the numbers of female creators and creators of color who contributed programming. This was fueled by research and the continuing work of media advocates. Columbia University's *Latino Media Gap* study, UCLA's *Hollywood Diversity Report*, and other studies confirmed the continuing underrepresentation of Latina/os in television.[7] The findings were amplified in news stories and at times linked to industry protests, such as #OscarsSoWhite, of the entrenchment of white hegemony in the media industries.[8] The Multi-Ethnic Media Coalition and National Hispanic Media Coalition continued to actively push on these issues, as did the writers' and directors' guilds and industry players such as Christy Haubegger. Then an executive in charge of Multicultural Business Development at Creative Artists Agency (she is currently Executive Vice President and Chief Enterprise Inclusion Officer, and Head of Marketing & Communications at WarnerMedia), Haubegger advocated through a variety of industrial initiatives for the hiring and promotion of Latina/o and other writers of color to positions of greater status and responsibility. Some television networks and streaming outlets likely felt pressure to show that they cared to do something about Latina/o invisibility by greenlighting a pilot or series with a major Latina or Latino character or giving a Latina/o writer-producer a chance to create and run a series.

Together, these shifts encouraged networks and streaming media outlets to more often seek out and value Latina/o-centric programming. The CW greenlit *Jane the Virgin* (2014–19), an adaptation of the Venezuelan telenoleva *Juana la Virgen* (2002), to critical and popular success. While helmed by a non-Latina, Jennie Snyder Urman, her writing team included several Latina/o writers, and star Gina Rodriguez became a co–executive producer and later an executive producer of the series. *Telenovela* (2015–16), spearheaded by Eva Longoria, *Queen of the South* (2016–21), *One Day at a Time*, *Vida*, and *On My Block* followed in the late 2010s. Latina and Latino writer–executive producers and series with Latina/o lead characters continued to be a rarity, but their numbers were slowly growing. In addition to the professionals already mentioned, they included Peter Murrieta (*Wizards of Waverly Place* [2007–12], *Welcome to the Family* [2013], *Cristela* [2014–15], *Superior Donuts* [2017–18], and *Mr. Iglesias* [2019–]); Danielle Sanchez-Witzel, who has worked in various writing and executive producer roles and was the executive producer for *The Carmichael Show* (2015–17); René Echevarria, with a busy career of series creation and production that has included *The 4400* (2004–07), *Terra Nova* (2011), and *Carnival Row* (2019–); and Cynthia Cidre (*Cane* [2007], *Dallas* [2012–14], and *Blood and Oil* [2015]). Well-known Latina/o actors Eva Longoria, America Ferrera, and Gina Rodriguez also joined George Lopez, Jennifer Lopez, and Salma Hayek in the ranks of executive producers through forming production companies that supported and produced new series, while their celebrity usefully helped their pitches to catch the attention of network programmers.[9] The new wave of Latina creators, like the Latino showrunners of the 2000s, served as cultural translators for white viewers, still a large portion of the audience.[10] However, in the 2010s, their storytelling could privilege and foreground Latina/o viewers. These narratives also reflect their creators' feminist, hybrid identities, bringing material to television story worlds that would have in the past been considered too risky or potentially off-putting for national and global audiences.

Breaking in with Humor: Cristela Alonzo and *Cristela*

ABC's *Cristela*, which aired in 2014 and 2015, was unique for giving an up-and-coming performer and writer a central role as star and also in the writer's room. Cristela Alonzo, a Texas-born Mexican American actress, comedian, and writer, had spent several years as a stand-up comedian and television writer. She had a chance to quickly rise up the television writing-producing ladder when given the opportunity to cocreate and star in *Cristela*. ABC's past track record with *George Lopez* and *Ugly Betty* may have convinced executives that greenlighting a series led by a performer still relatively unknown nationally would be worth the gamble.

Growing up in the Texas border town of San Juan, Alonzo began her love for television when she was encouraged by her mother, an immigrant from Mexico raising four children, to watch television and stay away from the negative influences in their neighborhood.[11] She subsequently grew up fascinated with both Spanish-language and English-language programming, especially sitcoms. When she later studied theater and trained as an actor, and quickly realized there were few interesting roles written for Latinas, this spurred her interest in writing them. Her career in stand-up included touring with Carlos Mencia and other male comedians, and extensive time on the college comedy circuit.[12] Alonzo later wrote for individual seasons of *Mind of Mencia* (2005–08) and *Ladies Room Diaries* (2011–12) while continuing her stand-up career in Los Angeles. Her accolades (she was named one of "10 LA Comedy Acts to Watch in 2014" and "One of 13 Funny Women to Watch in 2014" by *LA Weekly* and *Cosmopolitan*, respectively) illustrate that her comedy career was taking off when she was given the offer by producer Becky Clements to cowrite (with Kevin French) and star in her own series.[13]

There were several challenges to getting the script greenlit for a season pickup, however. All of the networks passed on their original pilot script. Alonzo found the process of pitching to them eye-opening as well. Executives thought the stories of her life growing up in a working-class family in South Texas were far too sad and stereotypical to become the backbone of an appealing sitcom.

They're [the family is] blue collar. We all live under one roof. I'm the aunt. I don't date. I want to explore the relationship, the role of the aunt and how she's the second mother to these kids. Because that was my life. And the comedy comes in certain sad things. . . . I had pitched an idea where there's an episode where we couldn't afford to pay the electric bill. So we had to have hurricane lamps and have a camp out. Which is what my family did when we were younger. We would have the oil hurricane lamps . . . we would just sit around. And it was hot in South Texas, so sometimes we'd sit near a window or outside just to get a breeze. And we would just laugh. We had a little radio, a plastic red radio from Radio

Shack, and we would listen to this radio station, and we would just laugh and hang out. And I wanted to have that episode and really show how even in sad times we were so happy because we had each other. But I also wanted to make a statement about how in this time it was nice to be unplugged from everybody and actually be plugged in with each other. I was pitching ideas like that. And when I finished pitching, one of the executives said, "Eehhh; it sounds really sad."[14]

She found many executives were interested only in narratives centered on middle-class Latina/os. This reaction was echoed in the experience of a former student of mine who interned in comedy pilot development at one of the major networks in the early 2010s. After extolling a script that was among the best of dozens that she had read, she was told that it wouldn't be approved because it included working-class Latina/o characters, which would be viewed by audiences as stereotypical.

ABC greenlit the *Cristela* pilot script, but chose later not to produce it. This wasn't the end of the story, however. Alonzo, French, and Clements decided to take the unusual step of using the penalty money of $500,000 (far less than the usual pilot budget of at least $1 million) from ABC to produce the pilot themselves.[15] "We just felt they weren't getting

Figure 6.1. Cristela Alonzo in a publicity photo with the cast of *Cristela* (2014–15). From left: Jacob Guenther, Carlos Ponce, Maria Canals-Barrera, Alonzo, Terri Hoyos, Gabriel Iglesias, and Isabella Day.

it, that something was missing in [the network's imagined] translation from script to stage," she told *Variety* in a 2014 interview.[16] Alonzo was very involved in the casting and production. Because of their limited budget they shot it multi-camera, on a sound stage. While this cheaper, once popular mode of production had become rare, Alonzo had great fondness for the multi-camera sitcoms she had watched as a child. She also felt a series on a broadcast network, perhaps a good home for a multi-camera sitcom, would be more likely to be watched by Latina/o viewers.

The pilot introduces the audience to Cristela Hernandez, an ambitious law student in an unnamed, large Texas city who needs to secure an internship at a law firm, and also to convince her sister and brother-in-law to let her live with them, their kids, and the sisters' mother a bit longer so that she can afford to take the internship. She's not always treated well while she interviews at a law firm led by a mildly racist older white man, but she takes it in stride, even when another applicant, a young blonde woman, mistakes her first for a janitor, and next for the parking attendant. When the woman asks her for "validation," Cristela, undaunted, cuts the woman off, brightly saying, "I think you've been validated enough!" The laugh track makes it clear that she's getting the last word. Cristela's mother and brother-in-law, similarly, give her a hard time; she's bold and funny in how she responds to these and other challenges. Alonzo and the other writers drew from her stand-up routines in jokes about how poor her family was and how her mother discouraged her children from having ambitions for fear they would end up disappointed. For instance, the pilot includes a moment when Cristela and her mother, Natalia, reminisce about Natalia taking her as a young girl to see the biggest house in the nicest neighborhood in their home town. "If you work hard and do well in school," they intone together, "you're going to clean that house!" Cristela finishes mirthfully, having heard it many times before. The true punch line for viewers aware of Alonzo's star text is that Alonzo instead ended up on stage, capably performing for admiring audiences.

When Alonzo, Clements, and French presented the pilot for the networks in 2014, the initial response was discouraging, however. Only one network executive, from ABC, showed up. (A FOX representative had sent a tepid email that implied the pilot was likely not as funny as Kevin

Hart's sitcom and so was not of interest. The implication seemed to be that they had already filled their quota of "ethnic shows.") ABC tested it and found the audience response was extremely positive; it was the strongest reaction they had gotten for a test pilot in the last five or six years, Alonzo was told. ABC decided to pick up the series.

In our August 2018 interview, Alonzo noted that while she was often credited publicity as a showrunner of the series, her title was initially under contention. ABC offered her the title of supervising producer, which does not signal creator credit nor confer creative agency. She fought it; ultimately Alonzo was credited as cocreator and an executive producer, alongside Hench, Clements, and executive producers Marty Adelstein and Shawn Levy. However, much to her consternation, Alonzo found that her veto power over the writing team's ideas was often questioned. The team of thirteen writers was mostly male and white; in addition to Alonzo, there were two Latino writers, one Latina writer, and another non-Latina female writer.[17] The other Latina was later let go by the other executive producers without consulting with Alonzo. The racial and gender makeup of the team thus put added pressure on Alonzo to have to advocate for stories she believed in. After all, the series was named *Cristela*!

> I had a lot of problems with the writers on my show because they thought I was very difficult. But they would pitch these stories, and I'm like—just not that, guys. Just not that. And I remember one day, and it wasn't all of them, one day, I finally got angry and said, "Hey, I know that for you this is just a job. But the name of my show is *Cristela*. I'm Cristela. So when this show is done, when they cancel it, when it's all forgotten and everything, you guys go and work on different shows. I, for the rest of my life, will always have to answer questions about the show. This could be the only shot I ever get. That's why I'm seen as quote-unquote difficult, because this show is about my life. And the fact that you guys don't understand that I don't get these story lines probably means that they're inauthentic."[18]

While she was pleased with much of the material they included in the episodes, particularly those centered on Mexican American cultural traditions like a Christmas *tamalada* (an episode written primarily by

Alonzo), she often was at odds with the other writers. She also had had to fight for the production to take on a Latino writing trainee from McAllen, Texas (adjacent to her home town of San Juan), who had gone through the Disney/ABC writers' fellowship program. "I said, I want this guy on my show because he understands the culture that I grew up with. He is that culture. So we gave him a job on my show. . . . It [the resistance she faced] frustrates me. Diversity writers are free. . . . Why wouldn't you want more voices available?"[19]

While Alonzo was touted extensively by ABC as the first Latina writer-showrunner-star, she had to battle with them also over series promotion. The network at first wanted to promote the series in a manner that betrayed a lack of understanding of the series and its audience. The initial poster was a closeup of her face; she was inexplicably wearing a quinceañera crown. "And every point in the quinceañera crown, in the tiara, had a letter from my name: C—R—I—S—T—E—L—A. And the logline was, 'Meet Cristela, the new reina of comedy.'" Feeling that it misrepresented her and that it could be perceived as clichéd pandering to Latina/o viewers, she argued that it should be changed, but the marketing team and network were initially unwilling to do that. Threatening to walk from the production made no difference. Finally, she tried another tack, of noting that a fellow comedian, Anjelah Johnson, had been promoted similarly, in a homecoming crown, six months earlier. They finally relented. The final poster used the same photo, with the tiara and *reina* reference removed.

Atypically, ABC also purchased no billboards for the series in Los Angeles. Instead, they promoted *Cristela* on bus benches in city suburbs. Clearly, class- and language-based presumptions about Latina/o viewers—and that *Cristela* would not appeal to non-Latina/os—played into these promotional buys. They also promoted the series through Spanish-language media outlets such as *People en Español*, despite the fact that English-dominant Latina/os and non-Latina/os would be its primary audience. Alonzo finally pushed to appear on ABC news and daytime talk shows such as *Good Morning America* and *The View* so that she could promote the show to English-speaking viewers.

From Alonzo's perspective, asking *People en Español* to promote *Cristela* amounted to asking a minute segment of the potential audience for a seal of approval. She found that it instead resulted in complaints;

Figure 6.2. Cristela Alonzo in ABC's eventual promotional poster for *Cristela*.

Latina/os were at times the show's fiercest critics. Some complained about Cristela's mother being too unsupportive or about depicting her character's family as having economic struggles. Alonzo noted this could feel like a criticism of her own childhood.

> That's the story of my life. My mom was that woman. My sister was that character. And I am that character. So why are you looking for this stereotype and dismissing it when you're missing the bigger picture? I was thinking about it in the long run. And other people, other Latinos, were saying, "Why is it so stereotypical? Why is the family poor?" I was like, I was poor. My family was poor. And that was a thing I had with the networks and studios, too.[20]

As I mentioned in relation to the pushback Paul Rodriguez experienced to his comedy and the *a.k.a. Pablo* series in the 1980s, an expectation to represent one's ethnic community only through aspirational images ("images of uplift") is a conundrum that many Latina/o comedians and other comedians of color have faced over time.[21] This dynamic is one that white performers typically don't experience; their transgressive comedy isn't viewed as standing in for white culture as a whole. Luckily for Alonzo, many other viewers responded positively to the series and its characters, especially to the eponymous Cristela.

Despite its potentially lowbrow status as a multi-camera sitcom, the issues addressed in *Cristela* include a range of serious issues, among them the marginalization of Mexican Americans and working-class families in schools, discrimination among Latina/os in relation to class status and skin color, and gendered expectations for Latina girls and women. Cristela poked gentle fun at herself and her family, alternating between charged, emancipatory humor and more light-hearted subjects such as her football fandom. Like *George Lopez*, *Cristela* regularly underscored and made fun of white privilege, as well as reclaiming insults disparaging poor and Mexican American families. At the same time, as Guillermo Avila-Saavedra argues about *George Lopez* and other Latino (male) television comedy of the 2000s, the series expresses a loyalty to the US and the American Dream, which could speak to both Latina/o and non-Latina/o viewers.[22] Cristela is always striving—to be respected by her boss and by her family, to become a lawyer, and correspondingly to be financially independent.

While she doesn't pointedly call herself a feminist, Cristela subtly challenges entrenched gender norms and inequities in almost every episode. She has no concern with getting married any time soon, ultimately telling her sister that she doesn't want her life as a wife and mother. She also constantly encourages her young niece to challenge what she's told about girls' possibilities—for example, telling her that cheerleaders are bimbos and that she can play soccer herself instead. The series played with this thematic tension at times, through emphasis on a suitor (comedian Gabriel "Fluffy" Iglesias, now the star of *Mr. Iglesias* [2019–]) who never takes no for an answer, and on Cristela's interest in pleasing others—particularly her boss. Alonzo also challenged Hollywood norms of beauty and idealized femininity through presenting herself as uninterested in outside standards for either, as when she happily dressed as a dumpy, mustachioed John Oates on Halloween (in "Hall-Oates-Ween"), all while radiating an exuberant charm.

While Alonzo was praised by television critics for her performance, and the series achieved passable ratings, ABC canceled it after one season. She was subsequently offered other series opportunities but passed on all of them, as she didn't want to be in the same position without executive producer status or creative agency. While she plans to return to television in the future, she noted to me in 2018 that she had shifted her priorities to put her energy into practical work for Latina/o communities and helping to get out the Latina/o vote. After having supported the campaigns of Beto O'Rourke and Joaquin Castro in 2018 and 2020, respectively, Alonzo performed on January 16, 2021, as a part of the America United festivities preceding President Biden and Vice President Kamala Harris's inauguration.

Cristela Alonzo's experiences with *Cristela* provide important illustrations of the industrial mindset that got in the way of Latina/o, and particularly Latina, cultural production at the broadcast networks even in the evolving industry landscape of the mid-2010s. Having been given the opportunity to leapfrog to executive producer status like George Lopez, Alonzo nevertheless faced challenges in this role. Even while ABC used *Cristela* to brand itself as nurturing diverse voices, it kept the series at a consistently lower budget than *Black-ish* and *Fresh Off the Boat* and initially promoted it only to a Spanish-speaking audience. While Alonzo's opportunity with *Cristela* was an important first, it illuminated the many ways in which the broadcast networks had not evolved enough for a Latina creator to flourish.

Ditching the "Let's Appeal to Everyone" Approach: Gloria Calderón Kellett and *One Day at a Time*

In *One Day at a Time*, there are moments that are rich with Cuban American specificity. Lydia, the grandmother, enticing her daughter Penelope to eat some home-cooked *ropa vieja*, which, despite her initial protests, she can't resist. Dynamic and loving family interactions, with words in Spanish interspersed in conversation without thought (or subtitles), alongside modern terms such as "Latinx" and "gender non-binary." Subtle references to Cuban history and music, to strong Bustelo coffee, to Latinx pride ("Latinx" being the show's preferred label), and other cultural signifiers make it clear that this is a modern, multigenerational Cuban American family. Gloria Calderón Kellet was the cocreator and co–executive producer of *One Day at a Time*, alongside Mike Royce; the series also was executive produced by Norman Lear and Brent Miller through Lear's Act III Productions. A remake of Lear's 1975–84 series, about a white divorced mother and her two teen daughters, it relates the stories of a divorced Cuban American mom who is a veteran and a nurse, her two children, and her Cuban mother, who all live under one roof.

I learned in an interview with Calderón Kellett that she began her career in television as an actress, after getting degrees in communication and theater. She also trained as a playwright, receiving multiple playwriting awards, and performed stand-up comedy. When she later tried to get work as an actress, she was frustrated that "all of the roles that [she] auditioned for were stereotypes." Not willing to always play the "gangbanger's girlfriend" or sister, she decided to break into television writing to create opportunities for other Latinas. As she noted at the *One Day at a Time* panel at the ATX Television Festival in 2018, without an agent or manager, she trained herself in television writing. One of the things that she would do is go to the Los Angeles branch of the Paley Center for Media (a public center dedicated to showcasing television, broadcasting and media history), where she would watch old TV shows to break them down and figure out how they were written. Her first job was as a staff writer on *Quintuplets* (2004–05). She later worked her way up as a writer, story editor, and finally co-producer on *How I Met Your Mother* (2005–14). From there she worked as a supervising producer for series such as *Rules of Engagement* (2007–13), *Devious Maids* (2013–16), *Mixology* (2014), and *iZombie* (2015–19). Lear then offered her a chance to be a showrunner with *One Day at a Time*. She was happy to find that Lear and her co–executive producer, Mike Royce, were very supportive. Even so, she had to labor to make Netflix executives understand that the Alvarezes needed to be depicted with cultural specificity. She wanted to push back against the usual "let's appeal to everyone [pan-Latino] approach," which had resulted in bland and uninteresting characters and narratives in the past.[23] As she stated in an interview with NBC News, "I would hope that it would resonate with somebody because I was being honest."[24]

What does creating a series with Cuban American specificity in mind look like in practice? Among other things, it involved decisions that ranged from the theme song ("This is It," the show's original theme song, performed by Cuban American singer Gloria Estefan) and props (Café Bustelo coffee, Goya products, the grandmother's pictures of the Pope), to casting and staffing the writers' room. While *One Day at a Time*'s casting was not confined to Cuban American and Cuban actors, the production attempted to keep the narrative content and aesthetic choices in line with Cuban American experience. To this end, half of the writing team is Latina/o, including Cuban American, Puerto Rican, Salvadoran, and Argentinian writers. The series' approach to storytelling arguably became a key to its popularity with its fans. The episodes take pains to deeply develop storylines about family members' emotional lives—for example, to explore the depression that Penelope experiences as a veteran who spent time in combat—as well as to offer gentle laughs and loving moments, as Penelope and Lydia work to guide strong-willed, activist-minded Elena and perpetually cool but sweet Alex through their teen years. A focus on intersectional identities is highly integrated into the show, as Elena's focus on her sexual orientation is central to the first season, alongside sensitive attention to how Lydia's experience as a first-generation Cuban immigrant has given her a radically different experience in the United States than that of her daughter and grandchildren. It all contributes to a nuanced narrative that strongly conveys a Cuban American sensibility. Culturally sincere storytelling is convincingly conveyed here.

The remake was first conceived by Lear as the story of a Mexican American family. He announced it in January 2015, not long after Gina Rodriguez's Golden Globe award for *Jane the Virgin*; he partnered initially with Televisa, then later with Sony Television as the project was in development. A few months later, in July 2015, Lear said that he was pursuing the project because Latina/os were so seldom depicted on television. "I just love the idea because I don't see enough of that representation on the air," he noted. "I don't see it any place. There isn't enough of it, and I think it's a rich idea."[25] Lear appears to have learned from his experience with *a.k.a Pablo*, in that he hired Calderón Kellett as an executive producer and supported her creative agency. To reflect Calderón Kellett's West Coast Cuban American background and childhood memories, they made the family Cuban American.

The narrative keeps one facet of the original series' story line, in that it focuses on a divorced woman and her children. (In the 1970s production, Bonnie Franklin played the mother to teenage daughters played by Mackenzie Phillips and Valerie Bertinelli.) In all other ways, it's an original story in its own right. The mother, Penelope Alvarez (played by a terrific Justina Machado), is a veteran struggling to regain a sense of normalcy and learn to date again after a divorce. She's raising Elena, a teen daughter questioning her sexuality, and Alex, an astute and sensitive pre-teen son. It also adds her Cuban mother, Lydia, played with dramatic humor by Rita Moreno, and a young, hipster Canadian landlord (Todd Grinnell) as the show's "Schneider." One of the narrative's many compelling elements is its exploration of the ways the various family members identify and live their lives based on their Cuban American and Cuban identities, in intersection with other aspects of their lives.

The series quickly won over critics and viewers with its warmth, smart writing, and good humor, qualities for which Norman Lear's programming has been known for decades and which were important to Calderón Kellett as well. Critics for *Variety*, *The New York Times*, and other outlets praised it as one of the ten best series of 2017, with the series' cultural specificity often singled out. Monica Castillo at *The New York Times*, for instance, praised the series' "joyful" storytelling about Cuban American and immigrant experience. Calderón Kellett responded:

Figure 6.3. The Alvarez family in *One Day at a Time* (2017–20), lauded both for its smart and culturally aware humor and for its portrayal of a loving family. The cast included, from the back left, Isabella Gomez, Rita Moreno, Justina Machado, and Marcel Ruiz.

Well, that's just my experience. Really, my house is not a sad place ever. We feel so blessed, we feel so grateful. We have a really good time. In the media, Latino families are always in crisis—there's gang violence, people weeping. That's just not what I know it to be. I wanted to reflect my experience, too, and to throw that in the ring. It seems a lot of people relate to that, too.[26]

One Day at a Time's narrative found warm humor in how a strong and uncompromising single mom and her modern family met challenges, focusing in season one on teenage Elena's coming out as a lesbian and Penelope making peace with her symptoms of PTSD; the later seasons turned to topical issues related to Latina/o experiences in the Trump era. For example, "The Turn," the second-season opener, sensitively addresses the impact of rising anti-Latino sentiment and the complex topic of colorism in Latina/o families and communities. In the episode, Penelope learns that her son, Alex, had been told "go back to Mexico" by other boys and has begun getting called slurs like "beaner" and "wetback." As his mother describes, Alex is a "beautiful shade of caramel," and he's treated very differently than fair-skinned Elena, who realizes to her chagrin that, despite her activist orientation, she's often perceived as white. Penelope and the family struggle with how to respond to these realities and the mixed degrees of racism that Latina/o family members sometimes face, culminating in their uncompromising and triumphant standoff in an ice cream shop with a guy who tells the family to quiet down their "fiesta." The episode prompted praise and discussion in a variety of news outlets for aptly sending up these timely issues and addressing the complexities of Latina/o identity with style and affection.

While the series gained publicity from its positive reviews, Calderón Kellett learned that many potential viewers were unaware of it and took

Figure 6.4. A scene from *One Day at a Time*'s "The Turn," in which Elena (Isabella Gomez), Lidia (Rita Moreno) and Penelope (Justina Machado) watch Alex's baseball game—with Cuban flourishes. The episode comedically tackles the topic of skin color and the amount of racism individual Latina/os experience.

it upon herself to do interviews and other press whenever possible. She began developing a sizable social media presence, promoting the show and responding occasionally to then-President Trump's anti-Latino and anti-immigrant rhetoric and policies. The show's first three seasons appeared to have had a highly enthusiastic, but perhaps small audience; it's impossible to know its size because Netflix does not share information about the numbers of viewers its series garner. In fact, Netflix ultimately kept the viewing numbers even from Calderón Kellett, Lear, and the other executive producers.[27] Each season there seemed to be a danger that the series would be canceled, spurring viewer campaigns to encourage Netflix to renew it. Even so, Netflix canceled it after its third season, claiming the audience just wasn't large enough.[28] Disappointed fans took to social media to protest. For months, the producers shopped the series to other networks, a complex proposition because Netflix's online dissemination model and contracts specified that it could not be exhibited in particular outlets, which speaks to the vulnerability of Latina/o series when a streaming outlet loses interest. Finally, it was picked up by Pop (also known as Pop TV), a streaming network of ViacomCBS. Its fourth season began airing episodes on Pop, TV Land, and Logo in March 2020, when the production and airing of new episodes was put on hold because of the COVID-19 pandemic. An animated series special, "The Politics Episode," was its last episode to air, on June 16, 2020. The series then was canceled by Pop in November 2020.

It's useful to consider the series' transition from Netflix to Pop, prior to the intrusion of the pandemic, as illustrative of Latina/o television in recent years. *One Day at a Time*'s cancellation by Netflix initially appeared indicative of the industry's lack of sustained support for Latina/o programming. However, Netflix subsequently greenlit three new Latina/o-led series, *Mr. Iglesias* (2019–), *Gentefied* (2020–), and *Selena: The Series* (2020–), showcasing the growing diversity of subject matter addressed in new Latina/o series and the entrance of a number of new Latina/o creators and writers in the industry. We can learn from this that the viability of the Latina/o audience has reached a level that encourages the greenlighting of programming, even while some cancellations may come quickly as well.

Pop's decision to pick up *One Day at a Time*, possible in the age of expanded media platforms, also illustrates a forward-thinking and creatively expansive mindset among *some* television executives, particularly working for digital outlets, when it comes to Latina/o narratives and storytelling. Notably, the fact that the Alvarezes are a Latina/o family was not mentioned directly in Pop's publicity about the series pickup. As Brad Schwartz, president of the cable network, said in a statement,

> How amazing it is to be involved with this brilliant and culturally significant series that deals with important themes one minute while making you laugh the next. If *Schitt's Creek* [2015–20] has taught us anything, it's that love and kindness always wins. Pop is now the home to two of the most critically praised and fan-adored comedies in all of television, bringing even more premium content to basic cable. We couldn't be more proud to continue telling heartwarming stories of love, inclusion, acceptance and diversity that pull on your emotions while putting a smile on your face.[29]

I interpret Schwartz at the time as presuming that audiences already know (and presumably care) that *One Day at Time* features the story of a Cuban American family. The fact that he chose instead to highlight the richness of the storytelling, its humor, and the emotions it elicits underscored its appeal to audiences of all backgrounds.[30] This is a far cry from how Latina/o series were perceived in previous decades.

Claiming Space for *Chingona* Storytelling: Tanya Saracho and *Vida*

In my estimation, the closest that we've come to television created in the spirit of *haciendo caras*, or Latina and Latinx storytelling that is soulful and honest to Latina and Latinx experience (I use Latinx here because Saracho does), has been Tanya Saracho's drama *Vida* (2018–20). This is the first time that a television series has been written and produced in a manner that so concertedly privileges a youthful, culturally hybrid and queer Latina perspective, which makes it feel both familiar and revelatory to its fans. Viewers of the series excitedly shared the news of a new season about to drop with the fervency of our older *tias* calling each other in the 1970s to quick, turn on the TV, because Henry Darrow, Rita Moreno, or Freddie Prinze was on a late-night talk show. The triumph of *Vida* showcased the possibilities for and the continued precarity of Latina/o television, given that it was recently canceled. Saracho's career path, and her work to promote Latina/o television storytelling, also illustrates how Latina/o cultural producers are working to lift each other up and change the dynamics of isolation and exclusion that Latina/o writers often encountered in the industry in the past and sometimes still encounter today.

Vida, adapted from "Pour Vida," a short story by Richard Villegas Jr., is centered on two Mexican American sisters who return to Boyle Heights in East LA after their mother has passed away. Estranged from each other and from the working-class Mexican American neighborhood where they grew up, they're forced to question their prior assumptions when they learn that their mother had been married to a woman and owned a bar unofficially catering to LGBT Latina/os. As they navigate their belonging in the rapidly gentrifying neighborhood, they come to terms with their own secrets, sexual choices, and life goals. After it launched with a six-episode first season in 2018 and as seasons two and three were released in 2019 and 2020, *Vida* received critical acclaim for its intricate and engaging storytelling, for illuminating aspects of Latinas' lives that have traditionally never been seen on television, and for its honest and warm depiction of Latinas and queer Latina/os in Los Angeles. For example, *Los Angeles Times* writers Carolina A. Miranda and Vera Castaneda, in describing their fandom of the show, cited its uniquely textured view "that is resolutely Latina."[31] And critic Roxanne Sancto noted that "Vida dives into the cultural make-up of this Californian Latin-community without leaving one stone uncovered."[32] In these and other reviews, the writing has been held up as exceptional. As Sophie Gilbert wrote for *The Atlantic*, "*Vida* isn't special only because it's putting underrepresented American stories on screen. It's special because it's doing it so well, mining the epic drama and the discrete experiences of its characters' lives to create something that's elaborate, distinct, and beautiful all at the same time."[33] *Vida* was cited as one of the best series of 2018 by *Variety*, NPR, *Vulture*, *Indiewire*, and *RogerEbert.com*, and of 2019 by *Time*, *The Atlantic*, *Vox*, and other media outlets.

The greenlighting of *Vida* by Starz underscores how networks could choose to nurture not just Latina/o series but Latina/o storytelling, as well as how the rise of a handful of Latina/o television professionals to executive status is helping to catalyze change within the industry. *Vida's* development was part of a multi-year effort by Starz to develop as many as three Latina/o series and their creators.[34] The Starz programming executive who directly oversaw these efforts was Marta Fernandez. Now president of Macro Television Studios, she was and is one of a minute number of Latina/o television executives at this level in the industry able to encourage programming development and greenlight new series in 2021.[35]

With support from Fernandez, Saracho was given an opportunity to create *Vida*, and later an overall deal to develop other programming for Starz, based in large part on her prior critical and creative successes as a writer. As Saracho has related in interviews, she was born in Sinaloa, Mexico, but grew up in both Mexico and McAllen, Texas, after her parents divorced, in an upbringing that bridged American and Mexican identities. After studying theatrical writing and performance, she moved to Chicago to pursue a career as an actress and playwright. Similar to both Alonzo and Calderón Kellett, she was inspired to write because of the lack of interesting Latina roles. With Coya Paz, she cofounded Teatro Luna in 2000 as a forum for Latina characters and stories that they weren't seeing elsewhere; they created and produced a number of popular performances such as *Machos, Dejame Contarte (Let Me Tell You), The María Chronicles*, and *S-e-x-Oh!*. Saracho subsequently branched off on her own as a playwright. Over the years, she received numerous awards for her plays, including *Our Lady of the Underpass*; a young adult adaptation of Sandra Cisneros's *The House on Mango Street*; *El Nogalar*, an adaptation of Chekhov's *The Cherry Orchard*; and *Mala Hierba (Bad Weed)*. She also had written for television series such as *Girls* (2012–17), *Looking* (2014–16), and *How to Get Away with Murder* (2014–20) by the time she met with Starz executives. In addition to her work as a playwright and screenwriter, Saracho has a long history as a *chingona* (Mexican American slang that loosely translates as a "badass," pushy woman) organizer and public advocate, nurturing Latina/o voices and advocating for more nuanced and meaningful representation. In addition to cofounding Teatro Luna, Saracho founded the Alliance of Latinx Theater Artists, which aims to foster Latina/o theater in Chicago. More recently she and Gloria Calderón Kellett have spearheaded the Untitled Latinx Project, which began as a support organization for female Latinx creatives in the media industries and now has branched into taking on an advocacy role as well.

In her work on *Vida*, Saracho's Latina-centric (and *chingona*-centric) vision has been instrumental to how the narrative is brought to remarkably vivid life. As she noted in a 2017 interview about her work as a playwright, "You know how Jill Soloway [now Joey Soloway, creator and showrunner of *Transparent* (2014–19)] is talking about the female gaze? I'm interested in the Latina gaze for the foreseeable future."[36] Saracho diverges here from the academic usage of the term, as in Jillian Baez's scholarship on Latinas' media reception practices.[37] Saracho's "Latina gaze" uses the term instead to describe her gaze and aesthetic as a storyteller, which foregrounds Latina perspectives and counters previous patterns of misrepresentation.

To illuminate Saracho's aesthetic and narrative strategies linked to this approach, I examined *Vida*'s first season episodes. The Latina gaze as enacted by Saracho begins with her unfettered creative vision and agency. It was of vital importance that Saracho was sought out by Marta Fernandez at Starz and supported fully as a series creator and executive producer. Remarkably, this had not happened for a Latina writer or producer of television programming for adults to the same degree prior to *Vida*. Saracho was given the authority and agency to hire the staff writers that she wished as well as to hire the production heads in charge of the cinematography, sound, and editing of the series. Saracho hired an all-Latina/o/x writing team, including mostly female writers and several queer writers. In the first season, this team consisted of Evangeline Ordaz, Mando Alvarado, Jennifer Castillo, Chelsey Lora, Santa Sierra, and Nancy Mejía. This allowed for a rich collaborative process typically possible only for white male writers, in this case for writing a Latina and queer-centric narrative. As Saracho noted in an interview with Pilot Viruet, "There's a cultural or gender shorthand that I haven't had [in past shows] because usually I'm the only or one of two females in the room."[38] She also hired female professionals in all of the production head positions. The look of the series, for instance, was overseen by Carmen Cabana, an Afro-Colombian cinematographer who previously had shot second unit for *Narcos* (2015–17), while Brienne Rose, the music supervisor, makes an enormous impact with songs by Latina/o and *chingona* musical artists like Maluca, Jarina De Marco, Selena, and Chicano

Batman. In addition, the series has been directed by directors of color and female directors, including many Latina directors. This has resulted in a series that looks, sounds, and feels Latina and Latinx-centric. In a public discussion I was able to have with Saracho and a few of the members of the writing team, she soundly credited Fernandez for encouraging and protecting her choices in this regard.

Beyond this foundation, a number of narrative strategies are distinct to *Vida*'s storytelling. First, the series centers complicated and well-developed Latina protagonists. Sisters Emma and Lyn Hernandez (played compellingly by Mishel Prada and Melissa Barrera) are deeply flawed, and only gradually do we come to see and understand them fully. As Saracho described at a *Vida* panel sponsored by the National Association of Latino Independent Producers (NALIP) at the 2018 Sundance Film Festival, "The roles are kind of ugly and complicated and flawed. That's something as Latinx, that we haven't gotten to do on television."[39] Their Mexican American identities are just a small part of who they are, a reflection of how Latina/os actually live their lives.

Latina heterogeneity is also highlighted in the diversity of Latina characters who become Emma and Lyn's friends, lovers, nemeses, and coworkers throughout the season. The story features women of differing personalities, ages, class status, body type, language preference, sexual orientation, and national origin group, to name a few of the ways in which they differ, and they sometimes clash dramatically in relation to their differences. We see this at first in the sister's alienation in their old neighborhood. When Emma and Lyn return after their mother's death, they're viewed at first as outsiders, and they likewise see the neighborhood as a place to leave as quickly as possible. This is seen in "Episode One," when they encounter Marisol, dressed in chola fashion, whom they knew as children in their neighborhood and school. An anti-gentrification activist, Mari is protesting a white hipster vlogger extolling the affordable virtues of a Mexican *birria* café in the neighborhood to her followers. To Mari, Emma and Lyn, with their fair skin and expensive clothes, must also be gentrifiers. Lyn realizes the woman is "little Mari," the sister of a guy she had dated for years, and tries to talk to her, only to be disdained as a *puta* and "white-tina." While the sisters come to a kind of peace with Mari in later episodes, class and other divisions that exist within Latina/o communities are put on display in this and

Figure 6.5. Emma (Mishel Prada) and Lyn (Melissa Barrera) in their initial confrontation with Mari (Chelsea Rendon) after they've returned to their East Los Angeles neighborhood in *Vida*.

other moments throughout the narrative. They feel no perfect sense of belonging within their community or even harmony within their family. The emphasis on Latina heterogeneity and community fault lines also underscores moments of recognition and misrecognition between and among Latinas and that centers their resulting feelings of belonging, community, or alienation.

Just as significantly, *Vida* keeps the focus squarely on the Latina protagonists through narrative developments rooted in their bodies and choices around their embodied experiences and emotional self-care through such things as exercise, sex, praying, and *curanderismo* (practices of folk healing and self-care). For example, Emma and Lyn's decisions about sexual and romantic relationships are foregrounded in the narrative. As reviewer Sophie Gilbert noted, "*Vida* is replete with graphic sex scenes, almost all of which serve a distinct purpose. Emma and Lyn's sexuality is key to understanding them as characters, and sex, in the show, is rarely just about gratification."[40] We also witness Lyn and Emma's decisions regarding how to dress and present themselves in their

East LA neighborhood and how to grieve and find peace as they mourn their mother's death. One illustration of this occurs in episode five, when several neighborhood women visit to pray the rosary with Eddy (Ser Anzoategui), their mother's widow, so that they might all express their grief at Vida's passing. Eddy, while not religious, chooses to accept the caring gesture and pray with them; Emma, meanwhile, is uncomfortable and opts out. She instead tries to distract herself in the privacy of her own room with a vibrating sex toy, only to the find the noise and her knowledge of the women praying downstairs takes her away from her pursuit of her own kind of solace. In its emphasis on corporeal experience and knowledge, the series privileges the inner worlds of its Latina protagonists, whether in times of intense sadness and loneliness or in moments of happiness and closeness with others. These scenes situate the emotion and drama squarely in the bodies and bodily choices of the Latina protagonists, in a manner that is revelatory in its intimacy.

Just as important, the narrative focuses squarely on its Latina protagonists' strengths and resilience, highlighting an overriding *chingona* perspective throughout. We witness the sisters struggling with their own self-destructive coping mechanisms, reconnect with their history in the neighborhood, and begin to trust each other as they decide to keep the bar going as a refuge for LGBT Latina/os in the barrio. As their toughness and growing confidence become more central to the narrative, it was fitting that one of the Starz posters for season two showcased Prada and Barrera striding confidently, with the words "Operating on Chingona Level" featured prominently.

With respect to viewership, *Vida* succeeded in encouraging a fair number of Latina/o viewers to subscribe to Starz, at least long enough to binge-watch the series. The network-reported Latina/o viewership grew steadily since the show's premiere, but apparently not enough.[41] Despite *Vida*'s devoted fanbase and the critical success that it had achieved, Starz announced in March 2020 that it would not be renewed after its third season was released in late April 2020. Marta Fernandez had left the network in June 2019 to serve as president of Macro Television Studios; while it's hard to know whether her move had an impact on *Vida*, it likely played a role to lose its strongest network ally. Tanya Saracho, in a March 18, 2020, letter to the show's fans, expressed her pride in the third season and her sadness about the

Figure 6.6. A poster for *Vida's* second season featuring Mishel Prada and Melissa Barrera puts the show's emphasis on strong *chingonas* front and center.

cancellation. "This goodbye is too bittersweet for words," she stated in the letter, published in its entirety on Deadline.com. She continued:

> I'd be lying if I said I'm not sad about not getting back into that magical writers room to keep crafting our story. But after all, I got to tell the exact story I wanted to tell, exactly how I wanted to tell it, and that is rare in this industry. I leave steeped in gratitude. Thankful to Starz for not just allowing VIDA to happen, but for being great co-parents as we raised her together. And grateful for the collaborators whose careers we were able to launch: Latinx cinematographers, writers, actors—almost entirely female—who are now out there and in demand. What a beautiful family we built. And what a beautiful show.[42]

While *Vida* will not be returning for a fourth season, its success with critics, appeal to different but overlapping groups of viewers, and mentoring of young writers arguably provides a promising model for Latina and Latinx television storytelling.

Conclusions

In creating and developing *Cristela*, *One Day at a Time*, and *Vida*, Cristela Alonzo, Gloria Calderón Kellett, and Tanya Saracho, respectively, are among the small handful of creators given the opportunity to use the medium of television to tell stories about and for Latina/os in the late 2010s. Like Chicana and other Latina feminist performers, writers, and independent filmmakers in earlier decades, these women created exciting "new dramatic structures, new protagonists, new perspectives, and new ways of articulating, negotiating, and accommodating bilingual and bicultural audiences."[43] Their narratives reflected and reflect the worldview of Latina/o viewers in the late 2010s and early 2020s, who see themselves as simultaneously American and Latina/o/x, citizens and immigrants, marginalized and part of the mainstream.

These series were distinct from the Latina/o series of earlier eras in a number of ways. They aimed for cultural specificity and to appeal first to Latina/o viewers. These are American *and* Latina/o/x stories, featuring complicated and flawed protagonists that embrace rather than downplay their radical hybridity. Notably, these series' routine feminist challenges to traditional norms of gender, family, and sexuality also set them apart from those of earlier decades. In an entertaining manner, they enlighten and educate viewers on these topics. From a scholarly perspective, they subtly impart what Anita Tijerina Revilla has described as *mujerista* (from *mujer* [woman]: women-centric) pedagogies, centered on "commitment to creating social change through Chicana/Latina resistance to subordination . . . coupled with warmth, love, and fun."[44] While Tijerina Revilla was describing the strategies of Latina high school activists, it's also an apt description of the narrative approaches and ideological takeaways of *Cristela, One Day at a Time*, and *Vida*, which use humor and take up feminist and culturally hybrid stances to talk back to misogynist, anti-Latino, homophobic, and classist discourses in their story worlds and in US communities in recent years. They model the claiming of Latina and Latinx agency and empowerment, disrupting gendered and racialized paradigms in the process.

With respect to their contributions and influence more broadly, Alonzo, Calderón Kellett, and Saracho also have worked to demystify television writing and producing and to demythologize the industry and make it more accessible for Latina/o writers coming after them. Alonzo does so in her autobiography, *Music to My Years: A Mixtape Memoir of Growing Up and Standing Up*,[45] and in guest appearances in which she talks frankly about her career and the setbacks she encountered. Calderón Kellett and Saracho in turn regularly contribute time to organizations like NALIP, which provides training and networking opportunities to Latina/o media professionals, as I'll address further in this book's conclusion. Alonzo, Calderón Kellett, and Saracho also have embraced the responsibility of serving as community leaders. They regularly take to social media to comment on Latina/o representation and issues of concern to Latina/o communities in this political era. As noted earlier, Alonzo, in addition, has devoted time and energy to supporting Democratic campaigns and causes. The social outreach of all three professionals can be understood as part of their ongoing creative careers, but even more as about aiming to lift their communities up, in television and outside the industry.

Conclusion

"Dear Hollywood": The Ongoing Struggle for Latina/o Television

I've learned a great deal during this years-long study of Latina/o television since the 1950s and the stalemates and more recent battles over Latina/o access, self-representation, and creative agency in television programming and production. As a result of the histories I uncover in the previous chapters, Latina/o agency in envisioning and producing television narratives—and the linked consequence that I describe as Latina/o cultural citizenship—is a possibility in recent years that would not have been imaginable in the medium's first decade. Even so, I'm left with frustration and optimism in equal measure as I look ahead.

I'll begin with the frustration, which initially moved me to begin this study. In 2021, there are only a small handful of continuing series that focus on Latina/o perspectives and communities, even within the currently overstuffed landscape of hundreds of series airing and streaming on broadcast and cable networks and digital media outlets. While *Gentefied*, *Los Espookys*, and *Selena: The Series* have gained critical buzz and rapt viewers, highly popular series *Vida* and *On My Block* have been canceled. ABC's *The Baker and the Beauty* (2020) and *United We Fall* (2020) were canceled before they could develop a following, while the Big Four networks still offer only occasional Latina/o characters sprinkled among their programming's ensemble casts. Perhaps most importantly, there is still only a minute number of Latina/o creative professionals with the status to create and executive produce a television series at this time. A small handful of series and creators thus are being asked to represent the dramatically diverse swathe of Latina/o Americans who compose almost one-fifth of American viewers. As a result, Latina/o inclusion in US English-language television can feel like an elusive dream that is promised, yet always out of reach.

Why are Latina/o viewers, narratives, and creators still being over-looked? One of the answers was provided by Texas state Representative Joaquin Castro in *Variety* in an August 2020 guest column poignantly titled "Latinos Love Hollywood, but Hollywood Hates Latinos." In the column, Castro points out that because of age-old patterns of Latina/o erasure on screen and in media industry employment, "It's clear that many Americans have a fundamental misunderstanding of who Lati-nos are."[1] They often still hold incorrect assumptions about their Latina and Latino neighbors in their cities and country, as do many television executives and creative personnel. It's surprising to still have to say: We don't fit into one box. A recent example that put this overdue point in bold relief was the assumptions that drove the two 2020 presidential campaigns' conflation of all Latina/os under the umbrella of the "Latino vote," reinforced by a dearth of Latina/o journalists and news sources. Both Democrats and Republicans may have been chagrined to learn later that they had overlooked the actual diversity of US Latina/os with respect to their concerns, motivations, and eventual votes. Television similarly has been stuck in a rut of characterizations and narratives re-inforcing narrow perceptions of Latina/os and in the common exclusion of Latina/os from creative professional circles, resulting in a failure to depict the diversity of our histories, experiences and viewpoints.

These frustrations as felt by Latina/o television and film writers was evinced in their recent public response to the media industries. On Oc-tober 15, 2020, 270 Latina and Latino showrunners and writers, includ-ing Lin-Manuel Miranda, Tanya Saracho, Gloria Calderón Kellett, Steven Canals, Roberto Aguirre-Sacasa, Marco Ramirez, and Linda Yvette Chávez, released an "Open Letter to Hollywood" over social media and to *Deadline*, linked to the hashtag #EndLatinXclusion.[2] The idea for the letter was credited to Untitled Latinx Project, a support organization for Latina television creatives founded by Saracho, which aims to unite the Latina/o creative community and increase Latina/o-created narratives. In the letter, which began "Dear Hollywood," these professionals called attention to the ongoing roadblocks that they and other Latina/o/x cre-atives face to getting their projects greenlit, to gaining employment and furthering their careers, and to getting opportunities to write and pro-duce personal and nuanced narratives in film and television. "As Latinx Showrunners, Creators, TV and Feature Writers, we are incensed by the continued lack of Latinx representation in our industry, especially among the Black and Indigenous members of our community," they stated in the letter's second paragraph.[3] They continued,

> Our stories are important, and our erasure onscreen contributes to the persistent prejudice that prevents real change in this country. This prejudice is not as overt as the one that keeps immigrant children in cages and separates families at the border, or as violent as the racism that is killing our Black, Brown, and Indigenous community members at the hands of police. But when we are onscreen, we're often relegated to stereotypes and villains.[4]

The writers went on to underscore the harmful impact of Latina/o erasure and misrepresentation, seen in such negative consequences as the tragic El Paso Walmart shootings in 2019 and other hate crimes. "We are tired," they charged, of the industry fallacy that there is a lack of Latina/o writers to hire, and of the resulting repetitive pattern of "being painted with the same brush." Finally, the writers highlighted what can and must be done to rectify the exclusion of Latina/os in television and film writing. Their suggestions included greenlighting Latina/o projects by Latina/o creators, working to tell more diverse Latina/o narratives, promoting Latina/o writers to positions with higher levels of responsibility and creative agency, and hiring Latina/o creatives on non-Latina/o projects as well. Their letter concluded strongly with an exhortation to the industry and fellow creatives to finally enact real change.

This entreaty by Latina/o creators and writers themselves highlights the need to hold the industry accountable for the continued dearth of Latina/o television and creatives supported to envision and produce the narratives that we want, need, and deserve to see on our screens. This is intimately linked with an industry mindset, that we Latina/os at times buy into without realizing, that Latina and Latino-focused narratives will not be interesting, universal, or appealing to US or global audiences.

While the industry is slow to change, social and political shifts are afoot that will challenge and are challenging these notions. For one thing, Latina/o Millennials are now 24 percent of the young adult audience. Partly as a result, notions of universal American stories are at times now centering Latina/os, without calling attention to Latina/o content as "special". The greenlighting and success of series such as *On My Block* on Netflix and *Los Espookys* on HBO (as opposed to HBO Latino) are useful cases in point. As Tara Yosso points out, our previous notions of cultural capital in the US can be usefully reframed with the question of *whose* culture is being valued.[5] This turns hegemonic thinking on its head, to respect and value the riches of experience and knowledge gained in Latina/o families and cultural communities. The valuing of Latina/o cultures (and in this discussion, television narratives), which I would argue we're beginning to witness, revolutionizes how we envision US television story worlds and the value that Latina/o writers and creators contribute to them. In an overlapping development, more Latina/os are entering screenwriting programs and film schools than ever before, and as I learn from my students every day, they have no plans to be marginalized or blocked from telling and sharing their stories. An earthquake is beginning to rumble underfoot.

Thus, we have reasons to feel optimistic as well. Another arena in which we're witnessing a blossoming is in the growth and complexity of Latina/o narratives that will be part of the future of television programming. In particular, we're moving beyond "identity based" narratives and those that primarily retell stories of Latina/o immigration (which in the past may have added to misperceptions of all Latina/os as recent immigrants). Latina/o/x television is also breaking out of the its rut in the sitcom genre, in narratives with roots in genres where previously we were never seen, such as in the cases of the absurdist comedy/horror/fantasy series *Los Espookys* and the dreamy, rotoscoped science fiction/young adult drama *Undone* (2019–).

The narrative complexity of Latina/o television also is increasing. The success of series such as *George Lopez, Ugly Betty, One Day at a Time*, and *Vida* can be attributed in part to the intricacy and emotional layers of these narratives, to the extent that they acknowledge pain and disappointment felt by the protagonists, in addition to moments of humor, joy, and personal connection. I liken these narratives' inclusion of moments of personal loss and cultural discord to what scholars of jazz and blues music, English folk music, and Irish music call "bent" or "blue notes," musical elements of a dissonant tone.[6] Unsurprisingly, in music these notes have often been interpreted as expressive of submerged sadness or pain, likely part of the appeal to fans of these musical genres. More and more, we are witnessing television series that acknowledge and feature the blue notes of US Latina/o histories and contemporary life. As I noted in this manuscript, Latina/o family histories are not typically those of the American Dream, even while they are truly American stories. Cultural sincerity in Latina/o TV narratives thus often might entail not just elements that make us laugh and care about the characters, but also attention to the pain we've learned to live with as members of a stigmatized group, and to anxieties regarding whether and how we fit within the mashup of disparate cultures and identities that compose the Latina/o and national imaginaries. We cannot deny that living as a Latina/o in the United States involves pain as well as pleasures; shiny, only-happy stories of model minorities feel insulting in the face of these realities. This is how and why it matters to "make face" with our own truths and blue notes, and why audiences are noticing and flocking to the shows that do.

These trends of more complex and compelling television centering Latina/o perspectives and characters have not uncoincidentally developed alongside the growth of Latina/o writers' and creatives' alliances and organizations in the industry and outside of it, with the founding of groups such as NALIP and Untitled Latinx Project. In my interviews I learned of ways in which Latina/o creatives especially in the last decade have been forming support groups, hiring and mentoring more junior professionals, sharing helpful workplace *chisme* (gossip) and job announcements, and working to together hold the industry accountable. Latina creative professionals in particular have spearheaded and modeled these important efforts.

All of these trends are evident in The Latinx TV List, launched in 2019, which selects and showcases ten unproduced pilot scripts each year felt to be exceptional and most worthy of being greenlit and produced. The project is modeled after The Black List, an annual list since 2005 of the "most liked" unproduced film scripts of the year ("Black" is a reference to being blacklisted, as in not put into play in Hollywood, rather than to the race of the screenwriters). The Latinx TV List is currently a collaboration of NALIP, the Latin Tracking Board (a support organization for Latina/o media executives and staff), the journal *Remezcla*, and Untitled Latinx Project. In 2020, the scripts on The Latinx

TV List ran the gamut of genres, showcasing their writers' impressive originality and creativity. The protagonists of the 2020 pilots include a teenager on the US–Mexico border who has to convince others that a new life form has grown in a sewage spill, a Nuyorican pulled into the world of international espionage in a highly unusual fashion, the impersonator of a CGI Instagram celebrity who has to cope with the actual celebrity encouraging fans to commit suicide, a couple in Cuba during Fidel Castro's revolution, a post-apocalyptic cockroach, a closeted bisexual barber who has to learn to be a father to his estranged six-year-old daughter, and a young Mexican actress in 1929 Hollywood hoping to leave an abusive past behind as she stars in a Spanish-language version of *Dracula* (based on Lupita Tovar's life story).[7] I would eagerly watch any and all of these series, which dramatically break away from long-term patterns of presenting Latina/os in all of the old and tired ways.

These promising narratives and countless other, equally idiosyncratic and exciting stories are what we can look forward to watching and experiencing in the years ahead, if Latina/o children are encouraged to pursue careers as writers, creative professionals and media executives and if the television industry works to allow greater access, training, and opportunities for Latina/os to enter, thrive, and become leaders in the industry. I'm reminded of the Mexican saying "*Cada cabeza es un mundo*": "Each mind is a world of its own." Each Latina, Latino, and Latinx writer and creative professional given opportunities to share their stories and truths will reveal new worlds to us and new dreams to dream. We should not accept less.

ACKNOWLEDGMENTS

As my research for *Latino TV: A History* has spanned more years than I ever expected, my list of people to thank for helping me imagine, conduct research for, improve, and complete it has grown. The support of a great many people has been instrumental in helping me to make this journey.

My work home in the Department of Radio-Television-Film at the University of Texas at Austin has been a dream job with respect to offering me the chance to teach courses specific to my research interests in Latina/os and media, to co-found and lead the Moody College of Communication's Latino Media Arts & Studies Program from 2017 to 2020, and to work with so many talented and committed undergraduate and graduate students who help me remember on a continuous basis why a book on Latina/o television representation and television creators is important. I'm grateful for my kind, whip-smart colleagues in RTF, Mexican American & Latina/o Studies, and Latino Media Arts & Studies, many of whom offered helpful feedback on early versions of the manuscript and who encouraged me to not give up when the project's end seemed out of reach. A special shout out to Mirasol Enríquez, who has been an incredible friend and collaborator. Alisa Perren, Caroline Frick, Wenhong Chen, Karma Chavez, Kathy Fuller-Seeley, Charles Ramírez Berg, Suzanne Scott, and Rachel González-Martin also have been stalwart friends, colleagues, and supporters who helped me complete this project. The Moody College of Communication and Center for Mexican American Studies also provided invaluable support in the form of research leaves that allowed me to devote concerted time to this project and to take needed research trips to Los Angeles and Washington, DC.

My research was also strengthened by my colleagues in Latina/o media studies and in television and film studies at other universities, who shared useful feedback and provocative questions with me when their academic departments invited me to present my pieces of my research and when we met while presenting on and attending the same panels at academic conferences. These included talks I presented for the Film and Media Studies Department at University of Kansas, the Transborder Studies Colloquium Series at Arizona State University, the Cinema Studies Program at University of Tennessee, and the Latinx Digital Media Virtual Seminar Series at Northwestern University. Early versions of several of this book's chapters were also shared at Society for Cinema and Media Studies, Race and Media, and Latina/o Studies Association conferences, as well as with the Latinx Media Studies Research Group at UT Austin. Thank you all, for your encouragement, astute insights that strengthened my work, and for setting the bar high and inspiring me with your own awesome research. Rather than risk leaving out a name, I've chosen to offer all of you (you know who you are!) a collective and heartfelt thanks.

I also want to thank the creative professionals who generously shared their time and personal stories with me about their experiences in the television and film industries in interviews that were instrumental to my research. These individuals include (alphabetically) Cristela Alonzo, Gloria Calderón Kellett, Enrique Castillo, Natalie Chaidez, Henry Darrow, Luis C. Garza, Mike Gomez, Dan Guerrero, Christy Haubegger, Bel Hernandez, Brenda Herrera, Ruth Lansford, Dennis Leoni, Luisa Leschin, Ruth Livier Nuñez, Katie Elmore Mota, Peter Murrieta, Rick Najera, Dyana Ortelli, Susan Racho, Luis Reyes, Dailyn Rodriguez, Paul Rodriguez, José Luis Ruiz, Tanya Saracho, Pepe Serna, Jesús Treviño, Ligiah Villalobos, JoAnne Yarrow, and Richard Yniguez. I was lucky that several of these professionals also helped me connect with others in the "Latinowood" community, and helped me settle in in Los Angeles in my time there. As I note in my introduction, this book serves as a testament to these individuals' determination, talent, and resilience in the face of an often unwelcoming and soul-crushing work climate.

I have many people also to thank for their assistance with my library research and with the publication of this book. This includes several archivists and library staff who made my time in their libraries and archives worthwhile. I was assisted in my research over the years by Martin Gostanian at the Paley Center for Media, Mark Quigley and the other staff at the UCLA Film & Television Archive, Kevin Kern at the Walt Disney Archives, the staff of Special Collections at the UCLA

Library, the staff of the UCLA Chicano Studies Research Center, the Television Collections staff at the Library of Congress, and the staff of the Wisconsin Center for Film and Television Research.

The editors and other staff at NYU Press also deserve special thanks. I would like to thank my editor, Eric Zinner, for his belief in this project over these many years, and series editors Jonathan Gray, Aswin Punathambekar, and Adrienne Shaw and NYU Press staff Furqan Sayeed, Martin Coleman, James Harbeck, and Dolma Ombadykow for helping to shepherd the book from start to finish. I am grateful as well to the anonymous reviewers who offered invaluable advice that strengthened my research and conception of this project in their reviews of early and later drafts of the manuscript.

Finally, I want to thank my family and close friends who buoyed me during the most difficult parts of this process, and who endured my many absences when I was busy with some aspect of the project. I want to first thank Tom Hackett, my partner during the research and much of the writing of the book, for his steady support over these many years, his meticulous editing suggestions, and for always encouraging me to take this project seriously, in countless conversations that we had about the work in progress.

My father, Rodney Caudle, who married my mother, born Verónica Beltrán, in 1948—both taking this leap before they could speak each other's language—passed away during my years of research devoted to this project. This was just a few short years after my amazing and inspirational mother's passing. She of all people in my life modeled what it means to live life with *ganas*, the drive and determination to not let others define you, and to work tirelessly to meet one's goals; I have no doubt that this book would never have been written without her influence. My father also was a maverick in his own way; he taught me about diligence and approaching the world with wide-open eyes, which has served me well in this project. I have fond memories of sharing quiet times and getting to know him better during my early research for this book. He had been an avid reader who shifted to television as his vision deteriorated; we watched countless hours of TV series together, including some of those that I discuss in this book. He loved asking "How's the book coming? Is it done yet?" to tease me and also show me his support. I wish he were still here so I could tell him, "It's done!" I also want to give a shout

out to my brother, Don, and my nieces, Ani and Sophie, who always help me have fun and stay connected to the vast world outside of academic research and teaching. Sophie's intense love for *Jane the Virgin* gave me more confidence about this project when my spirits were flagging. I'm sorry that I didn't get to interview Gina Rodriguez this time around, but maybe next time, Soph! My sister Anita, brother David, and sister-in-law Linda, and my awesome *primas* and other relatives in El Paso also have lifted my spirits and supported me through this time. Finally, I want to thank my good friends Becky Lentz and Karin Wilkins, who have in particular helped me in countless ways during this last year, who help me laugh when I need it most, and who are always there for me.

APPENDIX

Interviews with Media Professionals

Alonzo, Cristela. Personal interview. San Antonio, TX. August 16, 2018.

Calderón Kellett, Gloria. Phone interview. April 24, 2018.

Castillo, Enrique. Personal interview. Baldwin Hills, CA. September 17, 2017.

Chaidez, Natalie. Phone interview. June 13, 2018.

Darrow, Henry. Phone interview. April 26, 2018.

Garza, Luis C. Personal interview. Los Angeles, CA. April 9, 2018.

Guerrero, Dan. Zoom interview. February 4, 2021.

Haubegger, Christy. Phone interview. April 24, 2018.

Hernandez, Bel. Personal interview. Baldwin Hills, CA. April 8, 2018.

Herrera, Brenda. Personal interview. Los Angeles, CA. September 16, 2017.

Lansford, Ruth. Personal interview. Playa del Rey, CA. June 21, 2017.

Leoni, Dennis. Personal interview. Chatsworth, CA. February 9, 2018.

Leschin, Luisa. Personal interview. Toluca Lake, CA. February 10, 2018.

Mota, Katie Elmore. Skype interview. August 24, 2015.

Murrieta, Peter. Phone interview. August 6, 2018.

Najera, Rick. Personal interview. North Hollywood, CA. April 13, 2018.

Nuñez, Ruth Livier. Skype interview. June 21, 2017.

Ortelli, Dyana. Personal interview. Burbank, CA. April 11, 2018.

Racho, Susan. Phone interview. February 22, 2018.

Reyes, Luis. Personal interview. Pasadena, CA. February 8, 2018.

Rodriguez, Dailyn. Personal interview. Los Angeles, CA. April 10, 2018.

Rodriguez, Paul, and Mike Gomez. Personal interview. Los Angeles, CA. September 16, 2017.

Ruiz, José Luis. Personal interview. Los Angeles, CA. April 11, 2018.

Ruiz, José Luis, and Jesús Treviño. Personal interview. Los Angeles, CA. February 8, 2018.

Saracho, Tanya, Lindsey Villarreal, and JoAnne Yarrow. Facilitated public conversation as part of Moody Movie Club event, Moody College of Communication, University of Texas at Austin. Virtual event on Zoom. July 23, 2020.

Serna, Pepe. Phone interview. December 19, 2017.

Treviño, Jesús. Personal interview. Austin, TX. November 3, 2016.

Villalobos, Ligiah. Phone interview. March 2, 2018.

Yniguez, Richard. Personal interview. Studio City, CA. April 10, 2018.

NOTES

1 Throughout the book I use "Latina/o" to refer to men and women of Latin American descent in the United States. In addition, I use "Latina" or "Latino" when making gender-specific references, and "Latinx" in chapter 6 in reference to contemporary media professionals and audiences that prefer this gender-fluid term, popular since the mid-2010s. I also use "Chicana/o," "Chicano," and "Chicana" similarly when referring to Mexican Americans who identify by this particular label, and "Puerto Rican," "Nuyorican," and terms specific to other Latina/o national origin groups when relevant. In these choices I aimed to be mindful of the terminology used in the historical era illuminated in specific chapters. I also chose to use "Latino" in the book title because it's the most recognized term among Latina/o Americans who are not academics, to encourage readership beyond an academic audience.

2 Charles Ramírez Berg traced the origins of these patterns of representation in early and classical Hollywood film, in *Latino Images in Film: Stereotypes, Subversion, and Resistance* (Austin: University of Texas Press, 2002), 66–86. Sadly, these sorts of images are not hard to spot even in late 2010s and 2020 television series and films.

3 Writers Guild of America West, *WGAW Inclusion Report 2020* (Los Angeles: WGAW, 2020); Nicholas Jones et al., "Improved Race and Ethnicity Measures Reveal US Population is Much More Multiracial," *US Census Bureau*, August 12, 2021, census.gov.

4 See Renato Rosaldo, "Cultural Citizenship, Inequality, and Multiculturalism," in *Latino Cultural Citizenship*, ed. William V. Flores and Rina Benmayor (Boston: Beacon Press, 1997); Jillian M. Báez, *In Search of Belonging: Latinas, Media, and Citizenship* (Urbana: University of Illinois Press, 2018).

5 Hector Amaya, *Citizenship Excess: Latina/os, Media, and the Nation* (New York: NYU Press, 2013).

6 Gloria Anzaldúa, *Making Face/Making Soul: Haciendo Caras: Creative and Critical Perspectives by Women of Color* (San Francisco: Aunt Lute Books, 1990), xv.

7 Anzaldúa, *Making Face/Making Soul*, xv.

8 For more on sincerity as a useful construct for exploring the writing and performance of narratives of people of color and other marginalized groups in the United States, see John L. Jackson, *Real Black: Adventures in Racial Sincerity* (Chicago: University of Chicago Press, 2005), and A. J. Christian, "Camp 2.0: A Queer

Performance of the Personal," *Communication, Culture and Critique* 3 (2010): 352–376.

9 Kristal Brent Zook, *Color by Fox: The Fox Network and the Revolution in Black Television* (New York: Oxford University Press, 1999).

10 This seminal scholarship includes Chon Noriega, *Shot in America: Television, the State, and the Rise of Chicano Cinema* (Minneapolis: University of Minnesota Press, 2000); Angharad Valdivia, *Latina/os and the Media* (Cambridge: Polity, 2010); Berg, *Latino Images in Film*; Isabel Molina-Guzmán, *Dangerous Curves: Latina Bodies in the Media* (New York: NYU Press, 2010); Dolores Inés Casillas, *Sounds of Belonging: U.S. Spanish-language Radio and Public Policy* (New York: NYU Press, 2014); and María Elena Cepeda, *Musical ImagiNation: U.S.-Colombian Identity and the Latin Music Boom* (New York: NYU Press, 2010), among others.

11 Research documenting the underrepresentation of Latina/os in television story worlds and employment includes studies by S. Robert Lichter and Daniel Amundson, *Don't Blink: Hispanics in Television Entertainment* (Washington, DC: Center for Media and Public Affairs, 1996); Allison Hoffman and Chon Noriega, *Looking for Latino Regulars on Prime-Time Television: The Fall 2004 Season*, SCRC Research Report 4 (Los Angeles: UCLA Chicano Studies Research Center, 2004); Dana E. Mastro and Elizabeth Behm-Morawitz, "Latino Representation on Primetime Television," *Journalism and Mass Communication Quarterly* 82, no. 1 (Spring 2005): 110–130; Dana Mastro and Alexander Sink, "Portrayals of Latinos in the Media and the Effects of Exposure on Latino and Non-Latino Audiences," in *Race and Gender in Electronic Media: Content, Context, Culture*, ed. Rebecca Ann Lind (New York: Routledge, 2017), 144–160; Frances Negrón-Muntaner et al., *The Latino Media Gap: A Report on the State of Latinos in U.S. Media* (New York: Center for the Study of Ethnicity and Race, Columbia University, 2014); and Darnell Hunt et al., *Hollywood Diversity Report 2020* (Los Angeles: UCLA College of Social Sciences, 2020).

12 Horace Newcomb and Paul M. Hirsch, "Television as a Cultural Forum: Implications for Research," *Quarterly Review of Film Studies* 8, no. 3 (1983): 45–55.

13 Charo was born Maria del Rosario Mercedes Pilar Martínez Molina Baeza in 1951 in Murcia, Spain. A renowned flamenco guitarist, she moved to the United States with her first husband, bandleader Xavier Cugat. Charo recorded guitar albums for five decades and also became an actress and popular talk show guest.

14 Freddie Prinze was known to be of Puerto Rican and Hungarian descent, while Robert Hegyes was of Hungarian and Italian heritage. Erica Gimpel is Slavic and African American.

15 William H. Frey, "The US Will Become 'Minority White' in 2045, Census Projects," *Brookings* (Washington, DC: Brookings Institute, 2018), brookings.edu.

16 Hunt et al., *Hollywood Diversity Report 2019*.

17 Casillas, *Sounds of Belonging*; Arlene Dávila, *Latinos, Inc.: The Marketing and Making of a People*, updated ed. (Berkeley: University of California Press, 2012).

18 Adam Jacobson, "Spanish or English? Try Both for Reaching Hispanic Viewers," *Radio + Television Business Report* , January 28, 2020, rbr.com.

19 Mark Hugo Lopez, Jens Manuel Krogstad, and Antonio Flores, "Key Facts about Young Latinos, One of the Nation's Fastest-Growing Populations," Pew Research Center (Washington, DC: Pew Research Center, 2018), pewresearch.org.

20 In 2018, Mexican Americans were 61.9 percent of Latina/os, a drop from 65.7 percent in 2008. "Table B03001. Hispanic or Latino Origin by Specific Origin. 2018 American Community Survey 1-Year Estimates" (Washington, DC: US Census Bureau, July 1, 2018), data.census.gov.

21 Martha Menchaca's research on how Southwestern communities with large Mexican American populations evolved into systems of social apartness provides useful insights into how Mexican Americans historically were excluded from the nascent film industry. Menchaca, *The Mexican Outsiders: A Community History of Marginalization and Discrimination in California* (Austin: University of Texas Press, 1995).

22 Both the film and television industries have been shown in studies and historical accounts to have been closed to diverse employment in this period. For further information, see Maryann Erigha, *The Hollywood Jim Crow: The Racial Politics of the Movie Industry* (New York: NYU Press, 2019), and Michele Hilmes, *Radio Voices: American Broadcasting, 1922–1952* (Minneapolis: University of Minnesota Press, 1997).

23 In 1974, the first year for which these statistics were kept, only 36.5 percent of Hispanics had completed high school and 5.5 percent had completed a four-year college degree. "Table A-2. Percent of People 25 Years and Over Who Have Completed High School of College, by Race, Hispanic Origin and Sex: Selected Years 1940 to 2019," CPS Historical Time Series Tables (Washington, DC: US Census Bureau, 2019). As William Vélez documents, segregated "Mexican" schools predominated in the Southwest. Such schools were found to offer an inferior education that encouraged school dropout and prepared students only for manual and domestic labor positions. Vélez, "The Educational Experiences of Latinos in the United States," in *Latinas/os in the United States: Changing the Face of América*, ed. Havidán Rodríguez, Rogelio Saénz, and Cecilia Menjívar (New York: Springer, 2008), 129–148.

24 Some examples include Anthony Quinn's role as Luis "Mountain" Rivera in the teleplay adaptation of *Requiem for a Dream* (1956) on *Playhouse 90* (1956–61), and Katy Jurado as Sister Monica in the adaptation of *Four Women in Black* (1957), which aired on the same series.

1. 1950S

1 Stuart Hall, "New Ethnicities," in *Black Film, British Cinema* Document 7 (London: British Film Institute/Institute for Contemporary Arts, 1988). Reprinted in *Stuart Hall: Critical Dialogues in Cultural Studies*, ed. David Morley and Kuan-Hsing Chen (London: Routledge, 1996), 441–449.

2 The most popular television genres in the early 1950s included the variety show, the family-focused situation comedy, and the anthology drama, as noted by Michele Hilmes in *Only Connect: A Cultural History of Broadcasting in the United States* (Boston: Wadsworth, 2013).

3 Gary A. Yoggy, "Prime-Time Bonanza! The Western on Television," in *Wanted Dead or Alive: The American West in Popular Culture*, ed. Richard Aquila (Urbana: University of Illinois Press, 1996), 160–161.

4 Yoggy, "Prime-Time Bonanza!" 161.

5 As Monica Muñoz Martinez points out, a number of popular media narratives such as *The Lone Ranger* (1949–57 on television) valorized the Texas Rangers, who in fact were instrumental in the persecution of and violence against Mexican Americans and other Americans of color in the 1910s. Martinez, *The Injustice Never Leaves You: Anti-Mexican Violence in Texas* (Cambridge, MA: Harvard University Press, 2018).

6 It is now presumed that Latina/os were undercounted in 1950 because there was no racial or ethnic category for Mexican Americans or other Latinos, only "Spanish mother tongue" and "Spanish surnamed." See Frank Hobbs and Nicole Stoops, *Demographic Trends in the 20th Century* (Washington, DC: US Census Bureau, February 2002).

7 Launched by Raoul A. Cortez, the first Spanish-language television station in the United States, KCOR-TV (now KWEX-TV), began to broadcast in San Antonio, Texas in 1955.

8 For more on how the Latina/o audience and consumer market were constructed and viewed in these years, see Dávila, *Latinos, Inc.*, and Clint C. Wilson II, Félix Gutiérrez, and Lena M. Chao, *Racism, Sexism, and the Media: Multicultural Issues into the New Communications Age*, 4th ed. (Thousand Oaks, CA: Sage, 2012).

9 Television Westerns reached their peak of popularity in 1959, when eight of the top ten-rated shows were Westerns. See J. Fred MacDonald, *Who Shot the Sheriff? The Rise and Fall of the Television Western* (New York: Praeger, 1986).

10 See for instance Rodolfo Acuña, *Occupied America: A History of Chicanos*, 8th ed. (New York: Pearson, 2014); Vicki L. Ruiz, *From Out of the Shadows: Mexican Women in Twentieth-Century America* (New York: Oxford University Press, 2008); Eric Avila, *Popular Culture in the Age of White Flight: Fear and Fantasy in Suburban Los Angeles* (Berkeley: University of California Press, 2006).

11 Scholars who document this social history include Neil Foley, Elizabeth R. Escobedo, and Manuel G. Gonzales. See Foley, *Mexicans in the Making of America* (Cambridge, MA: Harvard University Press, 2014); Escobedo, *From Coveralls to Zoot Suits: The Lives of Mexican American Women on the World War II Home Front* (Chapel Hill: University of North Carolina Press, 2013); and Gonzales, *Mexicanos: A History of Mexicans in the United States* (Bloomington: Indiana University Press, 2009).

12 He also has a half-Mexican girlfriend. In a macabre twist, when he finds she's been cheating on him, he tricks the other man into murdering her.

13 Notably, one of the film's two directors, Raoul Walsh, was of partial Spanish descent and had directed Mexican revolutionary leader Pancho Villa and Mexican actress Dolores del Río in past films; these experiences may have influenced the portrayal. Baxter won an Academy Award for his performance and recreated the role four times in sequels.

14 This character, named Gordito (Spanish for "Fatty") and later Pancho, was played over the years by Chris-Pin Martin, Martin Garralaga, and Leo Carrillo, who were Mexican and Yaqui American, Dominican, and Spanish American, respectively.

15 Frederic Ziv, interview with Karen Herman, Archive of American Television (October 23, 1998), www.emmytvlegends.org.

16 It aired on Mutual Network radio stations from 1942 to 1945, on Don Lee Network stations from 1946 to 1947, and in general syndication from 1947 to 1956. Morleen Getz Rouse, *A History of the F. W. Ziv Radio and Television Syndication Companies: 1930–1960*, PhD diss. (University of Michigan, 1976).

17 Daniel Herbert Levoff, *The Radio and Television Production and Promotion of The Cisco Kid*, PhD diss. (Ohio State University, 1970), 28.

18 Frederic Ziv cited in Rouse, *A History of the F. W. Ziv Radio and Television Syndication Companies*, 120.

19 Ziv cited in Levoff, *The Radio and Television Production and Promotion of The Cisco Kid*, 11.

20 Berg, *Latino Images in Film*.

21 These writers included Elizabeth Beecher, Betty Burbridge, and Louise Rousseau. "*The Cisco Kid* (1950–1956) Full Cast and Crew," Internet Movie Database, www.imdb.com.

22 David William Foster, "Of Gay Caballeros and Other Noble Heroes," in *Good Bandits, Warrior Women, and Revolutionaries in Hispanic Culture*, ed. Gary Francisco Keller (Tempe, AZ: Bilingüe Press, 2010), 23–44.

23 The history of the Mexican *charro*, typically an elite of Spanish (and never indigenous) heritage and privilege, further linked Cisco to the Latin Lover. For more on *charrería*, closely tied to Spanish colonialism in Mexico, see Kathleen Mullen Sands, *Charrería Mexicana: An Equestrian Folk Tradition* (Tucson: University of Arizona Press, 1993).

24 Shilpa Davé, *Indian Accents: Brown Voice and Racial Performance in American Television and Film* (Champaign: University of Illinois Press, 2013), 2–3. Davé builds on the seminal research of Michele Hilmes, particularly her work in *Radio Voices*, on the construction of ethnic and racial notions through accent and dialogue in radio narratives.

25 Leo Carrillo as Pancho in particular contributes to this effect. Outside his roles as an actor, Carrillo (correctly pronounced "Car-il-yo," the Spanish, rather than Mexican pronunciation) was an individual of status and note in California; his wealthy family had a long history as Spanish settlers and political leaders. Carrillo also was fair-skinned and spoke perfect English when not in character. Pancho was a performance with little grounding in his life.

26 Jose Gonzalez-Gonzalez, who grew up performing in his family's Las Perlitas act in Southwest Texas, began his television and film career with his role on *The Cisco Kid*. His brother, Pedro Gonzalez-Gonzalez, also was a nationally recognized comic actor after appearing on Groucho Marx's *You Bet Your Life* (1947–61) in 1953.

27 Levoff, *The Radio and Television Production and Promotion of* The Cisco Kid.

28 Nash Candelaria, "The Day the Cisco Kid Shot John Wayne," in *The Day the Cisco Kid Shot John Wayne* (Tempe, AZ: Bilingual Press/Editorial Bilingüe, 1988).

29 Kay Sanford cited in Rouse, *A History of the F. W. Ziv Radio and Television Syndication Companies*, 131.

30 The original Zorro narrative was adapted from "The Curse of Capistrano" by Johnston McCully, which appeared in installments in *All-Story Weekly* in 1919. "A Brief Zorro History," *The Vintage Library*, www.vintagelibrary.com. Other popular narratives said to have influenced the series are Alexandre Dumas's 1844 novel *The Three Musketeers* and Baroness Orczy's play and novel *The Scarlet Pimpernel* (1803 and 1805, respectively), both adventure dramas with plenty of swordplay.

31 Gerry Dooley, *The Zorro Television Companion: A Critical Appreciation* (Jefferson, NC: McFarland & Co., 2005).

32 Dooley, *The Zorro Television Companion*, 47.

33 The character's full name was Demetrio Lopez Garcia, which should have made the character's abbreviated name Sgt. Lopez, rather than Sgt. Garcia, however.

34 According to Carey McWilliams's research and writing, Californians idealized the period when Spain controlled the territory, imagining this period as the "fantasy heritage" and true foundation of modern Californian identity. McWilliams, *North from Mexico: The Spanish-Speaking People of the United States*, 3rd ed.; 2nd ed. updated by Matt S. Meier, 3rd ed. updated by Alma M. García (Santa Barbara, CA: Praeger, 1948/2016).

35 McWilliams, *North from Mexico*, 17.

36 McWilliams, *North from Mexico*, 16.

37 While this story was factual, Baca became known later in his life as a teller of tall tales, making it difficult to establish the truth of some of the legend that came to surround him. Biographies of Elfego Baca include Kyle Crichton, *Law and Order, Ltd.: The Rousing Life of Elfego Baca of New Mexico* (Santa Fe, NM: Sunstone Press, 2008); Howard Bryan and Rudolfo A. Anaya, *Incredible Elfego Baca: Good Man, Bad Man of the Old West* (Santa Fe, NM: Clear Light Press, 1993); Larry D. Ball, *Elfego Baca in Life and Legend* (El Paso: Texas Western Press, 1992); Robert J. Alvarado, *Elfego Baca, Destined to Survive* (Santa Fe, NM: Sunstone Press, 2013); and the autobiography *Here Comes Elfego!* (Albuquerque, NM: Vinegar Tom Press, 1970).

38 *The Many Lives of Robert Loggia*, film short, Walt Disney *Legendary Heroes* DVD Bonus Material (Burbank, CA: Buena Vista Home Entertainment, 2005).

39 *Nine Lives of Elfego Baca* files, Walt Disney Archives, Burbank, California.

40 Stan Jones, "The Nine Lives of Elfego Baca," by Richard Dehr and Frank Miller, Disneyland Records, 1958.

41 The real-life Elfego Baca later shared that the shack that he hid in had a floor several inches below ground level, which allowed him to be safe from the bullets that riddled it.

42 In the *Albuquerque Evening Democrat*'s account of the trial in Bernalillo County, New Mexico, cited by biographer Howard Bryan, the jurors are listed; all have Spanish surnames. Howard Bryan, *The Incredible Elfego Baca: Good Man, Bad Man of the Old West* (Santa Fe, NM: Clear Light Publishers, 1989), 46.

43 This episode aired two weeks later, October 17, 1958.

44 Ferenc Morton Szaz, "A New Mexican 'Davy Crockett': Walt Disney's Version of the Life and Legend of Elfego Baca," *Journal of the Southwest*, 48, no. 3 (Autumn 2006): 261–274.

45 Joe Reddy, "Walt Disney Presents, 1958–59," press release, Walt Disney Productions (September 3, 1958).

46 Albert Colegrove in the *Washington DC News* and *San Francisco News*, for instance, stated "he was born and raised in Kanas, and was of Spanish descent. When he grew up he went to New Mexico in the 1870s and became a sort of Robin Hood, going around righting wrongs" (*Washington DC News*, March 30, 1958). In contrast, the *Houston Chronicle* was one of the few newspapers that described Baca as "a man of Latin American descent" (September 25, 1958), noting that the story took place in the southwest near the Mexican border. The only newspaper mention that I found that described Elfego Baca as Mexican American was in the San Mateo, California, *Times & News Leader*, September 19, 1958. The California newspapers the Venice *Vanguard* and Glendale *News Press* called Robert Loggia a "Young Latin" in their headlines. Clippings file for *Nine Lives of Elfego Baca*, Walt Disney Archives, Burbank, California.

47 J. G. O'Boyle, "'Be Sure You're Right, Then Go Ahead': The Early Disney Westerns," *Journal of Popular Film and Television* 24, no. 2, Special Issue: Walt Disney (1996): 69–81, 78.

48 O'Boyle, "'Be Sure You're Right, Then Go Ahead,'" 78.

49 There are no preserved materials on performers' appearances as Elfego Baca at Disneyland in the Disney Archives, however.

50 Roberto, Carmelita, and Arturo Gonzalez of The Gonzalez Trio performed at Disneyland from the mid-1950s through 1966 or 1967, according to online discussions by former visitors to the theme park. See "The Gonzalez Trio," www.davelandweb.com.

51 Disneyland Main-Gate Map (Walt Disney Productions, 1958).

52 See for instance Kathy Merlock Jackson and Mark I. West, eds., *Disneyland and Culture: Essays on the Parks and their Influence* (Jefferson, NC: McFarland, 2010); Janet Wasko, *Understanding Disney: The Manufacturing of Fantasy* (Cambridge: Polity, 2001); and J. P. Telotte, *Disney TV* (Detroit: Wayne State University Press, 2004).

53 Alan Bryman, *The Disneyization of Society* (London: Sage, 2004), 131.

54 *Rural Migration News* staff, "The Bracero Program," *Rural Migration News* 3, no. 2 (April 2003).

55 Jason Mittell, "The Great Saturday Morning Exile: Scheduling Cartoons on Television's Periphery in the 1960s," in *Prime Time Animation: Television Animation and American Culture*, ed. Carol Stabile and Mark Harrison (New York: Routledge, 2003): 33–54, 43.

2. 1960S–70S

1 See Chon Noriega, *Shot in America*; Lillian Jiménez, "Moving from the Margin to the Center: Puerto Rican Cinema in New York," in *The Ethnic Eye: Latino Media Arts*, ed. Chon Noriega and Ana M. López (Minneapolis: University of Minnesota Press, 1996), 22–37; Rosa Linda Fregoso, "Chicana Film Practices: Confronting the 'Many-Headed Demon of Oppression,'" in *Chicanos and Film: Representation and Resistance*, ed. Chon A. Noriega (Minneapolis: University of Minnesota Press, 1992), 168–182; and Jesús Salvador Treviño, *Eyewitness: A Filmmaker's Memoir of the Chicano Movement* (Houston: Arte Publico Press, 2001).

2 See Noriega, *Shot in America*.

3 Lyndon B. Johnson, "Remarks Upon Signing the Public Broadcasting Act of 1967," in *Public Papers of the Presidents, Lyndon B. Johnson 1967: Book II* (LBJ Presidential Library, November 6, 1967), www.lbjlibrary.org.

4 Ralph Engelman, *Public Radio and Television in America: A Political History* (Thousand Oaks, CA: Sage, 1996).

5 See *The Ford Foundation 1968 Annual Report* (New York: Ford Foundation, 1968); *The Ford Foundation 1969 Annual Report* (New York: Ford Foundation, 1969); *The Ford Foundation 1970 Annual Report* (New York: Ford Foundation, 1970), www.fordfoundation.org.

6 In the mid- to late 1960s a spate of impassioned and sometimes destructive protests were carried out by African Americans in Detroit, Michigan, and Newark, New Jersey, and other cities, often sparked by police violence toward members of their community. They were referred to in the mainstream news media as "race riots." President Lyndon B. Johnson ultimately appointed the Kerner Commission to investigate the causes of and potential solutions for these protests. For an overview of this history, see Alice George, "The 1968 Kerner Commission Got It Right, but Nobody Listened," *Smithsonian Magazine*, March 1, 2018, smithsonianmag.com.

7 The Civil Rights Act of 1964 helped to set the stage for the establishment of the Equal Employment Opportunity Commission (EEOC) in 1965. While the EEOC held hearings with the film studios and conducted research in 1969, ultimately pronouncing that the studios and networks were systemically discriminating against people of color in their hiring practices, the commission lacked in the ability to force them to make changes. This was made clear when the Justice Department refused to file a suit against the industry. Instead, the studios and networks made promises to voluntarily improve diversity among their employees,

then didn't follow through. See David E. James, *The Most Typical Avant-Garde: History and Geography of Minor Cinemas in Los Angeles* (Berkeley: University of California, 2004), 502, note 6.

8 It also supported research and experiments on the thorny issue of enabling stations to air the same program at the same time around the country in those days before digital and satellite technologies. See *The Ford Foundation 1967 Annual Report* (New York: Ford Foundation, 1967) and *The Ford Foundation 1968 Annual Report*.

9 For instance, in 1971, NMAADC and Justicia partnered with the League of United Latin American Citizens (LULAC) and the National Latino Media Council to challenge the FCC licenses of a number of California television stations to argue for more responsiveness to local Latina/o communities, for the removal of Frito-Lay's "Frito Bandito" commercials, which focused around an incorrigible Mexican thief of Fritos corn chips, and for an end to actor Bill Dana's Jose Jiménez character, which they felt depicted Mexican Americans as foolish and unintelligent. Noriega, *Shot in America*; Francisco J. Lewels Jr., *The Uses of the Media by the Chicano Movement: A Study in Minority Access* (New York: Praeger, 1974). As noted later in this chapter, activists in New York City also staged a sit-in at WNET to push for the station to serve the Latina/o community. In contrast, CARISSMA and Nosotros advocated for industry employment and other opportunities. James, *The Most Typical Avant-Garde*, 312.

10 Gilbert Pompa cited in Lewels, *The Uses of the Media by the Chicano Movement*, 67.

11 Lewels, *The Uses of the Media by the Chicano Movement*.

12 Similar schisms are evident in the manifestos of Chicano filmmaker collectives from the same period. See for example Cine-Aztlán's "Ya Basta Con Yankee Imperialist Documentaries!" and Francisco X. Camplis's "Towards the Development of a Raza Cinema," both in *Chicanos and Film*, ed. Chon Noriega.

13 Lewels, *The Uses of the Media by the Chicano Movement*, 75; Noriega, *Shot in America*, 82.

14 A new Center for EthnoCommunications was established in 1996 as part of UCLA's Asian American Studies Center. See Antonio Campos, "A New Generation of Storyteller Emerges, *University of California News* (May 18, 2021), universityofcalifornia.edu.

15 For more on the original Ethno-Communications Program and its impact, see Noriega, *Shot in America*.

16 Tragically, the videotaped episodes of this series, like most public television programming of these years, were taped over in the making of other productions at KCET. Only the first episode of *Canción de la Raza* has been archived at the UCLA Film and Television Archive.

17 E. B. Eiselein's "Television and the Mexican American" was not published in *Public Telecommunications Review* until 1974, for instance. "Television and the Mexican American," *PTR: Public Telecommunications Review* 2, no. 1 (February 1974): 13–18.

18 Richard S. Scott, MD, and Charles R. Allen, "Cancion de la Raza: An ETV Soap Opera," *Television Quarterly* 8, no. 4 (Fall 1969), 24–38.

19 Scott and Allen, "Cancion de la Raza," 37.

20 The cast of *Canción de la Raza* included Tina Menard as Bernarda, the mother; Mike De Anda as Miguel, the father; Richard Yniguez, Robert De Anda, Priscilla-Ann Garcia, as siblings Roberto, David, and Maria Elena; and Efrain Ramirez as David's friend Chuy.

21 Richard Yniguez's busy acting career continued with guest roles in early 1970s series and included starring roles in the TV movie *The Deadly Tower* (1975), the films *Boulevard Nights* (1979) and *What's Cooking?* (2000), and the TV series *Ohara* (1987) and *Babylon 5* (1998).

22 Richard Yniguez, interview with the author, Studio City, CA, April 10, 2018.

23 Scott and Allen. "Cancion de la Raza," 27.

24 Scott and Allen. "Cancion de la Raza," 27–28.

25 Cited in Carolyn See, "PTV Knocks on a Ghetto Door," *TV Guide* (January 18–24, 1969), 27.

26 For more about the high school walkouts, see Mario T. García and Sal Castro's *Blowout! Sal Castro and the Chicano Struggle for Educational Justice* (Durham: University of North Carolina Press, 2014), and Margarita Berta-Ávila, Anita Tijerina Revilla, and Julie López Figueroa, eds., *Marching Students: Chicana and Chicano Activism in Education, 1968 to the Present* (Reno: University of Nevada Press, 2011).

27 Scott and Allen, "Cancion de la Raza," 35.

28 Scott and Allen, "Cancion de la Raza, 34–36.

29 *Ford Foundation 1969 Annual Report.*

30 Jesús Treviño and José Luis Ruiz both described the resources they had to work with as they produced their public affairs shows as merely "two chairs and a camera" in interviews with the author in 2017 and 2018.

31 Ralph Engelman, *Public Radio and Television in America: A Political History* (Thousand Oaks, CA: Sage, 1996).

32 Dozens of black-themed and black-led series were produced and aired by local PBS stations, local network affiliate stations, and national networks in these years, vastly outnumbering series for Latina/o audiences. Many are still on the air. Some of the best known are *Black Journal/Tony Brown's Journal* (1968–2008), which began on PBS, moved to a broadcast network and later back to PBS; *Soul!* WNET New York, 1970–73; *Like It Was*, WABC New York, 1968–; *Say Brother/ Basic Black*, WGBH Boston, 1968–; *Black Horizons*, WQED Pittsburgh, 1968–; and *Black Omnibus*, nationally syndicated, 1972–73. See Devorah Heitner, "List of Black-Produced shows Nationwide, from 1968 on," *Thirteen: Media with Impact* (February 27, 2009), www.thirteen.org.

33 See for example Noriega, *Shot in America*; Joshua Glick, *Los Angeles Documentary and the Production of Public History, 1958–1977* (Berkeley: University of California Press, 2018); James, *The Most Typical Avant-Garde.*

34 "The Best of '¡Ahora!'" *KCET*, 2019, video, 22:20, www.kcet.org.

35 Jesús Treviño, interview with the author, Austin, TX, November 3, 2016.

36 Treviño, interview with the author.

37 "The Image: Part 1," *¡Ahora!* prod. Jesús Treviño (Los Angeles: KCET-TV), DVD. Aired on KCET Los Angeles in 1970.

38 *Che!* had cast Egyptian actor Omar Sharif as Argentine guerrilla leader Ernesto "Che" Guevara.

39 Very little scholarship had been conducted on Latina/o representation in Hollywood film at this point in time, as Chicana/o and Latina/o studies and film studies were not yet established disciplines at universities.

40 These meetings in San Antonio included representatives from five different community centers, San Antonio's Model Cities program, and VISTA, as well as staff from KCET.

41 Frank Duane, "A People and a Program," in *Broadcasting and Social Action: A Handbook for Station Executives* (Washington, DC: National Association of Educational Broadcasters, 1969), 33.

42 Duane, "A People and a Program," 35.

43 Duane, "A People and a Program," 34.

44 "'Periodico' Planned to Meet Needs of Mexican Americans," *San Antonio Express and News*, November 17, 1968.

45 Gradillas cited in Wes Marshall, E. G. Eisenlein, John Thomas Duncan, and Raúl Gamez Bogarín, *Fiesta: Minority Television Programming* (Tuscon: University of Arizona Press, 1974), 54.

46 Marshall et al., *Fiesta*, 93.

47 Marshall et al., *Fiesta*, 94.

48 Yasmin Ramirez, *Taller Boricua and the Puerto Rican Art Movement in New York*, tallerboricuatimeline.wordpress.com.

49 Taller Boricua, "Realidades Revisited Panel Discussion pt. 1 / July 6, 2019," *Taller Boricua/Puerto Rican Workshop Inc.*, July 22, 2019, YouTube video, 1:38:48, www.youtube.com.

50 Humberto Cintrón, "The '70s: Bold and Fearless," *THIRTEEN*, January 31, 2013, streaming video, 1:28:03, www.pbs.org.

51 Noriega, *Shot in America*, 150.

52 Cintrón cited in Christopher Bell, *East Harlem Remembered: Oral Histories of Community and Diversity* (Jefferson, NC: McFarland Press, 2012), 193.

53 Beatrice Berg, "Television," *New York Times*, December 17, 1972.

54 Taller Boricua, "Realidades Revisited Panel Discussion pt. 1."

55 Bell, *East Harlem Remembered*, 194.

56 George Maksian, "Realidades for & by Puerto Ricans," [New York] *Sunday News*, December 17, 1972.

57 Beatrice Berg, "Anglos Can Watch, Too," *New York Times*, December 17, 1972.

58 Taller Boricua, "Realidades Revisited Panel Discussion pt. 1."

59 David Diaz worked at WNBC-TV from 1978 to 1993, as a senior correspondent at CBS 2 TV News from 1993 to 2005, and is now a Distinguished Lecturer at City University of New York. J. J. Gonzalez was employed at WCBS in 1972; it has not been possible to discern how his career progressed.

60 José Luis Ruiz and Jesús Treviño, interview with the author, February 8, 2018.

61 For instance, a 1973 episode of *Reflecciones* on media stereotyping included interviews with actors Ricardo Montalbán and Alma Beltrán, discussion of the work of Chicano media advocacy groups and of why stereotypes are harmful, footage of a workshop sponsored by Latina/o actors' advocacy group Nosotros, and an interview with a Hollywood casting director.

62 Treviño, interview with the author.

63 Ruiz and Treviño, interview with the author.

64 Notably, a number of male producers made feature films in the next stage of their careers, while the female producers who got their start on the same series moved mostly into documentary and short film production. Rosa Linda Fregoso points to male dominance of the Hollywood film industry and unequal access to funding as having likely influenced these differing trajectories. Fregoso, "Chicana Film Practices."

65 Treviño cited in Noriega, *Shot in America*, 50.

66 Noriega, *Shot in America*, 152.

67 Ruiz and Treviño, interview with the author.

68 Other national organizations that supported the arts, including the National Endowment for the Arts and the National Endowment for the Humanities, began to fund Chicana/o and Latina/o media projects, as Ford and the CPB were less likely to do so. Treviño and Ruiz, who submitted and supported a great many proposals for films and television projects in these years, noted that the staff at NEA and NEH were often "people from Kennedy's era that came to Washington with all the dreams and hopes of the country changing [in a progressive fashion]," as Ruiz noted. These individuals were supportive of Latina/o media projects and often helped in a variety of ways behind the scenes to get them made. Ruiz and Treviño, interview with the author.

69 Noriega, *Shot in America*, 144, drawing on Astor.

70 The Chicana/o movement lost steam because of variety of reasons, including internal fissures, transitions to other goals such as founding Chicana/o studies programs at universities and efforts to focus on political elections in some parts of the country, and FBI intimidation of and interference with some activist groups. For further information, see Mario T. García, ed., *The Chicano Movement: Perspectives from the Twenty-First Century* (New York: Routledge, 2014).

71 Reagan's appointed FCC chair, Mark Fowler, dismantled many of the FCC regulations that were intended to ensure that television and radio stations served the public interest of citizens and communities. These policy changes included extending station licenses from three years to five, abolishing limits on the amount of advertising included with programming, and eliminating the "fairness

doctrine," which had encouraged stations to include contrasting points of view in their news reporting.

72 Ruiz and Treviño, interview with the author.

73 Ruiz and Treviño, interview with the author.

74 Jesús Salvador Treviño, "Latinos and Public Broadcasting: The 2% Factor," *Jump Cut* 65 (April 1983).

75 Pedro Pietri, *Puerto Rican Obituary* (New York: Monthly Review Press, 1973).

76 Task Force on Minorities in Public Broadcasting, *A Formula for Change: A Report of the Task Force on Minorities in Public Broadcasting* (Washington, DC: Task Force on Minorities in Public Broadcasting, 1978).

77 Treviño, "Latinos and Public Broadcasting."

78 The CPB offered a grant of $1.7 million for the production of *Oye Willie*, which was pitched as a 10-part series. It began with a direct grant to what was described as the "Latino TV Broadcasting Service" in a brief news piece by Les Brown, *New York Times*, October 27, 1979.

79 Yolanda Broyles-González, "What Price Mainstreaming? Luis Valdez' Corridos on Stage and Film," *Cultural Studies* 4, no. 3 (1990): 281.

80 Marshall et al., *Fiesta*, 94.

3. 1970S

1 See Norman Mailer, "The White Negro," *City Lights* (Fall 1957), reprinted in *Dissent* (June 20, 2007), www.dissentmagazine.org; Jack Kerouac, *On the Road*, 5th ed. (New York: Penguin Books, 1999); Alyssa Cokinis, "Beaten White," *Beatdom* (October 28, 2015), on Jack Kerouac and the Beats' romanticization of black culture; Joel Dinerstein, *The Origins of Cool in Postwar America* (Chicago: University of Chicago Press, 2017); Rebecca Walker, *Black Cool: One Thousand Streams of Blackness* (Berkeley, CA: Soft Skull Press, 2012).

2 For more on how television news programs neglected to cover news linked to the Chicana/o Movement, see Randy Ontiveros, "No Golden Age: Television News and the Chicano Civil Rights Movement," *American Quarterly* 62, no. 4 (2010): 897–923.

3 I learned in interviews with Latina/o actors that most had to endure the challenge of never getting to see a script in advance of an audition for a small role, instead getting the "sides" right before they had to perform for casting personnel. They also might be told to ad-lib dialogue on the spot into Spanish, among other indignities. The Screen Actors Guild unfortunately did not provide concrete support in the 1970s and early '80s to its Latina/o members who asked for the condemnation of the discriminatory practices they encountered, which also included auditions that directed actors to read for roles based strictly on signs that read "English" and "Spanish."

4 See Kathryn C. Montgomery, *Target: Prime Time: Advocacy Groups and the Struggle over Entertainment Television* (New York: Oxford University Press, 1989), and Noriega, *Shot in America*.

5 "Chicanos' Question: What about Us?" *Broadcasting*, June 28, 1971.

6 I learned from Latina/o creative professionals working at that time that the networks also began to work to contain and disarm potential public advocacy groups. Their tactics included hosting dialogues with group leaders, providing financial support for specific projects such as award shows, working exclusively with one group they deemed the least challenging (often Nosotros), and hiring group representatives as "technical consultants," as was the case with ABC's arrangement with Justicia's Paul Macias and Ray Andrade. Montgomery, *Target: Prime Time*, 51–74.

7 Enrique Castillo, for instance, recounted a time in 1971 when some Paramount executives attempted to offer him a major role in *The New Centurians* (1972) after his theatrical group performed at the Inner City Cultural Center in Los Angeles. He wasn't present, and his fellow theatrical group members rejected it on his behalf, underscoring that they and Castillo had no desire to work within Hollywood. At the time they considered members of the actors' advocacy group Nosotros to be sellouts in contrast to their own stance. Interview with the author, Baldwin Hills, CA, September 17, 2017.

8 Lansford's widow, Ruth Lansford, shared that her husband also often submitted series episode scripts that included Mexican American or other Latino characters; almost always, these characters would be changed to a "white" ethnicity or simply omitted in the producers' process of bringing the episode to the small screen. In some cases, he was told this was because "Latinos can't act"; thus it would be too difficult to cast the role as written. Interview with Ruth Lansford, Playa del Rey, CA, June 21, 2017.

9 Interview with Ruth Lansford.

10 *Fantasy Island* (1977–84) is excluded from this list; despite the casting of Mexican actor Ricardo Montalbán in the title role of Mr. Roarke, Latina/o cultural identity is never foregrounded in the series.

11 Darrow was already a television star, having played the popular character of Mano "Manolito" Montoya in the Western adventure series *The High Chaparral* (1967–71) in the late 1960s. Born Enrique Delgado Jiménez in New York City and raised in Puerto Rico, the Nuyorican actor had just changed his stage name from Delgado to Darrow, in hopes of finding more acting opportunities, when he was sought for *The High Chaparral*.

12 See Aniko Bodroghkozy, *Groove Tube: Sixties Television and the Youth Rebellion* (Durham, NC: Duke University Press, 2001) for more background on how the young adult audience influenced television programming in this period.

13 For more discussion of programming in this period that aimed to address social issues and appeal to progressive-minded young adults, see Todd Gitlin, *Inside Prime Time*, 2nd ed. (New York: Pantheon Books, 1994); and David Marc, *Comic Visions: Television Comedy and American Culture* (Boston: UnwinHyman, 1989).

14 Sierra appears to have been the busiest Latina/o actor of the genre, as he also played Det. Sgt. Chano Amenguale, a driven and emotional Puerto Rican detec-

tive, in the first two seasons of *Barney Miller* (1975–82), a Jewish radical in a dramatic episode of *All in the Family* that addressed anti-Semitic violence, and Dr. Tony Menzies, the main character of a short-lived series about a hospital emergency team, *AES Hudson Street* (1978). Most Latina and Latino actors were not as lucky in television in this decade.

15 Gitlin, *Inside Prime Time*.

16 Notably, the diverse city (perhaps Albuquerque, New Mexico, where the series was shot) is presented as generally peaceful and contemporary. Mayor Thomas Jefferson Alcala as portrayed by Quinn is dignified and compassionate to a fault. His Anglo deputy mayor, played by Mike Farrell prior to his starring role on *M*A*S*H*, sometimes needed to keep him from getting overly focused on individual citizens' problems to the extent that he neglected running the city as a whole, however. Mayor Alcala had occasional, white love interests, but these romances never seemed to progress. In all, the narrative was fairly dull.

17 At this point Anthony Quinn had already twice won Oscars for Best Supporting Actor and twice been nominated for Best Actor.

18 Tim Brooks and Earle F. Marsh, *The Complete Directory to Prime Time Network and Cable TV Shows, 1946–Present*, 9th ed. (New York: Ballantine, 2007).

19 Producer John Rich had a long career in television and had worked on *All in the Family*, while Clement and La Frenais had experience in British television comedies.

20 Fuentes's prison buddies are Jewish, African American, and white Southern. As the wittiest, Fuentes is their leader. "I'm only here due to tragic circumstances," he deadpans. "I got caught" ("Old Fish, New Fish"). He makes the most of life in prison, such as through seeking a job as a prison chef. The humor was often based on cultural jokes. For instance, Fuentes's accent was fodder for laughs: "I want to be a chif," he says. "A chef?" he's asked. "Yeah, a chif," followed by laugh track ("Old Fish, New Fish"). Perez's casting was likely encouraged by Freddie Prinze's stardom after *Chico and the Man*'s 1974 debut; Perez's bright and sarcastic style, exaggerated accent, and mustache are reminiscent of Prinze.

21 In "I'll Never Forget What's Her Name," Puerto Rican film star Rita Moreno was brought in as Hector's visiting Aunt Rosa Dolores. Rosa Dolores, who believes she's destined for fame despite lacking talent as a performer, later admits she's there to borrow money from Hector. The episode focused so heavily on Rosa Dolores that it's apparent the writers were looking for a way to overhaul the series. Moreno, who played the (very popular) grandmother in the rebooted *One Day at a Time* (Netflix and Pop, 2017–20), also starred in multiple comedy pilots in this period that never progressed. She plays a character similar to Aunt Rosa Dolores in a 1978 CBS pilot with the working title of *The Rita Moreno Show*. In it, she's a hotel employee and former showgirl who unexpectedly inherits the hotel and has to learn to manage it. A second *Rita Moreno Show* pilot cast her as a daffy receptionist and aspiring performer always seeking her big break. It was one of the few pilots I was able to access to view. It's quite funny, and Moreno is fully in

command of her absurd character. A decade later, in the unaired CBS pilot *Rita* (1987), Moreno as the protagonist is a toy designer forced to take stock of her dissatisfaction with her life.

22 Brooks and Marsh, *The Complete Directory to Prime Time Network and Cable TV Shows*. After its cancellation, it was replaced in the summer of 1976 with ABC's *Viva Valdez*, addressed later in this chapter.

23 While episodes are no longer available to view, a CBS promo spot emphasizes comedy and connections to social relevance as the main selling points. As a white male announcer notes in voiceover accompanying a photo of the cast, "Popi, who holds three jobs to support two kids and still makes you laugh, premieres Tuesday right after *Good Times*" (CBS *Popi* bumper).

24 Preproduction choices for *Popi* likely contributed to the show's failure. Elizondo laments that he had urged the production team to hire non-professional child actors; in retrospect he felt the children hired were uninterested in their work, which led to stress on the set and hurt the series. Although Elizondo had also urged the hiring of Latino writers, he was told the industry "didn't have them." A few Latina/o writing assistants and trainees were hired instead. They were not adequately prepared to impress in these positions, according to Elizondo, and thus were not able to use them as springboards to other jobs.

25 Brooks and Marsh, *The Complete Directory to Prime Time Network and Cable TV Shows*. Ironically, ABC slotted it into *The Man and the City*'s former time slot on the prime-time schedule. It aired twelve episodes before it was canceled in September 1976.

26 Wohl cited in Paul Henniger, "Chicano Family Gets Series Try," [Salem, Oregon] *Statesman Journal*, May 30, 1976.

27 *Viva Valdez* pilot script. Available in the Frank Shaw Papers, located in the UCLA Libraries' Special Collections.

28 Howard Albrecht, *See You in Nairobi: How Work Become Fun—The Second Time Around: Adventures in the Laugh Trade* (Bloomington, IN: AuthorHouse, 2005), 249.

29 Tom Stempel, *Storytellers to the Nation: A History of American Television Writing* (New York: Continuum, 1992).

30 Mishkin cited in Stempel, *Storytellers to the Nation*, 151–152.

31 Carmen Zapata cited in Wesley Hyatt, *Short-Lived Television Series, 1948–1978: Thirty Years of More than 1,000 Flops* (Jefferson, NC: McFarland & Co., 2003), 250.

32 Wohl cited in Henniger, "Chicano Family Gets Series Try."

33 Mishkin cited in Stempel, *Storytellers to the Nation*, 152.

34 Mary Beltrán, *Latina/o Stars in U.S. Eyes: The Making and Meanings of Film and TV Stardom* (Urbana: University of Illinois Press, 2009).

35 Beltrán, *Latina/o Stars in U.S. Eyes*. The original script is archived in the James Komack files, Wisconsin Center for the History of Film and Television, University of Wisconsin-Madison.

36 Beltrán, *Latina/o Stars in U.S. Eyes*.

37 "'Chico and the Man' New TV Offering Next Season," UPI newswire article, *The* [Fort Wayne, IN] *Journal—Gazette*, June 30, 1974.

38 "'Chico and the Man' New TV Offering Next Season."

39 See for example Cecil Smith, "Chico, Man Smash Hit," syndicated column that ran in *The Scrantonian*, November 10, 1974.

40 In a video made by the National Association of Latino Independent Producers (NALIP) in 2009 in connection with an award they gave him for Pioneer Achievement for Advocacy, Andrade discusses his childhood experience of having to sleep at the boxing gym where he trained as having provided some of the inspiration for the premise of *Chico and the Man*. I attempted to interview Ray Andrade as a part of this research. He unfortunately didn't respond to my request.

41 Justicia press release, January 30, 1974. The contact information on the last page lists Ray Andrade as contact.

42 Beltrán, *Latina/o Stars in U.S. Eyes*.

43 Beltrán, *Latina/o Stars in U.S. Eyes*, citing Lee Winfrey, "TV News Gets Break in Equal Time Denial," *Philadelphia Enquirer*, September 30, 1974.

44 Smith, "Chico, Man' Smash Hit."

45 Freddie Prinze, *Looking Good!* Audio CD of Prinze's comedy act (Columbia, 1975; Collectables, 2000).

46 Harry Waters, "Hot Hungarican," *Newsweek*, November 11, 1974; "The Prinze of Prime Time," *Time*, September 30, 1974; Tom Burke, "The Undiluted South Bronx Truth About Freddie Prinze," *Rolling Stone*, January 1975; Bill Davidson, "Get Out of Here and Take Your Flies with You," *TV Guide*, November 23, 1974; Rosemary Edelman, "'Pobrito,' It Ain't Easy Being a Star," *TV Guide*, February 15, 1975; Edwin Miller, "Call Me a Hungarican!" *Seventeen*, October 1974; "Chico's Wild Ways!" *Sixteen*, March 1975; "Freddie Prinze Out the Window," *Playboy*, May 1974.

47 Vahac Mardirosian, "Chicano Educators Object: Under Fire: Chico and the Man," *Los Angeles Times*, October 4, 1974.

48 Cited in Frank Torrez, "Man in the Middle," *Los Angeles Herald-Examiner*, October 8, 1974.

49 "KNBC-TV License Challenged by Chicanos," *Brooklyn Belvedere Comet*, November 21, 1974.

50 Alicia Sandoval and Paul Macias, "'Chico and the Man': Some Chicanos Are Not Amused," *Los Angeles Times*, October 24, 1974.

51 These changes were revealed in the "Veterans" episode, which aired November 8, 1974.

52 This was in fact the norm on all of the "socially relevant" series of this era, but was increasingly criticized by ethnic media advocacy groups and others.

53 Memorandum from Warren Murray to Robert Howard, December 5, 1974, NBC. *Chico and the Man* production files, Box 23, "Chicano Writers" folder, David L. Wolper Collection, USC Cinema and Television Library, University of Southern California, Los Angeles.

54 Memorandum from Warren Murray to Robert Howard, December 5, 1974.

55 Beltrán, *Latina/o Stars in U.S. Eyes*, 104.

56 Ron Friedman, interviews with John Dalton and Adrienne Faillace, Television Academy Foundation, November 7, 2016, and August 18, 2017, Writers Guild Foundation Collection, interviews.televisionacademy.com.

57 Noriega, *Shot in America*, 71.

4. 1980S–90S

1 The late Lalo Guerrero (1916–2005), a Tucson-born guitarist, singer, and song-writer, became known as the Father of Chicano Music in a career that spanned generations. His music included *corridos* about the struggles and triumphs of Mexican American heroes, ballads that brought audiences to tears, and comic songs that elicited laughter. Among his many awards, Guerrero received the National Medal of Arts from President Bill Clinton in 1997; he was the first Chicano ever to receive the nation's highest arts award. The documentary *Lalo Guerrero: The Original Chicano* (2006), produced by his son Dan Guerrero and Nancy De Los Santos, surveys and celebrates the life and career of this inimitable performer and Chicano leader.

2 Paul Rodriguez Jr. is a skateboarding star with lucrative endorsements and celebrity in his own right.

3 Antonio Flores, "2015, Hispanic Population in the United States Statistical Portrait" (Pew Research Center, September 18, 2017), www.pewresearch.org.

4 Chon A. Noriega, *Ready for Prime Time: Minorities on Network Entertainment Television*, Latino Policy and Issues Brief, no. 2 (Los Angeles: UCLA Chicano Studies Research Center, 2002).

5 Alonso was a former Miss Teenager World in 1971 and Miss World/Venezuela in 1975 before embarking on a singing and acting career. Her Hollywood film credits include *Moscow on the Hudson* (1984), *Extreme Prejudice* (1987), and *The Running Man* (1987).

6 Mexican American actress Jackie Guerra was discovered doing stand-up comedy. She is best known for portraying Selena Quintanilla's sister Suzette in *Selena* (1997), and she appeared in the PBS series *American Family* (2002–04). Greg Giraldo, of Colombian and Spanish descent, was educated at Harvard Law School. He passed the bar, but he quickly left his life as a lawyer for a career as a stand-up comedian on stage and in television. He died of an apparent accidental drug overdose in 2010.

7 Judine Mayerle, "A Dream Deferred: The Failed Fantasy of Norman Lear's *a.k.a. Pablo*," *Central States Speech Journal* 38, no. 3/4 (Fall-Winter 1987), 223.

8 The Latino films that premiered on PBS's *American Playhouse* (1982–96) included Jesús Salvador Treviño's *Seguin* (1982), Victor Villaseñor and Robert M. Young's *The Ballad of Gregorio Cortez* (1983), and Gregory Nava's *El Norte* (1983). Lindsey Law, who was vice president and executive producer of *American Playhouse*, played a decisive role in bringing these works to a national audience.

9 Fregoso, "Chicana Film Practices."

10 Ávalos was known at that time for being part of the acting ensemble on the PBS children's series *The Electric Company* (1971–77). The series, which premiered on February 10, 1983, was created by Sheldon Bull, who had worked on *M*A*S*H* (1972–83) and *Newhart* (1982–90).

11 The series was created by Michael J. Leeson (who had an Emmy for writing on *The Cosby Show*) and written by Leeson, Chris Cluess, and Stu Kreisman. It faltered at times from issues of tone, especially when it attempted to address how Dora's family was treated by death squads in El Salvador while still maintaining a traditional sitcom humor. It aired a season of thirteen episodes but was not renewed.

12 *Fort Figueroa* wasn't picked up as a series, and aired as a summer *CBS Playhouse* special. It was written by Carla Jean Wagner under the name C. J. Charles. The director, surprisingly, was Chicano playwright and filmmaker Luis Valdez. Valdez doesn't appear to have had creative input into the production, however.

13 Notably, only the white cast members were featured in most of the promotional photos found for *Fort Figueroa*.

14 Alonso was already a film star when *One of the Boys* was created and executive produced by Martin Cohan, Blake Hunter, and network impresario Fred Silverman; Silverman's company had signed Alonso to a development deal. Bob Leszczak, *Single Season Sitcoms of the 1980s: A Complete Guide* (Jefferson, NC: McFarland Publishing, 2016). A promotional photo for the series presents Alonso with her hair sexily tousled, in a black dress arranged so that she is almost falling out of it. It graced the cover of the *Philadelphia Inquirer*'s TV section when *One of the Boys* debuted, as it likely did in other newspapers. It illustrates a common approach of marketing Latinas primarily as objects of romantic and sexual desire in this period. It did little to sell the series, which was canceled after its six episodes aired.

15 *Sanchez of Bel Air* was created and executive produced by Dave Hackel and April Kelly for USA Network. It focuses on the Sanchez family and its recent life change. Ricardo Sanchez, a clothing manufacturer, is proud to have moved his family from East LA to tony Bel Air, but his wife, teen children, and mother struggle to varying comedic degrees with their new lives.

16 One of the few exceptions was Miguel, played Richard Coca, who snarkily describes his sister as a HAP—a "Hispanic American Princess"—when she worries what her new Bel Air classmates will think of her. His performance is a real standout in the pilot episode.

17 One of the consultants was Dolores Sanchez, publisher of a chain of Latino-oriented newspapers, a US commissioner on Unemployment Compensation, a board member of the Mexican American Legal Defense and Educational Fund, and an advocate with the networks for Latina/os. The other was Helen Hernandez, vice president for public affairs for Norman Lear's Embassy Television and president of the Imagen Foundation. In 1984, with the assistance of Norman Lear, Hernandez established Imagen Foundation. It aims to promote positive portrayals

of Latina/os and the employment and promotion of Latina/os as creative professionals and media executives.

18 Mayerle learned that the research carried out by the production's writers and Helen Hernandez included interviews with students at two Latina/o-majority high schools in East Los Angeles. They asked their interviewees about their views and goals, how they got along with their families and peers, and the importance of connection to a gang; from these interviews the writers began to formulate ideas for series episodes. The writers also read biographies and autobiographies by Mexican American authors, and arranged with the Los Angeles County Sheriff's Department to meet with local gang members, in their efforts to learn about "Mexican American life, consciousness, and culture." Mayerle, "A Dream Deferred," 228.

19 Bill Dana, a comedic actor of Hungarian Jewish descent, also held a key role in Latina/o television history in ongoing performances as the character José Jiménez that quickly became controversial. The absurd Bolivian character was featured on late night talk shows and, later, the *Bill Dana Show* (1963–65). Dana ultimately retired the character because of protests from Chicana/o and Latina/o activists.

20 *Qué Pasa, USA?* was a bilingual sitcom about a Cuban American family adapting to life in the US. Produced at Miami public television station WPBT, it aired on PBS stations from 1977 to 1980.

21 Mayerle, "A Dream Deferred," 228.

22 Paul Rodriguez, interview with Bill Dana and Jenni Matz, February 19, 2007, American Comedy Archives, 37.

23 Examples include George Lopez's executive producer roles on the series in which he starred, America Ferrera's executive producer status on *Superstore* and *Gentefied*, and Gina Rodriguez's executive producer status on *Jane the Virgin*, negotiatied after it became a success.

24 Dolores Sanchez cited in Mayerle, "A Dream Deferred," 229.

25 Norman Lear cited in Mayerle, "A Dream Deferred," 225.

26 *a.k.a. Pablo* premiered on March 6, 1984. Scheduled between *Foul Ups, Bleeps and Blunders* (1984–85) and *Three's Company* (1987–94) at 8:30 p.m. Tuesday nights, it struggled against NBC's highly popular *The A-Team* (1983–87). Brooks and Marsh, *The Complete Directory to Prime Time Network and Cable TV Shows.*

27 Rodriguez mentioned in interviews that he retired this joke years later because Latina/o advocates told him it recalled stereotypes of Latinos as gangsters. American Comedy Archives interview.

28 This episode aired March 27, 1984. It's not clear if Rivera was the sole writer, however. I was told in interviews with various television writers that getting credit as writer of a television episode had different meanings regarding authorship that varied by series and how the showrunner managed the writing team. For some series, all or most of the writers had input into each episode, but the showrunner offered each writer an individual episode for which they could claim sole credit.

For other series, the writers worked individually on separate episodes and so would clearly claim credit for the episodes on which they were the lead writer.

29 George Maksian, "ABC Shelving a.k.a. Pablo," [New York] *Daily News*, April 10, 1984. A television rating indicates the percent of all television households that tuned in to a specific program, while a television share indicates the percent of households watching television tuned in to a specific program.

30 Paul Rodriguez, American Comedy Archives interview, 38.

31 Perry Simon cited in Robert Sabal, "Television Executives Speak about Fan Letters to the Networks," in *The Adoring Audience: Fan Culture and Popular Media*, ed. Lisa A. Lewis. (New York: Routledge, 1992), 185–188, 187.

32 Scott Harrison, "From the Archives: Protests against California Proposition 187," *Los Angeles Times*, November 6, 2019.

33 Matt A. Barreto and Ricard Ramirez, "Anti-immigrant Politics and Lessons for the GOP in California," *Latino Decisions, Polls & Research* (September 20, 2013), latinodecisions.com.

34 For more on networks beginning to target working women in this time period, see Julie D'Acci, *Defining Women: Television and the Case of Cagney & Lacey* (Chapel Hill: University of North Carolina Press, 1994); and Bonnie J. Dow, *Prime Time Feminism: Television, Media Culture, and the Women's Movement since 1970* (Philadelphia: University of Pennsylvania Press, 1996).

35 Greg Braxton and Jan Breslauer, "Casting the Spotlight on TV's Brownout," *Los Angeles Times*, March 5, 1995; Yvette C. Doss, "Network TV: Latinos Need Not Apply," *Frontera* 1, no. 2 (1996): 20–21, 43.

36 For a more detailed overview of ethnic media advocacy efforts targeting the networks from 1992 to 2002, see Mary Beltrán, Jane Park, Henry Puente, Sharon Ross, and John Downing, "Pressurizing the Media Industry: Achievements and Limitations," in John Downing and Charles Husband, *Representing 'Race': Racisms, Ethnicities and Media* (London: Sage, 2005), 160–193.

37 Rounding out the cast, Diana Maria Riva, of Dominican American heritage, played a tacky and bawdy Latina secretary at the firm, while Gregory Sierra played Giraldo's tense, presumably Colombian barber father.

38 Notably, this involved dramatically changing the narrative and replacing the original star, Cuban and Jewish American performer Mel Gorham. Gorham had pitched the pilot as a Latina-centric narrative about a middle-aged woman who moves to New York to pursue her dream of becoming an actor. The original pilot reportedly was based loosely on Gorham's own life. Gorham hams it up in the lead role, with a broad Cuban accent and silly (but funny) repartee, as a souvenir store clerk in Miami convinced to make the move by a man robbing the store. In New York she looks up an old friend, finding instead her friend's dumped boyfriend. Undeterred, she begins her new life, now friends with the dumped boyfriend. NBC dropped most of this premise and replaced Gorham with Constance Marie, a Mexican American actress, now known best as George Lopez's wife Carmen on *George Lopez*. The network reportedly based their decision on a

test screening. Brian Lowry, "Troupers Are Easily Trumped When Actors Flood the Market," *Variety*, May 30, 2013.

39 *Frannie's Turn* was created by now-veteran writer-producer Chuck Lorre, in partnership with Carsey Werner Productions. Frannie Escobar is given a cranky husband, a difficult mother-in-law, a daughter getting engaged who may be pregnant, and a sweet but dim-witted son. Episodes focused on such story lines as Frannie and her husband Joe bickering over the kitchen sink, grandmother Rosa insisting she has seen a saint, and the fallout when their son reports he's failing Spanish. Cuban-born Italian American actor Tomas Milian played Frannie's husband Joe.

40 *Four Corners* (1998) was created by David Jacobs and produced by Jacobs and Michael Filerman; both had worked previously on *Dallas* (1978–91) and *Knots Landing* (1979–93). It premiered February 24, 1998. While CBS was the first network to simulcast a series in English and Spanish, Columbia Pictures Television, producers of the Paul Rodriguez sitcom *Trial & Error* (1988), a decade earlier had offered a Spanish language translation of its March 15, 1988, episode that aired on several Spanish-language radio stations, a first for a television production and distribution company. "Columbia TV Gets Mucho Responses to 'Trial & Error' Spanish Radio Feed," *Television/Radio Age*, April 4, 1988.

41 The ratings and share for the *Four Corners* premiere were 6.9 and 11. John Carmody, "The TV Column," *Washington Post*, February 27, 1988.

42 Culture Clash was founded in San Francisco in 1984 by José Antonio Burciaga, Marga Gómez, Monica Palacios, Richard Montoya, Ric Salinas, and Herbert Siguenza and has seen multiple changes in its troupe membership over the years. The troupe is known for political and social satire via comedic performance.

43 *Culture Clash* sketches included "'90s Chicano Activist Meets Che Guevara," a spoof of *Stand and Deliver*, and a biting "Word of the Day" segment (with words such as *pendejo*, *gabacho*, and *hijole* taught by guest stars such as Edward James Olmos, Jimmy Smits, and Dolores Huerta). *House of Buggin'* included inspired sketches such as "The Chicano Militant Minute" and an affectionate *West Side Story* battle scene spoof.

44 Braxton and Breslauer, "Casting the Spotlight on TV's Brownout."

45 Jackie Guerra, *Under Construction: How I've Gained and Lost Millions of Dollars and Hundreds of Pounds* (New York: New American Library, 2006), 8.

46 Guerra, *Under Construction*, 46.

47 Sorkins had executive produced the hit series *The Golden Girls* (1985–92) and worked on *Laverne & Shirley* (1976–83).

48 Guerra, *Under Construction*, 48.

49 Guerra, *Under Construction*, 50.

50 Since Guerra played the character of Gordie on *American Family* in 2002, she appears to have left acting. Efforts to reach her through social media and my contacts in the industry for an interview were not successful.

51 Jackie Guerra in Pero Like, "Latinas that Slay: Jackie Guerra," *Buzzfeed*, June 2017, streaming video, 1:31, https://www.buzzfeed.com/bfmp/videos/19012.

52 Jackie Guerra in "Latinas that Slay: Jackie Guerra."
53 Rick Najera, *Almost White: Forced Confessions of a Latino in Hollywood* (New York: Smiley Books, 2013), 125. To prove these executives wrong, Najera wrote *Latinologues*, a series of monologues featuring Latina/o actors skewering Hollywood stereotypes. After a successful run on Broadway in 2005, it had multiple national tours.
54 See Beltrán, *Latina/o Stars in U.S. Eyes*, for a more in-depth discussion of the significance of the term "crossover" as used to describe Latina/o stars in the 1990s.

5. 2000S

1 As I note in *Latina/o Stars in U.S. Eyes*, the boom in sales of Selena's music and memorabilia about her life and that of other Tejano music after her untimely death in 1995 was a major catalyst for the founding of *People en Español* and for other media efforts that began to capitalize on Latina and Latino stardom.
2 The WGA West documented in 2000 and 2005 that Latina and Latino writers were only 1.4 and 1.5 percent of employed film and television writers, respectively, in these years. "Table 1: Demographic Characteristics of the WGAW Current Membership, Employed and Unemployed Writers, 2005 and 2000," *2007 Hollywood Writers Report* (Los Angeles: Writers Guild of America West, 2007).
3 Among the studies that confirmed Latina/o underrepresentation in narrative programming in these years were Tomás Rivera Policy Institute, *Still Missing: Latinos In and Out of Hollywood* (Claremont, CA: TRPI, 2000); Children Now, *Latinowood and TV: Primetime for a Reality Check* (San Francisco: Children Now, 2000); and Noriega, *Ready for Prime Time*.
4 As was discussed in chapter 4, the four media advocacy groups that joined efforts under the umbrella of the Multi-Ethnic Media Coalition were the National Hispanic Media Coalition, the Asian Pacific American Media Coalition, American Indians in Film and Television, and the National Association for the Advancement of Colored People. For more on this history, see Beltrán et al., "Pressurizing the Media Industry."
5 These executive positions have since expanded into departments of network staff working toward inclusion and diversity goals in programming, employment, and practices. While in the 1990s and early 2000s, "diversity" was the watchword for these departments and their attempted reforms, "inclusion" began to be used to signal these goals by the 2010s. Sister networks within a larger conglomerate now often share an inclusion department. For example, Creative Talent Development and Inclusion (CTDI) serves the Walt Disney Television networks, which include ABC, FX, Freeform, and Disney Channel, in pursuing these goals.
6 Murrieta, who is of mixed Mexican and EuroAmerican heritage, would later go on to become executive producer for the wildly successful *Wizards of Waverly Place* (2007–12), which ran on the Disney Channel.

7 Nava, a Mexican American writer and director, is best known as a film director. He is known for films such as *El Norte* (1983), *My Family/Mi Familia* (1995), and *Selena: The Movie* (1997).

8 These included the FOX sitcoms *The Ortegas* (2003), an adaptation of the British comedy *The Kumars at No. 52*, starring Mexican and Sicilian American comedian Al Madrigal, and the sitcom *Luis* (2003), a star vehicle for Puerto Rican actor Luis Guzmán. CBS also briefly aired the family crime drama *Cane* (2007), led by Cuban American showrunner Cynthia Cidre.

9 Howard Rosenberg, "2 Families Worth Knowing," *Los Angeles Times*, July 1, 2002.

10 Mireya Navarro, "A Life So Sad He Had to Be Funny," *New York Times*, November 27, 2002.

11 A study by Martha Lauzen found that in 2017–18, the most recent years for which they gathered information, female writer-producers made up 27 percent of series creators. Moreover, the percentage of female series creators has never risen above 28 percent. Lauzen, *Boxed In 2017–18: Women On Screen and Behind the Scenes in Television* (San Diego: San Diego State University, Center for the Study of Women in Television & Film, 2018).

12 Alicia Gaspar de Alba illuminates how Chicano and Chicana artists' work was marginalized in US art museums and how Chicana artists were also initially marginalized by Chicano artists in *Chicano Art Inside/Outside the Master's House: Cultural Politics and the CARA Exhibition* (Austin: University of Texas Press, 1998).

13 Felicia Henderson aptly describes the male and white-centric climate of most television writers' rooms in "The Culture Behind Closed Doors: Issues of Gender and Race in the Writers' Room," *Cinema Journal* 50, no. 2 (2011): 145–152.

14 Luisa Leschin, interview with the author, Toluca Lake, CA, February 10, 2018.

15 These actors, including Dyana Ortelli, Enrique Castillo, Richard Yniguez, Pepe Serna, Bel Hernandez, and Luisa Leschin, shared stories of difficult situations that they had to navigate on television and film sets. Typically in television they had been cast in a one-episode guest starring role and had no agency to challenge how their character was developed or how they were treated on the set.

16 Blaustein and Chipperfield had been known particularly for writing for Eddie Murphy when he was a cast member of *Saturday Night Live* in the early 1980s.

17 Created in partnership with the WGA in 1990, the program has now been in existence for over 25 years. It provides an entrée to awardees into funded staff writer positions on a series. More recently, other writers' trainee programs include the National Hispanic Media Coalition's Television Scriptwriters Program, NBC Universal's Writers on the Verge, the CBS Writers Mentoring Program, Fox Writers Lab, and the HBO Access Writers Fellowship.

18 Luisa Leschin most recently was awarded the Norman Lear Writer's Award by the Imagen Foundation in 2019. Her writing credits include *Resurrection Blvd.* (2000–02), *George Lopez* (2002–07), *The Brothers Garcia* (2000–03), *Everybody Hates Chris* (2005–09), and *East Los High* (2013–17), and producing and co-

executive producing *George Lopez, Austin & Ally* (2011–16), and *Just Add Magic* (2015–).

19 These writers included but were not limited to Maria Elena Rodriguez, Luisa Leschin, and Nancy de los Santos on *Resurrection Blvd.*, Robert Aguilar Jr. on *Greetings from Tucson*, Dailyn Rodriguez, Michele Serros, Ann Serrano Lopez, and Valentina Garza on *George Lopez*, and Barbara Martinez Jitner on *American Family*.

20 Brett Martin, *The Sopranos: The Complete Book* (New York: Time Home Entertainment, 2007); Jerry Offsay cited in John Dempsey, "Showtime Shows 'Soul,'" *Variety*, December 16, 1999; Dennis Leoni cited in Richard T. Rodríguez, *Next of Kin: The Family in Chicano/a Cultural Politics* (Durham, NC: Duke University Press, 2009).

21 Levin cited in Scott Wible, "Media Advocates, Latino Citizens and Niche Cable: The Limits of 'No Limits'' TV," *Cultural Studies* 18: 1, 34-66.

22 Leoni's research materials, archived at the UCLA Chicano Studies Research Center, included the 1999 *Newsweek* "Latino USA" cover story, which featured Mexican boxer Oscar de la Hoya alongside other celebrities, and news stories about other Latino American boxers and their families.

23 Dennis Leoni, interview with the author, Chatsworth, CA, February 9, 2018.

24 The writers' room for *Resurrection Blvd.* included Leoni, Maria Elena Rodriguez, Luisa Leschin, Jorge Reyes, Rosemary Alderete, and Nancy De Los Santos, while its directors included Treviño, Sylvia Morales, Norberto Barba, Rosemary Alderete, and *Resurrection* actors Tony Plana, Elizabeth Peña, and Michael DeLorenzo. The crew also included casting director Bob Morones, film editor Juan Garza, costume designer Sylvia Vega-Vasquez, and publicist Luis Reyes.

25 Wible, "Media Advocates, Latino Citizens and Niche Cable," 51.

26 Peter Murrieta faced a similar challenge casting *Greetings from Tucson*. Notably, few Latina/o actors had had opportunities to gain experience and credits as it and *Resurrection Blvd.* were in pre-production, making it difficult to reassure the network if a showrunner wanted to cast a relatively unknown actor.

27 Wible, "Media Advocates, Latino Citizens and Niche Cable," 56

28 Kristal Brent Zook, "La Vida Local," *Washington Post*, June 25, 2001.

29 *Freddie*, based loosely on Freddie Prinze Jr.'s life, focuses on a young chef whose sister-in-law, niece, and grandmother suddenly move in with him. Notably, his Puerto Rican grandmother (played by Peruvian American Jenny Gago) only speaks Spanish in the narrative, which was subtitled for non-Spanish-speaking viewers. George Lopez assisted in getting the series getting off the ground through promoting the idea with ABC and encouraging his executive producer, Bruce Helford, to work on both shows simultaneously.

30 Constance Marie, *George Lopez* panel, William S. Paley Television Festival 2003, Paley Center for Media, March 8, 2003.

31 Helford and Borden had worked on such hits as *Roseanne* (1988–97) and *The Drew Carey Show* (1995–2004).

32 *George Lopez* panel, William S. Paley Television Festival 2003.

33 Bullock and Martin noted that they had been pursuing what Bullock described as the "bad idea" of developing a Latina/o *Beverly Hillbillies* series. Looking for a Jethro, they went to one of Lopez's performances at a comedy club in Austin, Texas. This is when the idea for *George Lopez* began. *George Lopez* panel, William S. Paley Television Festival 2003.

34 Masiela Lusha, who played George's daughter Carmen in the first five seasons of the series, was the lone exception, as she was Albanian American.

35 Paige Albiniak, "Lopez a Sleeper Hit," *Broadcasting and Cable*, April 12, 2008.

36 Failed telenovela adaptations over the years have included *Killer Women* (ABC, 2014), *Hollywood Heights* (Nick at Nite and Teen Nick, 2012), *Chasing Life* (ABC Family, 2014–15), *Fashion House* (mynetworktv, 2006), and *Desire* (mynetworktv, 2006).

37 Horta passed away in Miami in January 2020 after struggles with addiction and depression. See Seth Abramovitch, "The Secret Anguish of Silvio Horta: Demons and Hollywood Anxiety Plagued the Ugly Betty Creator," *The Hollywood Reporter Magazine*, January 15, 2020, www.hollywoodreporter.com.

38 See Juan Piñon, "*Ugly Betty* and the Emergence of Latina/o Producers as Cultural Translators," *Communication Theory* 21 (2011): 392–412. Mateu, who was Venezuelan American and grew up in Florida, saw opportunities in successfully adapting telenovelas for the US market. Silverman—who later ran programming at NBC from 2007 to 2009, then co-founded the production companies Reveille and Propagate—for his part saw a great potential for an ugly duckling story to appeal to multiple audiences.

39 Piñon, "*Ugly Betty*," 400.

40 Haas cited in Abramovitch, "The Secret Anguish of Sivio Horta." Among Horta's early television series were the horror comedy film *Urban Legend* (1998), the sci-fi series *The Chronicle* (2001–02), about a tabloid covering paranormal phenomena, and *Jake 2.0* (2003–04), about a computer technician transformed into a secret agent when his body is infected with nanobots.

41 Silvio Horta, interview with Nancy Harrington, *Television Academy Foundation: The Interviews*, October 13, 2013, interviews.televisionacademy.com.

42 Piñon, "*Ugly Betty*."

43 Horta, interview with Nancy Harrington.

44 Horta, interview with Nancy Harrington.

45 Horta, interview with Nancy Harrington.

46 Horta, interview with Nancy Harrington.

47 Isabel Molina-Guzmán, *Dangerous Curves: Latina Bodies in the Media* (New York: NYU Pres, 2010).

48 Butterflies, known for undergoing a metamorphosis from larva through chrysalis, became a motif *Ugly Betty* used heavily, visually and narratively, throughout the series' four seasons.

49 Molina-Guzmán, *Dangerous Curves*.

50 Magical realism is a style of storytelling that creates a realistic version of its world that includes some magical elements. It has been especially associated with Latin American authors, particularly Colombian novelist Gabriel García Márquez, and has been adopted by many other writers and media producers over the years.

51 Kathleen Rowe Karlyn, *Unruly Girls, Unrepentant Mothers: Redefining Feminism on Screen* (Austin: University of Texas Press, 2011).

52 Jennifer Esposito, "What Does Race Have to Do with *Ugly Betty*? An Analysis of Privilege and Postracial(?) Representations on a Television Sitcom," *Television and New Media* 10, no. 6 (2009): 521–535.

53 By this time, Ferrera was beginning to produce media content through her own production company, Take Fountain Productions. It began selling television series to networks in 2015. She also partnered with Charles King's Macro to help produce *Gentefied*.

54 Jennifer Lopez also had established Nuyorican Productions, which began to produce films and television series, in which she did not initially star, in the 2000s. Actors who followed suit include America Ferrera, Eva Longoria, and Gina Rodriguez.

55 Nina Tassler, who is Puerto Rican and Jewish, and Herb Scannell, who is of Puerto Rican and Irish descent, were the only network executives of Latina/o descent in these years. Tassler was senior vice president of drama programming for CBS, before being promoted to President of Entertainment in 2004, then Chairman from 2014 to 2015. She later founded PatMa Productions with producer Denise Di Novi. Scannell was the president of Nickelodeon and TVLand from 1996 to 2006, having earlier served as Director of Programming for Showtime/ The Movie Channel. In later years, he founded Next New Networks, served as president of BBC America, and as president of mitú Network until 2018. He currently is president and CEO of radio station KPCC.

56 This was related to me by a former student who worked as an intern in comedy development, reading pilot scripts for one of the Big Four networks in the summer of 2011.

6. 2010S

 1 Fidel Martinez, "Latinx Files: What will the future of Latinx television look like?" *Los Angeles Times*, February 4, 2021, www.latimes.com.

 2 Luiz Salles, "5 Ways to Connect with Hispanic Millennials," *Adweek*, February 21, 2019, www.adweek.com.

 3 As noted in this book's introduction, the numbers of Latina/o professionals employed as writers and showrunners have increased only slightly in the last few decades. In 2019–20, they were just 4.7 percent of working writers. Writers Guild of America West, *WGAW Inclusion Report 2020*. Women, meanwhile, are underrepresented among employed creative professionals in the industry. Their numbers increased slightly, to 31 percent of employed creatives, in 2018–19. Martha Lauzen, *Boxed In 2018–19: Women On Screen and Behind the Scenes* (San Diego: San Diego

State University, Center for the Study of Women in Television & Film, 2018). Considering this, Latinas have double the obstacles to overcome to break in.

4 I elaborate on this topic in "The New Hollywood Racelessness: Only the Fast, Furious (and Multi-Racial) Will Survive," *Cinema Journal* 44, no. 2 (Winter 2005): 50–67; "Fast and Bilingual: Fast & Furious and the Latinization of Racelessness," *Cinema Journal* 53, no. 1 (Fall 2013): 75–96; and with Camilla Fojas in "Introduction: Mixed Race in Hollywood Film and Media Culture," in *Mixed Race Hollywood*, ed. Mary Beltrán and Camilla Fojas (New York: NYU Press, 2008), 1–20.

5 Showrunners of color in 2011 included Veena Sud, who is of Indian and Filipino descent, and Tyler Perry, who is African American. None of the handful of showrunners were Latina/o.

6 Vittoria Rodriguez and Mary Beltrán, "From the Bronze Screen to the Computer Screen: Latina/o Web Series and Independent Production," in *The Routledge Companion to Latina/o Media*, ed. María Elena Cepeda and Dolores Inés Casillas (New York: Routledge, 2016), 156–170.

7 Negrón-Muntaner et al., *The Latino Media Gap*; Darnell Hunt and Ana-Christina Ramón, *Hollywood Diversity Report 2020: A Tale of Two Hollywoods* (Los Angeles: UCLA, 2020).

8 Copies of the *Hollywood Diversity Report*, conducted annually since 2014, can be obtained from UCLA's College of Social Sciences at socialsciences.ucla.edu/deans-initiatives/initiative-archive/hollywood-diversity-report/. Further information about the Annenberg Inclusion Initiative and Stacy L. Smith's research is located at annenberg.usc.edu/research/aii. Reggie Ugwu provides a useful overview of the movement in "The Hashtag that Changed the Oscars: An Oral History," *New York Times*, February 6, 2020.

9 To list their producing credits: George Lopez: (*George Lopez* [2002–07], *Saint George* [2014], and *Lopez* [2016–17]); Jennifer Lopez: (*The Fosters* [2013–18], *Shades of Blue* [2016–18]); and Salma Hayek" (*Ugly Betty* [2006–10], *Monarca* [2019–21]). They were joined in the 2010s by Eva Longoria: (*Devious Maids* [2013–16], *Telenovela* [2015–16], and *Grand Hotel* [2019]), America Ferrera: (*Superstore* [2015–21] and *Gentefied* [2020–]), and Gina Rodriguez: (*Diary of a Future President* [2020–]).

10 Piñon, "*Ugly Betty*."

11 Susan Dominus, "Cristela Alonzo Wants to Make America Laugh," *New York Times Magazine*, October 17, 2014.

12 Dominus, "Cristela Alonzo Wants to Make America Laugh."

13 This came about after she met Eric Rovner, a WME agent of Cuban and Jewish descent, through Stacy Mark, her WME stand-up comedy agent. Rovner recommended that she meet Clements. From the partnership with Clements, *Cristela* was born.

14 Cristela Alonzo, interview with the author, San Antonio, TX, August 16, 2018.

15 Nellie Andreeva, "Cristela Alonzo Latina Comedy from 21 Laps/Adelstein Lands at ABC with Penalty," *Deadline.com*, August 21, 2013, www.deadline.com.

16 Iain Blair, "10 Comics to Watch 2014: Cristela Alonzo Scores a First with ABC Sitcom," *Variety*, July 22, 2014, variety.com.

17 The *Cristela* writers included Peter Murrieta, Emelia Serrano, and Aaron Serna, in addition to Kay Cannon.

18 Alonzo, interview with the author.

19 Alonzo, interview with the author.

20 Alonzo, interview with the author.

21 Christine Acham describes such a dynamic with respect to audience reactions to Redd Foxx on *Sanford and Son* because the series focuses around a crochety junk yard owner who makes no overtures to move into the middle class. Acham, *Revolution Televised: Prime Time and the Struggle for Black Power* (Minneapolis: University of Minnesota Press, 2004).

22 For more on this strategy in the comedy of *George Lopez*, Carlos Mencia's *Mind of Mencia* (2005–08), and the sitcom *Freddie* (2005–06), see Guillermo Avila-Saavedra's "Ethnic Otherness versus Cultural Assimilation: Latino Comedians and the Politics of Identity," *Mass Communication and Society* 14, no. 3 (May 2011): 271–291.

23 Gloria Calderón Kellett, phone interview with the author, April 24, 2018.

24 Cited in Ana Sofía Peláez, "Meet the Woman Who Gave 'One Day At A Time' Its Bicultural, Latino Flavor," *NBC News*, January 26, 2017, www.nbcnews.com.

25 Norman Lear, cited in Jackie Strause, " 'One Day at a Time' Trailer: First Look at Norman Lear's Netflix Remake," *Hollywood Reporter*, December 7, 2016, hollywoodreporter.com.

26 Gloria Calderón Kellett cited in Monica Castillo, "I Saw My Cuban American Life in 'One Day at a Time.' Netflix Jilted It, and Me," *Washington Post*, March 16, 2019.

27 Lauren Alvarez, "Was Netflix Justified in Canceling 'One Day at a Time'?" *Forbes*, March 14, 2019.

28 They also announced around this time that because they cared about "showcasing diverse voices and perspectives," they were greenlighting three new series with Latina/o themes: *Mr. Iglesias* (2019–), featuring Cristela Alonzo's former costar Gabriel Iglesias and executive produced by her former producing partner Kevin French, *Gentefied* (2020–), and *Selena: The Series* (2020–).

29 Brad Schwartz cited in Sonia Rao, "Pop TV Picks Up 'One Day at a Time' Following Its Netflix Cancellation," *Washington Post*, July 27, 2019.

30 While *Viva Valdez* promised appeal to viewers of all backgrounds because of a "universal" story, it arguably wasn't a Mexican American narrative. This is a far cry from *One Day at a Time*, given its cultural sincerity in relating its narrative of various generations of a Cuban American family.

31 Carolina E. Miranda and Vera Castaneda, "Analysis: As 'Vida' is Renewed for a Second Season, two Latina writers debate what it does well and what it could do better," *Los Angeles Times*, July 24, 2018.

32 Roxanne Sancto, "Vida Season 2 Review—Operating on a Chingona Level," *Little White Lies*, May 28, 2019, lwlies.com.

33 Sophie Gilbert, "*Vida* Mines the Highs and Lows of Coming Home," *Atlantic*, May 25, 2019.

34 Then-Starz Chief Executive Officer (CEO) and President Chris Albrecht announced the initiative at a Television Critics Association event in January 2017. Albrecht held this position from 2010 to 2019. Prior to this, he was Chairman and CEO at HBO for two decades, greenlighting programming such as *The Sopranos* (1999–2007), *Six Feet Under* (2001–05), and *The Wire* (2002–08), and a former agent at International Creative Management (ICM) whose clients had included Keenan Ivory Wayans and Whoopi Goldberg.

35 Very few Latina/o media professionals fill these roles, especially at networks and television production companies not designated specifically for Latina/o viewers. Some of these new television executives include Cris Abrego, the co-CEO of Endemol USA; Enrique Guillen, Executive Vice President at NBC Universal; and Cat Rodriguez, Vice President of Unscripted Development and Programming at Lifetime. There is a much larger number of Latina/os in mid-level and entry-level executive positions.

36 Saracho cited in Garrett Anderson, "Expanding Upon the Canon of Latinx Plays: Spotlight on Tanya Saracho," *Breaking Character*, July 25, 2017, www.breakingchar actermagazine.com.

37 A term first used in media studies scholarship by Jillian Báez, the "Latina gaze" is a corrective to the canonical feminist film theory term, the "male gaze." Báez, *In Search of Belonging*. Introduced by Laura Mulvey in "Visual Pleasure and Narrative Cinema," *Screen*, October 1975, the "male gaze" refers to the common construction of women in Hollywood films in a manner that presumes a heterosexual and white male viewer, with female characters existing "to be looked at" by male characters and male film spectators. The concept was soon critiqued for neglecting to consider active female characters and the impact of race, sexual orientation, and other factors in character construction and reading practices.

38 Saracho cited in Pilot Viruet, "How Starz's 'Vida' Created a Safe Space to Explore Latinx and Queer Stories," *Hollywood Reporter*, May 4, 2018, www.hollywoodre porter.com.

39 Saracho cited in Kiko Martinez, "How First-time Showrunner Tanya Saracho Got Her Queer Latinx Series Greenlit by Starz," *Remezcla*, February 6, 2018, www .remezcla.com.

40 Gilbert, "*Vida* Mines the Highs and Lows of Coming Home."

41 BWW News Desk, "Award-winning Original Series VIDA Earns Third Season on Starz," *Broadway World*, June 3, 2019, broadwayworld.com.

42 Tanya Saracho cited in Dominic Patten, "Starz Says Adios to 'Vida'; GLAAD Media Award Winner to End with Third Season," *Deadline*, March 18, 2020, deadline .com.

43 Alberto Sandoval-Sánchez, *José, Can You See? Latinos On and Off Broadway* (Madison: University of Wisconsin Press, 1999), 122.

44 Anita Tijerina Revilla, "Muxerista Pedagogy: Raza Womyn Teaching Social Justice through Student Activism," *High School Journal* 87, no. 4 (April–May 2004): 80–94, 84.

45 Cristela Alonzo, *Music to My Ears: A Mixtape Memoir of Growing Up and Standing Up* (New York: Atria Books, 2019).

CONCLUSION

1 Joaquin Castro, "Latinos Love Hollywood, but Hollywood Hates Latinos," *Variety*, August 18, 2020, variety.com.

2 Dino-Ray Ramos, "Latinx Creators Sign Open Letter to #EndLatinXclusion in Hollywood: 'We Are Tired,'" *Deadline*, October 15, 2020, deadline.com.

3 Untitled Latinx Project, "Open Letter to Hollywood," *Latinx Project*, October 15, 2020, 1–3, www.latinxproject.org.

4 Untitled Latinx Project, "Open Letter to Hollywood," 1.

5 Tara Yosso, "Whose Culture Has Capital? A Critical Race Theory Discussion of Community Cultural Wealth," *Race, Ethnicity, and Education* 8, no. 1 (2005): 69–91.

6 David Evans, *Big Road Blues: Tradition and Creativity in the Folk Blues* (Berkeley, CA: Da Capo Press, 1982).

7 National Association of Latino Independent Producers, "Announcing the Inaugural TV List Writers!" *NALIP*, June 29, 2020, www.nalip.org.

INDEX

Page numbers in *italics* indicate Photos and Figures.

ABOUT THE AUTHOR

MARY BELTRÁN is Associate Professor of Media Studies/Radio-Television-Film and Mexican American & Latina/o Studies at the University of Texas at Austin. She is the author of *Latina/o Stars in U.S. Eyes: The Making and Meanings of Film and TV Stardom* and coeditor with Camilla Fojas of *Mixed Race Hollywood*.

Lightning Source UK Ltd.
Milton Keynes UK
UKHW041901211221
396016UK00001B/46